PRAISE FOR
Emotionally Healthy Discipleship

"A new generation of leaders must help the church take up her prophetic role as a community that bridges racial, cultural, and class barriers in Christ. Scazzero's *Emotionally Healthy Discipleship* shows us a biblical and proven way to get there."

Dr. John M. Perkins
Founder & President Emeritus
John & Vera Mae Perkins Foundation
Christian Community Development Association

The Emotionally Healthy Discipleship Course

By Peter And Geri Scazzero

A proven strategy that moves people from shallow discipleship to deep transformation in Christ.

PART 1

Introducing people to a transformative spirituality with God.

Emotionally Healthy Spirituality
- Eight-session DVD video study with leader support resources
- Workbook
- *Emotionally Healthy Spirituality Book*
- *Emotionally Healthy Spirituality Day by Day*

PART 2

Practical skills to launch people into a transformative spirituality with others.

Emotionally Healthy Relationships
- Eight-session DVD video study with leader support resources
- Workbook
- *Emotionally Healthy Relationships Day by Day*

ALSO BY PETER SCAZZERO

The Emotionally Healthy Leader
The Emotionally Healthy Woman (with Geri Scazzero)

 emotionally
HEALTHY DISCIPLESHIP

ZONDERVAN®

Emotionally Healthy Discipleship

Moving *from* Shallow Christianity
to Deep Transformation

Peter Scazzero

ZONDERVAN
REFLECTIVE

ZONDERVAN REFLECTIVE

Emotionally Healthy Discipleship
Copyright © 2021 by Peter Scazzero

Requests for information should be addressed to:
Zondervan, *3900 Sparks Dr. SE, Grand Rapids, Michigan 49546*

Zondervan titles may be purchased in bulk for educational, business, fundraising, or sales promotional use. For information, please email SpecialMarkets@Zondervan.com.

ISBN 978-0-310-10951-8 (international trade paper edition)

ISBN 978-0-310-10950-1 (audio)

Library of Congress Cataloging-in-Publication Data

Names: Scazzero, Peter, 1956- author.
Title: Emotionally healthy discipleship : moving from shallow Christianity to deep
    transformation / Peter Scazzero.
Description: Grand Rapids : Zondervan, 2021.
Identifiers: LCCN 2020051967 (print) | LCCN 2020051968 (ebook) | ISBN 9780310109488
    (hardcover) | ISBN 9780310109495 (ebook)
Subjects: LCSH: Spiritual formation. | Discipling (Christianity)
Classification: LCC BV4511 .S375 2021 (print) | LCC BV4511 (ebook) | DDC 248.4--dc23
LC record available at https://lccn.loc.gov/2020051967 LC ebook record available at https://
    lccn.loc.gov/2020051968

Cover design: Faceout Studio
Cover photo: Vaks-Stock Agency / Shutterstock

Printed in the United States of America

22 23 24 25 26 27 28 29 30 31 32 /LSC/ 16 15 14 13 12 11 10 9 8 7 6 5

*To every pastor and leader in the world
who serves Jesus and his church.*

Contents

The Difficult Journey to Move Beyond Shallow Discipleship

My discipleship journey began at age nineteen when a friend invited me to a Christian concert, and I gave my life to Christ. I immediately joined the Christian fellowship on our university campus and attended Bible studies three to four times a week. I devoured Scripture for two to three hours a day. I shared the gospel with anyone and everyone and participated in every available discipleship program I could find.

The best word to describe me at that time was *voracious*—I was spiritually insatiable! I couldn't get enough of learning about Jesus. I was discipled in how to study Scripture, pray, share the grace of the gospel clearly, discover and use my spiritual gifts, and grow in God's heart for the poor and marginalized in the world.

After graduating college, I taught high school English and then joined the staff of InterVarsity Christian Fellowship, a ministry on university and college campuses. Those parachurch days added to my practical ministry skills and expanded my knowledge of Scripture.

I was so hungry for God that I began memorizing whole books of the Bible—Ephesians, Colossians, Philippians. But that was little compared to one of my coworkers who memorized the entire sixteen chapters of Romans!

This deep hunger to learn more led me to two leading seminaries in the United States, Princeton Theological Seminary and Gordon-Conwell Theological Seminary. I loved every moment of my three years there. I learned to study the Bible in its original languages, along with learning church history, systematic theology, and hermeneutics. It was a tremendous gift to learn from and be challenged by some of the best theologians in North America.

Six months before graduation, Geri and I were married. Then we moved to Costa Rica to learn Spanish. We moved in with a family of ten children for a year. None of them spoke English, and we didn't speak any Spanish. After our year, we returned to the United States. Then, in September 1987, we started New Life Fellowship Church in a working-class, multiethnic, primarily immigrant section of New York City.

I had leadership and speaking gifts. I loved sharing the gospel and teaching. I was in love with Jesus. And I considered myself rock solid in the faith and a mature believer.

But I was not.

SOMETHING WAS VERY WRONG

Our first worship service began with just a few people, but God moved powerfully in those early years and the church grew rapidly. Since I spoke Spanish, we began a Spanish congregation in our third year. By the end of the sixth year, there were about four hundred people in the English-speaking congregation, plus another two hundred and fifty in our first Spanish-speaking congregation. We had also planted two other churches.

God taught us a great deal about prayer and fasting, healing the sick, spiritual warfare, the gifts of the Holy Spirit, and hearing God's voice. People were becoming Christians, with hundreds beginning a personal relationship with Jesus Christ. The poor were being served in new, creative ways. We were developing leaders, multiplying small groups, feeding the homeless, and planting new churches.

But all was not well beneath the surface.

It seemed we were recycling the same immaturities and childish behaviors over and over, especially in the area of conflicts. With a commitment to bridge racial, economic, and cultural divides, our inability to engage in difficult conversations threatened to derail our community. What was most confusing, however, was the disconnect in some core members who were on fire for God and yet were experienced by others as judgmental, unsafe, and unenjoyable to be around.

Although I didn't realize it at the time, many of the things we were struggling with as a church were reflections of my own struggles and immaturities. My shallow discipleship was now being reproduced in those I led.

While the church was an exciting place to be, it was not a joy to be in leadership—especially for Geri and me. There was a high turnover among staff and leaders, most of which we ultimately attributed to spiritual warfare and the intensity of church planting in New York City. I was told these were the natural growing pains and fallout common to any large organization or business. But we weren't a business. We were a church.

However, Geri and I did know that something was missing. Our hearts were shrinking. Church leadership felt like a heavy burden. We were gaining the whole world by doing a great work for God, while at the same time losing our souls (Mark 8:36).

Something was deeply wrong. I secretly dreamed of retirement, and I was only in my mid-thirties. Despite ongoing spiritual checkups—no immorality, no unforgiveness, no coveting—I could not pinpoint the source of my lack of joy.

A CRAWL TOWARD A CRISIS

The bottom began to fall out when, in 1993–94, our Spanish-speaking congregation experienced a split, and relationships I considered rock solid suddenly disintegrated. I will never forget my shock the day I went to the afternoon Spanish service and two hundred people were missing. Only fifty people were there. Everyone else had gone with one of our Spanish-speaking pastors to start another congregation.

Over the next several weeks, what seemed like a tidal wave swept over the remaining members of that congregation. Phone calls exhorted them to leave the house of Saul (my leadership) and go over to the house of David (the new thing God was doing). People I had led to Christ, discipled, and pastored for years were gone. I would never see many of them again.

Suddenly, I found myself living a double life. The outward Pete sought to encourage the discouraged people who remained at New Life. "Isn't it amazing how God uses our sins to expand his kingdom? Now we have two churches instead of one," I proclaimed. "Now more people can come into a personal relationship with Jesus. If any of you want to go over to that new church, may God's blessings be upon you."

I lied.

I was going to be like Jesus (at least the Jesus I had imagined him to be), even if it killed me. It did—but not in a way that was healthy or redemptive.

Inside, I was deeply wounded and angry. These feelings gave way to hate. My heart did not hold any forgiveness. I was full of rage, and I couldn't get rid of it.

When I was alone in my car, just the thought of what had happened and the pastor who had initiated the split would trigger a burst of anger, a knot in my stomach. Within seconds, curse words would follow, flying almost involuntarily from my mouth: "You are a @#&%" and "You are full of $*#%."

MY FIRST CALL FOR HELP

"Becoming a pastor was the worst decision I've ever made," I told God in prayer.

I desperately searched for help. At last, a good pastor friend referred me to a Christian counselor. Geri and I went. It was March 1994.

I felt totally humiliated. Everything in me wanted to run. I felt like a child walking into the principal's office. "Counseling is for messed-up people," I complained to God. "Not me. I'm not that screwed up!"

Pausing and reflecting on the state of my soul was both frightening and liberating. At the time, I thought all my problems stemmed from the stress and complexity of New York City. I blamed Queens, my profession, our four small children, Geri, spiritual warfare, other leaders, a lack of prayer covering, even our car (it had been broken into seven times in three months). Each time, I was certain I had identified the root issue.

I hadn't. The root issues were inside me. But I couldn't—or wouldn't —admit that yet.

The next two years were marked by a slow descent into an abyss. It felt like I was going to be swallowed by a bottomless hole. I cried out to God for help, to change me. Yet, it seemed as if God closed heaven to my cry rather than answer it.

Things went from bad to worse.

I continued preaching weekly and serving as the lead pastor, but my confidence to lead had been thoroughly shaken by the split in the Spanish congregation. I hired additional staff and asked them to lead, which they did. Hadn't I failed miserably? Feeling they surely could do better, I let them begin rebuilding the church.

I attended leadership conferences to learn about spiritual warfare and how to reach an entire city for God. I attended "refreshing meetings" at other churches. If there was a way to soak in more of God, I wanted to find it. I attended an out-of-state prophetic conference where I received a number of encouraging personal prophecies. I intensified early-morning prayer meetings at New Life. I rebuked demons that were out to destroy my life. I prayed for revival. I sought counsel from numerous and nationally known church leaders.

I felt I was making progress personally. Perhaps it wasn't visible yet, but something was happening. At least I thought so. For Geri, however, things were as they had been throughout our marriage—miserable.

GERI QUITS THE CHURCH

In the second week of January 1996, Geri told me she was quitting the church. She was tired of feeling like a single parent raising our four daughters, and she was tired of the constant crises in the church. She calmly declared, "I'm leaving the church. This church no longer brings me life. It brings me death."[1]

I finally hit rock bottom. I notified our elders of my new crisis. They agreed to a one-week intensive retreat for us with some professional help to see if Geri and I could sort this out.

Within a few weeks, we went away to a Christian counseling center. Our hope was to step out of our current pressures and get some objectivity about the church. I hoped God would fix Geri; Geri hoped God would fix the church; we both hoped for a quick end to our pain.

We spent the next week with two counselors. This small, short-term Christian community was safe enough for us to give ourselves permission to speak our hidden feelings to one another.

What we did not anticipate was an authentic spiritual experience with God. For me, it began in the strangest way. Geri and I had talked late into the night. At about two o'clock in the morning, she woke me, stood up on the bed, and, with a few choice words, let me have it. For the first time, she told the brutal truth about how she felt about me, our marriage, and the church.

While Geri's explosion was painful, it was a liberating experience for both of us. Why? She had stripped off the heavy spiritual veneer of "being good" that kept her from looking directly at the truth about our marriage and lives.

I listened. She listened.

We looked at our parents' lives and marriages. I looked at New Life Fellowship honestly. The church clearly reflected dysfunctions from my family of origin.

Neither of us had ever sensed a permission to feel like this before.

What we discovered was that our discipleship, which we thought was authentic, was shallow—just a few inches deep. Although we had both been Christians for over seventeen years, the discipleship we knew and practiced had penetrated our personhood only superficially. With all my education and background in prayer and the Bible, it was quite a shock to realize that there were whole layers of my life that nevertheless remained untouched by God.

How could this be? I had done everything pastors and leaders had taught me about how to follow Jesus. I was faithful, devoted, absolutely committed. I believed in the power of God, Scripture, prayer, the Holy Spirit's gifts. How was it that my personal life and marriage, along with my leadership, got so stuck as I journeyed to follow Jesus? Where was the explosive power of God?

It felt as if something had died within me, especially as it related to my faith and my role as a leader. But this experience that initially felt like a death proved instead to be the beginning of a journey and the discovery of a relationship with God that would change our lives, our marriage, our family, our church, and thousands of other churches around the world.

I discovered that the problem wasn't the Christian faith itself but rather the way we had been discipled and were making disciples.

CLADDING DISCIPLESHIP

I've learned a lot about stonemasonry from my son-in-law, Brett. He took up the trade—one of the oldest in history—five years ago as an apprentice under a master mason and only recently moved on to his second level of training, that of a journeyman. He will remain a journeyman for seven or more years until he matures into a master stonemason. His entire training process could easily take ten to fifteen years!

Given the slow and costly process required to progress from apprentice to journeyman to master mason, it's no surprise that there are relatively few master masons. But when a master mason builds something, that structure can last thousands of years, even in severe weather conditions. We see this in the pyramids of Egypt, in medieval castles, and in well-made stone farmhouses in our day.

Because of the expense and time associated with mining, cutting, and transporting stone, and then hiring a master mason, the construction industry has developed cheaper alternatives over the years. To give people the look of real stone, builders often use a veneer called "cladding."

Cladding falls into two general categories—natural and synthetic.

Natural cladding is made by cutting large stones into light, one-to five-inch-thick slabs that are then placed over the exterior walls of a home or building. Geri and I recently installed stone cladding for a small area around our front door. It looks and feels like real, heavy stones that provide structural support for the house. People are impressed. But it is simply thin stone cladding attached as siding by workers without any masonry experience.

In contrast, synthetic cladding is made out of manufactured materials such as cement. It looks and feels like expensive natural stones, but without the higher cost of natural stone cladding (let alone the heavy stone used by master masons). Installation is fast and easy. Some brands even label their products as "do-it-yourself." Simply watch a brief YouTube tutorial and you're good to go.

At this point, you may be wondering why I'm waxing poetic about masonry and cladding. The answer is simple: *Much of discipleship in the church today is the spiritual equivalent of cladding.*

On the surface, everything looks like the real thing. Our people are upbeat and optimistic, filled with faith that Jesus will get them through crises and valleys. They are uplifted spiritually through moving worship experiences and dazzling messages. We highlight infectious testimonies. We see to it that our small groups and weekend gatherings are warm and welcoming and that there is a sense we are growing into the new things God wants to do in our midst.

The problem is that none of this is the heavy, load-bearing stone of Jesus's way of discipleship. It appears to be the real thing that will endure severe storms and the test of time, but it is not. Yes, our people participate in worship, listen attentively to sermons, and attend small groups. They often serve faithfully in various ministries and give financially. And yet, their transformation in Christ remains at the level of cladding, a thin veneer on a life that has yet to be touched beneath the surface.

Cladding discipleship surely describes the first seventeen years of my life as a Jesus-follower. Sadly, even though I looked good enough on the surface, I had large gaps in my discipleship and leadership. That was fine for a while because my gifts and zeal covered over a lot of what was missing beneath the surface. But before long, the thin veneer of my discipleship, along with that of our church, would be exposed for what it was.

THE HEAVY STONE OF EMOTIONALLY HEALTHY DISCIPLESHIP

Emotionally Healthy Discipleship is an invitation to radically shift toward the real thing, a discipleship that is heavy, load-bearing stone.

Yes, the process is raw, messy, and weighty. But, like true stonemasonry, it endures.

At its core, Emotionally Healthy Discipleship (EHD) is a biblical theology that, when fully implemented, informs every area of a church, ministry, or organization. It is a discipleship structure built with load-bearing stones so that people flourish even in the midst of crises and upheavals happening around them. More specifically, Emotionally Healthy Discipleship:

- Slows down our lives to cultivate a deep, personal relationship with Jesus amidst the hurry and distractions that routinely overload us.
- Offers guidelines to determine how much the values and goals of Western culture have compromised, or even negated, the radical call of Jesus to deny ourselves, take up our cross, and follow him.
- Makes provision for surrendering to, rather than fighting against, the gift of God's limits in our lives.
- Integrates sadness and loss into our following of Jesus. As a result we no longer miss out on the treasures God has buried within them.
- Provides clear criteria to measure spiritual maturity by how we are growing in our ability to love others.
- Connects how our family of origin and personal history influence our discipleship in the present. We no longer treat deep patterns and traumas from the past with a quick fix.
- Embraces weakness and vulnerability as core to accessing God's power and offering his love to the world.

Before I understood this, I, like most church leaders, simply worked harder and added new initiatives when people got stuck in their discipleship. I did not realize that the problem was in the way we made disciples and the quality of the materials we used. It was limited in its ability to get people unstuck in a number of areas in their lives. As a result, redoubling my efforts and doing the same things over and over but with more intensity, only led to greater confusion about why more effort bore so little long-term fruit.

It wasn't until I experienced a building-wide failure—personally and in our ministry—that I finally realized the problem was the materials themselves. What we needed was a whole new way of doing discipleship that worked beneath the surface of people's lives so they might experience a deep transformation and have a sustainable, long-term impact in the world as a result. We needed a model that was transformative.

Over the next twenty-five years, Geri and I and our team at New Life Fellowship Church embarked on a journey of research, study, and intentional personal growth. We sought wisdom and biblical principles by learning everything we could about transformation—family systems theory, monastic movements and spirituality, contributions from the global church, two thousand years of church history, historical theology, marriage and family studies, interpersonal neurobiology, ministry to the poor and marginalized, Quaker spirituality—just to name a few—while pastoring a local church in New York City.

Our goal was to move from the traditional discipleship model to a transformative one in which people experienced deep change. The graphics below demonstrate the contrast between the traditional model and the transformative model.

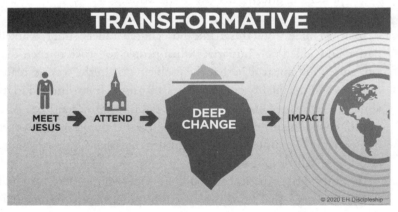

We have been implementing and improving this transformative model (which we call Emotionally Healthy Discipleship) for decades. Our church has served as fertile ground to live out and refine this in practical ways. It has served as a crucible as we engaged in the hard work of bridging barriers across race, class, and gender and lived together as a community with people from more than seventy-five nations.

We've also enjoyed the privilege of bringing Emotionally Healthy Discipleship to thousands of churches, both in North America and around the world. Valuable insights and feedback from these different contexts have shaped, nuanced, and sharpened what you will read in the pages that follow.

My hope in writing this book is that you will take the risk to build differently—both personally and in your church. Emotionally Healthy Discipleship offers a fresh lens, a paradigm shift, a vision to build a spiritual counterculture that informs every aspect of church and community life—including leadership and team development, marriage and single ministries, parenting, preaching, small groups, worship, youth and children's ministries, equipping, administration, and outreach.

Will implementing this be challenging? Absolutely. Will it take a lot of time? Most definitely. Will it be painful? Yes. But be assured of this. This journey with Jesus will be so fruitful that you will never be willing to settle for the thin veneer of cladding discipleship.

READING *EMOTIONALLY HEALTHY DISCIPLESHIP*

Writing *Emotionally Healthy Discipleship* has been a journey all its own. I wrote a first edition of this book eighteen years ago and titled it *The Emotionally Healthy Church.* If you've read any of the other books Geri and I have written since then, you know that God has sharpened and refined our thinking over the years. So much so that I knew simply updating *The Emotionally Healthy Church* would be inadequate to capture it all. An entirely new book was needed. Although this revised and updated edition retains some foundational content from the first edition, about 75–80 percent of it is new. If you read the first book years ago, you will encounter many new insights that have emerged in subsequent years of living this material.

I wrote every page of this book with you in mind. Whatever your role—lead pastor, church staff person, ministry leader, elder/deacon board member, small group leader, intern, denominational or parachurch leader, worship team member, administrator, support staff, missionary, or marketplace leader—I imagined you sitting across the desk from me as I wrote, both of us sipping cups of coffee. I love the church, and I understand how challenging and difficult it is to be a leader in today's world.

My hope is that you and your team will be stretched—spiritually, theologically, and emotionally—as you read.

My aim is nothing short of introducing you to a new way to do discipleship in the church. But it is important to note the old saying, "As goes the leader, so goes the church." We lead out of who we are more than what we do or say. So, while my focus is on the church as a whole, any significant change you hope to experience in your church necessarily begins with you and every other leader—staff and volunteer—in your church. That is how personal transformation impacts the congregation as a whole and then moves into the world.[2]

The chapters in this book are organized into two parts:

Part 1: The Current State of Discipleship
Part 2: The Seven Marks of Emotionally Healthy Discipleship

In Part 1, we'll explore the four primary causes of shallow discipleship: giving what we do not possess, severing emotional and spiritual maturity, ignoring the riches of the historical church, and defining success wrongly. You'll also have a chance to complete an emotional/spiritual maturity assessment to better understand where you're at in your own discipleship right now.

In Part 2, we'll examine the seven marks of Emotionally Healthy Discipleship: To be before we do, to follow the crucified—not the "Americanized"—Jesus, to embrace God's gift of limits, to discover the treasures buried in grief and loss, to make love the core measure of maturity, to break the power of the past, and to lead out of weakness and vulnerability. If we hope to multiply deeply transformed disciples and leaders, these theological realities must become part of the fabric of our lives and ministry cultures.

Finally, we'll consider a long-term strategy to help you implement Emotionally Healthy Discipleship into your church or ministry. That includes letting the change begin with you and your team, as well as practical guidance for leading your church.

As you read each page, I invite you to do so slowly. Allow the book to read you. In other words, invite the the Holy Spirit to challenge you with a vision of how your church and ministry might become a place of both transformation and far-reaching mission into the world for Christ. Stop along the way as God speaks to you. Perhaps you will want to journal. And most importantly, respond to God's invitations that will come to you along the way. Consider downloading the free discussion guide at www.emotionallyhealthy.org so you can discuss the book with your team.

My prayer for you is that God will meet you in new ways as you journey through these pages, equipping you and your ministry to lead from a place of transformation in ways that increasingly cause the earth to "be filled with the knowledge of the glory of the Lord (Jesus) as the waters cover the sea" (Habakkuk 2:14).

Part One

The Current State of Discipleship

Chapter One

The Four Failures That Undermine Deep Discipleship

In his bestselling book *The Man Who Mistook His Wife for a Hat*, Oliver Sacks tells the story of a woman who for decades lived in a family system that kept her stuck and immature.[1]

Madeleine arrived at St. Benedict's Hospital in 1980 at the age of sixty. She had been born blind and with cerebral palsy. Throughout her life, she had been protected, looked after, and babied by her family. What shocked Sacks, the neurologist responsible for her care, was that she was highly intelligent, spoke freely and eloquently, but could do nothing with her hands.

"You've read a tremendous amount," he noted. "You must be really at home with Braille."

"No, I'm not," she said, "All my reading has been done for me. . . . I can't read Braille, not a single word. I can't do *anything* with my hands—they are completely useless."

She held them up. "Useless godforsaken lumps of dough—they don't even feel part of me."

Sacks was startled. He thought to himself, *The hands are not something usually affected by cerebral palsy.* Her hands would seem to have the potential of being perfectly good hands—and yet they are not. Can it be that they are functionless—"useless"—because she had never used them? Had everything been done for her in a manner that prevented her from developing a normal pair of hands?"

Madeleine had no memory of ever having used her hands. In fact,

3

Sacks notes, "She had never fed herself, used the toilet by herself, or reached out to help herself, always leaving it to others to help her."

She lived, for sixty years, as if she were a human being without hands.

This led Sacks to try an experiment. He instructed the nurses to deliver Madeleine's food to her but to leave it slightly out of her reach, as if by accident.

He writes, "And one day it happened—what had never happened before: impatient, hungry, instead of waiting passively and patiently, she reached out an arm, groped, found a bagel, and took it to her mouth. This was the first use of her hands, her first manual act, in sixty years."

Madeleine progressed rapidly from there. She soon reached out to touch the whole world, exploring different foods, containers, implements. She asked for clay and started to make models and sculptures. She began to explore human faces and figures.

Speaking of her hands, Sacks writes, "They were, one felt, not just the hands of a blind woman exploring, but of a blind artist, a meditative and creative mind, just opened to the full sensuous and spiritual reality of the world."

Madeleine's artistry developed to the point that, within a year, she was locally famous as the "Blind Sculptress of St. Benedict's."

Who would have imagined that such a great artist and astonishing person lay hidden within the body of this sixty-year-old woman, who had not only suffered from multiple physical limitations but who had also been "disabled" by those who had thought they were caring for her?

It's a striking story in its own right but also illustrates a disturbingly similar dynamic at work in our churches. Too many people have been "babied" in their discipleship, to the point that they have become nearly disabled spiritually. As a result, they accept without question a faith that promises freedom and abundance in Jesus, and yet they never seem to notice how they remain imprisoned, especially in unbiblical ways of relating to themselves and others. They shrug their shoulders as if to say, "It's useless. I can't do anything about that. It's just the way I am."

This problem, which I refer to as shallow discipleship, isn't a recent one, but it has worsened and deepened over the years.[2] When I first came to faith forty-five years ago, a popular phrase used to describe the church was that we were one mile wide and one inch deep. Now, I would adjust it to say we are one mile wide and less than half an inch deep.[3]

That's not to say that there haven't been any attempts to turn this dynamic around. In fact, as I've worked with churches across the world, I've witnessed many heartening efforts to address our plight—prayer meetings for revival, intentional community life, renewed emphasis on Scripture reading, greater engagement in spiritual warfare, dazzling worship services, rediscovery of the supernatural power of God, increased involvement with the poor and marginalized, and more.

All are valuable. But none successfully address the fundamental question: *What are the beneath-the-surface failures that undermine deep discipleship and keep people from becoming spiritually mature?*

Over the last twenty-five years, I've had a chance to reflect long and hard on this question and on the discipleship systems that have kept people immature for so long. I've done this as the lead pastor for a local church and in my work around the world with different denominations and movements, in urban, suburban, and rural areas, and across racial, cultural, and economic divides. In the process, I've become convinced that implementing a robust and in-depth discipleship for our people requires that we address at least four fundamental failures:

1. We tolerate emotional immaturity.
2. We emphasize *doing for* God over *being with* God.
3. We ignore the treasures of church history.
4. We define success wrongly.

It's vital that we understand the background and implications of each failure. Why? Because apart from a clear understanding of the depth of our situation, we will not stick with the long-term solution required to fully address the widespread damage these failures are causing in our churches.

So let's get started, beginning with the roots of a discipleship system that too often results in people who are less whole, less human, and less like Jesus, rather than more whole, more human, and more like Jesus.[4]

FAILURE 1: WE TOLERATE EMOTIONAL IMMATURITY

Over time, our expectations of what it means to be "spiritual" have blurred to the point that we have grown blind to many glaring inconsistencies. For example, we have learned to accept that:

- You can be a gifted speaker for God in public and be a detached spouse or angry parent at home.
- You can function as a leader and yet be unteachable, insecure, and defensive.
- You can quote the Bible with ease and still be unaware of your reactivity.
- You can fast and pray regularly and yet remain critical of others, justifying it as discernment.
- You can lead people "for God," when, in reality, your primary motive is an unhealthy need to be admired by others.
- You can be hurt by the unkind comment of a coworker and justify saying nothing because you avoid conflicts at all costs.
- You can serve tirelessly in multiple ministries, and yet carry resentments because there is little personal time for healthy self-care.
- You can lead a large ministry with little transparency, rarely sharing struggles or weakness.

OUR FOUR FAILURES

1. **We tolerate emotional immaturity.**
2. We emphasize *doing for* God over *being with* God.
3. We ignore the treasures of church history.
4. We define success wrongly.

All of these are examples of emotional immaturity in action, and yet we don't see them as the glaring contradictions they are. Why? Because we have disconnected emotional health from spiritual health. Where did we get the idea that it's possible to be spiritually mature while remaining emotionally immature? The answer is multifacted, but let me focus here on two significant reasons.

Reason 1: We No Longer Measure Our Love for God by the Degree to Which We Love Others

Jesus repeatedly focused on the inseparability of loving God and loving others. When asked for the one greatest commandment, Jesus identified two—love God *and* love your neighbor as yourself (Matthew 22:34–40).

The apostle Paul made the same point in his first letter to the church at Corinth. He warned that great faith, great generosity, and even great spiritual gifts—without love—are worth *nothing* (1 Corinthians 13:1–3). In other words, if those around us consistently experience us as unapproachable, cold, unsafe, defensive, rigid, or judgmental, Scripture declares us spiritually immature.

The most radical expression of Jesus' teaching about love was also one of his most fundamental principles: "Love your enemies and pray for those who persecute you. . . . If you love those who love you, what reward will you get?" (Matthew 5:44, 46). For Jesus, enemies were not interruptions to the spiritual life, but often the very means by which we might experience deeper communion with God. That is one of the reasons he issued stern warnings such as, "Do not judge, or you too will be judged" (Matthew 7:1).[5] Jesus knew how easy it would be for us to avoid the difficult work of loving people.

Jesus radically reversed the teaching of first-century rabbis who stressed relationship with God at the expense of relationship with others. If you were in worship and realized someone had something against you, the rabbis taught that you should complete your worship to God (since God is always first) and then reconcile with the other person. Jesus turned that teaching upside down saying, "If you . . . remember that your brother or sister has something against you, leave your gift there in front of the altar. First go and be reconciled to them; then come and offer your gift" (Matthew 5:23–24).[6]

What Jesus taught and modeled was that our love for God was measured by the degree to which we love others. In fact, he was so clear about it that it would have been unthinkable for his followers to think otherwise. And yet, they did—and so do we.

Unfortunately, that kind of discipleship system was missing in my early discipleship and leadership development. The failure to measure my love of God by my love of others severely limited my spiritual and emotional growth for the first seventeen years of my Christian life. While I was disciplined in spiritual practices, the people closest to me (starting with my wife, Geri) did not experience me as more loving with each passing year. In fact, the more my leadership responsibilities increased, the more impatient and irritated I became at those who disagreed with me or slowed my efforts to expand God's kingdom.

Reason 2: We Elevate the Spiritual and Distrust the Emotional

Most Christians value the spiritual over every other aspect of our God-given humanity—the physical, emotional, social, and intellectual.

This prioritizing of the spiritual can be traced back to the influence of a Greek philosopher named Plato, who lived several centuries before Christ. His influence on a variety of leaders in church history continues to impact us today.[7] His message, which later became part of the thinking of those in the early church, was essentially, "The body is bad. The spirit is good." In other words, any aspect of our humanity that is not spiritual is suspect at best, including emotions. In fact, to be emotional is, if not sinful, at least less than spiritual.[8] This severely limits the acceptable sphere of our life in God to certain spiritual activities, such as praying, reading Scripture, serving others, or attending worship.

The problem is that we are far more than spiritual beings.[9] In Genesis 1:26–27, we learn we are made in God's image—that we are both whole and multifaceted. That wholeness certainly includes the spiritual aspect of who we are, but it also includes the physical, emotional, social, and intellectual dimensions as well.

FIVE ASPECTS OF BEING HUMAN

Unhealthy developments are inevitable when we fail to understand ourselves as whole people. For some reason, however, we persist in exalting the spiritual over the emotional. Over time, this unbiblical mindset has led to a view that regards emotions (especially sadness, fear, and anger) not just as less than spiritual, but as *opposed* to the Spirit. In the minds of many, shutting out emotions has actually been elevated to the status of virtue. Denying anger, ignoring pain, skipping over depression, running from loneliness, avoiding doubts, and denying sexuality has become an acceptable way of working out our spiritual lives.

Many Christian leaders I meet are emotionally numb. They have little to no awareness of their feelings. When I ask them how they feel, they may use the words "I feel," but what they report are only statements of fact or of what they think. Their emotions are in a deep freeze. Their body language, tone of voice, and facial expressions indicate that emotions are present, but they are not aware enough to identify them.

I witnessed this recently in a conversation with a pastor who was physically exhausted and emotionally depleted by the demands of his new ministry. With his face staring at the floor and his shoulders slumped, he recounted the stresses of the previous three months. When I invited him to listen to his feelings, and I suggested that God might be speaking to him through them, he looked at me as if I had two heads.

"What are you talking about?" he asked.

He had no way to connect what he was experiencing emotionally and physically to his leadership or his relationship with God.

Like so many others, this pastor was missing out on the rich dimension that opens up in our relationship with Jesus when we embrace emotions as an essential aspect of our humanity. In their book *The Cry of the Soul*, psychologist Dan Allender and theologian Tremper Longman III describe it this way:

> Ignoring our emotions is turning our back on reality; listening to our emotions ushers us into reality. And reality is where we meet God . . . Emotions are the language of the soul. They are the cry that gives the heart a voice. . . . However, we often turn a deaf ear—through emotional denial, distortion, or disengagement. . . . In neglecting our intense emotions, we are false to ourselves and lose a wonderful opportunity to know God.[10]

Unfortunately, the churches that shaped me were so emphatic on the sinfulness of my heart and emotions, I initally felt guilty about allowing myself to feel. I even wondered if I might be betraying the faith. But what I later discovered was that what I was actually betraying were the unbiblical beliefs the church had developed about emotions.

I firmly believed Jesus was both fully God and fully human. Yet, I rarely considered the humanity of Jesus—or my own humanity, for that matter. When I look back at my journal entries and written prayers from my early years as a Christian and pastor, they confirm that the Jesus I worshiped and followed was not very human at all.

Nor was I.

I ignored my human limits and ran myself ragged to do more and more for God. I regarded negative feelings such as anger or depression as anti-God and avoided them. I fell into the trap of living as if spending all day in prayer and the Word was more spiritual than cleaning the house, listening to Geri, changing the kids' diapers, or caring for my body.

The Jesus I worshiped was very much God and very little a human being. I somehow missed the stories that revealed how Jesus freely expressed his emotions without shame. He shed tears (Luke 19:41). He grieved (Mark 14:34). He was angry (Mark 3:5). He felt compassion (Luke 7:13). He showed astonishment and wonder (Luke 7:9).

For seventeen years, I ignored the emotional component in my seeking after God. The spiritual-only discipleship approaches of the churches and ministries that had shaped my faith had no theology or training to help me in this area. It didn't matter how many books I read or seminars I attended. It didn't matter how many years passed, whether seventeen or another fifty. I would remain an emotional infant until I acknowledged the emotional part of God's image in me. The spiritual foundation on which I had built my life, and had taught others, was cracked. And there was no hiding it from those closest to me.

FAILURE 2: WE EMPHASIZE *DOING FOR* GOD OVER *BEING WITH* GOD

One of the greatest challenges for every ministry leader is how to balance our *doing for* God and our *being with* him. In our efforts to serve God, most of us actually end up skimping on our relationship with him. We're in a perpetual state of hurry, battling to make the best use of every spare minute. We end our days exhausted from trying to meet the endless needs around us. Then our "free time" is filled with more demands in an already overburdened life.

Some of us are actually addicted—not to drugs or alcohol, but to the adrenaline rush of *doing*. We might read about the need to rest and recharge, but we fear how many things might fall apart if we did. So we just keep going. And in this hurried and exhausted state, we have little time or energy left to invest in our relationship with God, ourselves, or others. As a result, our own lives remain largely unchanged, and the only thing we have to give away to those we lead is our shallow discipleship.

> ### OUR FOUR FAILURES
> 1. We tolerate emotional immaturity.
> 2. **We emphasize doing for God over being with God.**
> 3. We ignore the treasures of church history.
> 4. We define success wrongly.

Over time, the privilege of leading others becomes instead a burden, one that does progressive violence to our own souls. The endless needs that routinely hurtle toward us leave us irritable. We become resentful. We feel stuck in a bad situation and disconnected from God.

This was how things were in my early years as a leader. I was overloaded with too much to do in too little time. Aside from message preparation, I took little time for reflection on Scripture, or for spending time in silence and stillness with God. I rarely reflected before God on my failures and weaknesses. Being with Jesus to simply enjoy him, apart from the purpose of serving other people, was a luxury I felt I could not afford.

Not only was my ability to *be with* Jesus compromised, so was my ability to be with myself and others. Think about it: How could I be in communion with other people when I wasn't in communion with myself? How could I be in a healthy relationship with others when I wasn't in a healthy relationship with myself? And how could I be in an intimate relationship with others when I wasn't intimate with myself?

The *doing for* versus the *being with* challenge of the spiritual life is not a new one, nor is it unique to ministry leaders. It's at least as ancient as Scripture itself, particularly in the iconic story of Mary and Martha.

[Martha] had a sister called Mary, who sat at the Lord's feet listening to what he said. But Martha was distracted by all the preparations that had to be made. She came to him and asked, "Lord, don't you care that my sister has left me to do the work by myself? Tell her to help me!"

"Martha, Martha," the Lord answered, "you are worried and upset about many things, but few things are needed—or indeed only one. Mary has chosen what is better, and it will not be taken away from her." (Luke 10:39–42)

Martha is actively serving Jesus, but she is missing him. Her life, in this moment, is defined by duty—by shoulds and have-tos, pressures and distractions. But her commitment to her duties has disconnected her from her love for Jesus. In fact, Martha's problem goes well beyond her momentary busyness. Her life itself is uncentered and fragmented. I suspect that even if Martha had taken the time to sit at Jesus's feet, she would still have been distracted. She is touchy, irritable, and anxious. One of the surest signs that her life is out of order is the fact that she even tells Jesus what to do: "Tell her to help me!"

Mary, on the other hand, is active in a different way. She sits at the feet of Jesus, listening to him. She is focused on *being with* Jesus, enjoying communion with him, loving him. She is attentive, open, taking pleasure in his presence. She is engaged in a slowed-down spirituality that prioritizes *being with* Jesus over *doing for* Jesus.

Mary has one center of gravity—Jesus. I suspect that if Mary had gotten up to help with the many household chores, she would not have been worried or upset by the same preparations that distracted her sister. Why? Because she slowed down enough to focus on Jesus and to center her life on him. That was her better choice.

When I first became a Christian, I was a lot like Mary. I fell in love with Jesus. I cherished my time alone with him reading the Bible and praying. Yet almost immediately, my *doing for* Jesus fell out of balance with my *being with* Jesus. I wanted to spend more time with him, but there was simply too much to do. My lopsided scale looked something like this:

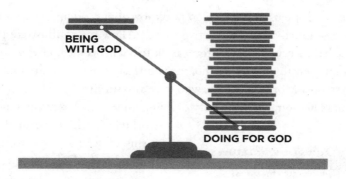

I often felt off center. I had been taught early on about the importance of quiet time or devotions to nurture my personal relationship with Christ, but it simply was not enough to overcome another message I had been taught—that I must be actively serving Jesus with my gifts, and doing a lot for him. The message to serve trumped the message to slow down for time with God.

When we disciple or lead others, we essentially give away who we are—specifically, who we are in God. We give who we are on the inside, we give our presence, we give our journey with Jesus. This means we can give away only what we possess, which is the life we actually live each day. How could it be any other way?

So what is it that we have to give away?

The answer for many of us is, not much. Work *for* God that is not nourished by a deep interior life *with* God will eventually deteriorate—and us with it.[11] Over time our sense of worth and validation gradually shifts from a grounding in God's love to the success or failure of our ministry work and performance. And that's when the peace, the clarity, and the spaciousness of our life with Christ slowly, almost imperceptibly, disappears.

FAILURE 3: WE IGNORE THE
TREASURES OF CHURCH HISTORY

Ignorance in any form—whether it be about finances, health, history, theology, or any other number of things—has the potential to exact a heavy toll in our lives and our disciple-making. Ignorance also has the power to shape us in ways we do not know about, often directing the course of our lives in destructive ways.[12] Allow me to illustrate this through the story of Tara Westover as she tells it in her memoir, *Educated*.

Tara grew up in rural Idaho, the youngest of seven children raised by extremist Mormon parents who were also survivalists. Her memoir recounts her long, painful story of living under her parents' paranoid worldview, which deemed all forms of secular education as evil and part of a larger government conspiracy to brainwash children and youth. So, Tara and her siblings were mostly homeschooled. It wasn't until she was seventeen that she decided she wanted a more formal education and learned enough through self study to take and pass the ACT test. After being accepted at Brigham Young University, Tara continued her journey of slowly filling in the gaps in her education—for example, she had never heard of significant historical events such as the Holocaust or the civil rights movement. After completing her undergraduate degree at Brigham Young, Tara went on to earn both a master's and a doctorate in intellectual history from Cambridge University.

> ### OUR FOUR FAILURES
> 1. We tolerate emotional immaturity.
> 2. We emphasize *doing for* God over *being with* God.
> **3. We ignore the treasures of church history.**
> 4. We define success wrongly.

This is how she describes the dramatic effect coming out of ignorance had on her:

> I had decided to study not history, but historians. I suppose my interest came from the sense of groundlessness I'd felt since learning about the Holocaust and the civil rights movement—since realizing that what a person knows about the past is limited, and will always be limited, to what they are told by others. I knew what it was to have a misconception corrected—a misconception of such magnitude that shifting it shifted the world.[13]

When I read this statement, I was stunned by the parallels between Tara's experience of being shaped by misconceptions about history and the ways in which the church has been shaped by ignorance of her own larger history. Those gaps in our understanding have led to misinformation and misconceptions that have misshaped our theology and our discipleship in significant ways. We have lost biblical treasures and suffered long-term consequences. That's the bad news.

The good news is that it's not a permanent condition. If we are willing to educate ourselves and allow our misconceptions to be corrected, it will "shift the world" as we know it, and move our churches forward in groundbreaking ways.

What are the truths that counter the misconceptions? There are three so large that they open a chest filled with spiritual treasures that truly shift our world. They are:

1. We are one stream within the larger river of God.
2. We are one global church with three branches.
3. We are one movement with our own dirty laundry and blind spots.

Let's begin with the source from which the other two follow—appreciating that we are one stream within the larger river of God.

Truth 1: We Are One Stream within the Larger River of God

I came to faith in Jesus Christ through the tradition of Protestant evangelicalism—more specifically, the Pentecostal stream of the church. The evangelical movement as a whole traces its roots back five hundred years to the Reformation initiated by Martin Luther. Over the centuries, it has been shaped by a host of Christian leaders and movements, including John Calvin, Jonathan Edwards, the Great Awakenings of the eighteenth and nineteenth centuries, Charles Finney, Sojourner Truth, William J. Seymour, Aimee Semple McPherson, and Billy Graham. The wonderful distinctives of this movement include:

- A commitment to lead people to a personal relationship with Jesus
- An emphasis on actively reaching the world with the gospel
- A deep conviction of the Scriptures as the Word of God
- A focus on the cross of Jesus Christ[14]

I love the evangelical stream in Christian history and would not be here writing or leading without it.[15] Yet, I have also suffered from the ways in which it has lost touch with the positive legacies and history of the larger church, one of which is the second of the four failures—emphasizing doing work *for* God over spending time *with* God. This led me to embrace the misconception that ministry productivity is equivalent to spiritual maturity. This resulted in years of building shallow Christ-followers and churches.

We need to get back to our roots—not just our roots as evangelicals but our roots as part of the global and historical body of Christ. This requires an openness to learning from Christians throughout the history of the church as well as from Christians around the world who may be very different from ourselves. And we can do so without losing the distinctives and gifts that our own tradition contributes to the larger church and her mission.

Truth 2: We Are One Global Church with Three Branches

There are three main branches[16] of the Christian church in the world today—Orthodox, Roman Catholic, and Protestant.[17] However, for the first 1,054 years of Christendom, there was only one church. When theological problems or divisions arose, bishops and leaders from the five major cities of the Roman and Byzantine empires—Alexandria, Rome, Jerusalem, Antioch, and Constantinople—gathered together to discuss them. These meetings became known as ecumenical or church-wide councils.[18] Their objective was to sort out thorny theological issues such as the Trinity and the nature of Jesus as both fully God and fully human.

The first council was held when the Roman emperor Constantine summoned bishops to the Greek city of Nicaea to settle doctrine for the entire church. This resulted in the Nicene Creed of AD 325. A second council of bishops met at Constantinople (present-day Istanbul) in AD 381 to revise and expand this document and to affirm what we now know as the final version of the Nicene Creed (see Appendix B).

What makes the Nicene Creed so important is that it has defined the bedrock of biblical Christian faith for over sixteen hundred years. The three main branches of the Christian church—Roman Catholic, Protestant, Orthodox—agree that this creed or "rule of faith" provides a foundation for the proper reading of Scripture. To this day, there are Christian churches around the world that recite the creed every week in worship. All three branches consider any person or group who disagrees with the Nicene Creed to be outside the boundaries of the Christian faith.

The Great Schism that ultimately divided the church struck in 1054. It had been building for centuries and had complex political, cultural, linguistic, and theological roots. The chart below offers an Orthodox perspective on the split and its impact on church history.[19]

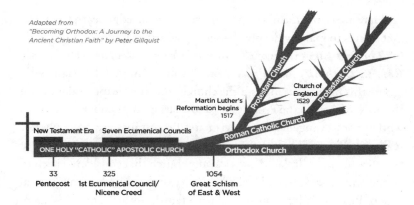

Adapted from
"Becoming Orthodox: A Journey to the
Ancient Christian Faith" by Peter Gillquist

Protestant Church

Protestant Church

Church of
England
1529

Martin Luther's
Reformation begins
1517

Roman Catholic Church

New Testament Era   Seven Ecumenical Councils

ONE HOLY "CATHOLIC" APOSTOLIC CHURCH   Orthodox Church

33
Pentecost

325
1st Ecumenical Council/
Nicene Creed

1054
Great Schism
of East & West

The Great Schism erupted when the bishop of Rome changed the Nicene Creed without consulting the other churches. In so doing, he declared himself infallible in matters of doctrine and faith. Leaders from the other cities excommunicated him. Then he excommunicated them. After that, where you lived geographically determined whether you were now part of the Eastern (Orthodox) or Western (Roman Catholic) church.

The schism was followed by the military Crusades of the Roman Catholic Church that began in the late-eleventh century. In retaking Jerusalem from the Muslims, the Crusaders also attacked and pillaged the Eastern churches along the way. The besieging and sacking of Constantinople's churches, convents, and monasteries in 1204 inflicted a deep wound that has not fully healed to this day. The Eastern and Western churches basically didn't speak to each other for over nine hundred years.

The later corruption and decline of the Roman Catholic Church led to a second great schism, which was the Protestant Reformation in 1517. Protestantism replaced the authority of the pope with the authority of Scripture. Now individuals were empowered to read and interpret the Bible on their own. That was a great breakthrough in that it gave people direct access to Jesus in Scripture. But it also resulted in a Protestant church that would go on to experience over three-hundred thousand splits in subsequent centuries. People could now easily break away to start their own churches without connection to the wider, historic church.

Here are two critically important truths we need to learn from this as it relates to making deeply changed disciples of Jesus.

The first 1,054 years of the church belong to all of us—Orthodox, Roman Catholic, and Protestant.[20] I meet many Christians who ignore this history, acting as if the church somehow leapt straight from the book of Acts to the Protestant Reformation. In their view, believers who are not evangelical or charismatic Protestants are probably not really Christians. They remain ignorant of the fact that the writers of the Nicene Creed declared heretical any church that considered itself to be the only true church. The early history of the church is an essential part of Protestant history—our church family—warts and all.[21]

We have much to learn from the brothers and sisters who came before us—especially those who are very different than us. The Protestant tradition is not the whole church. True believers are those who have a living relationship with Jesus Christ, trusting that he died for our sins and rose again to give us new life. They do not have to attend our church or belong to our tradition to have an authentic faith. There is much we can learn about God and the Christian life from Orthodox and Roman Catholic believers, even though every tradition—including our own—has its problems and differences.[22]

Truth 3: We Are One Movement with Our Own Dirty Laundry and Blind Spots

When I was in seminary, my classmates and I were taught church history, but primarily from a Protestant perspective that emphasized the problems and failures of the Orthodox and Roman Catholic traditions. In the process, we glossed over the treasures of these traditions and failed to reckon with our own dirty laundry and blind spots. Here are just a few examples.

- Martin Luther intensely disliked Jews and wrote essays against them that were later used by the Nazis to justify antisemitism. He also advised German nobles to slaughter rebelling peasants without mercy.
- Ulrich Zwingli, a Reformation pastor and theologian, condoned the torture and drowning of Anabaptists—some of them his own former students—because they believed in baptism by immersion.
- Jonathan Edwards and George Whitefield, leaders of the nineteenth-century Great Awakening, were both slaveholders. African American believers in our church have asked me if these men were really Christian.
- Many leaders of the Protestant Missionary Movement, along with a number of contemporary evangelical leaders, have failed in their marriage and family life. John Wesley, for example, couldn't live with his wife; their marriage was, by all accounts, deeply troubled.
- The great outpouring of the Holy Spirit in the Azusa Street Revival (1906) in Los Angeles split terribly over race.
- Moral failure among prominent church leaders has been part of our church reality for generations.

When Jesus says, "A good tree cannot bear bad fruit" (Matthew 7:18), he is making the point that what we do comes from who we are, that good fruit emerges naturally from deep and healthy roots. The bad fruit of continuous scandals indicates that something is profoundly wrong with the roots of our discipleship. One key contributor to our predicament is the isolation of our local churches, denominations, and movements. We are willfully and needlessly cut off from our rich history and the wisdom of the wider church.

When God looks at his church in the world, he doesn't see denominations, much less thousands of local churches fractured by a host of theological divisions. He sees one church that spans continents, transcends cultures, and has a long and rich history. We are part of this global and historical church even though we were born into it at a particular time in history, in a particular country, and in a particular Christian tradition.

As much as I love our branch of the church, I also recognize that Protestantism has a shadow. Our revivalist focus on individuals making a decision to receive Christ has led to a two-tier Christianity—believers and disciples. We now have large numbers of "believers" who have accepted Jesus as their Lord and Savior but who are not "disciples" following him. At the same time, our discipleship initiatives are top-heavy on renewing the mind through Scripture, but correspondingly weak in other critical components of a fully orbed, biblical spirituality—such as the practices of silence, stillness, solitude, and waiting on God.

If we are going to make disciples of Jesus who are healthy and whole, we must actively seek to learn from both our history and from Christians very different than us.

FAILURE 4: WE DEFINE
SUCCESS WRONGLY

For most of us, it is an absolute value—bigger is *always* better. We want bigger bank accounts, bigger influence, bigger social media platforms, bigger homes, bigger budgets, bigger profits, bigger staffs, bigger churches. Can you imagine a business, government agency, or nonprofit that *doesn't* try to grow and increase its reach? The logic is simple: If you aren't getting bigger, you are failing and potentially on your way to extinction.

> ### Our Four Failures
>
> 1. We tolerate emotional immaturity.
> 2. We emphasize *doing for* God over *being with* God.
> 3. We ignore the treasures of church history.
> 4. **We define success wrongly.**

So we should not be surprised that the church more or less does the same thing—we measure our success by the numbers, and bigger is always the goal. We measure increases in attendance, giving, small groups, and those serving in ministry. We count the number of conversions, baptisms, new programs, and church plants. If our numbers are increasing with more people participating in our ministry, we feel great and deem our efforts a success. If the numbers are decreasing, we feel despondent and consider our efforts a failure. I'm not saying that it's inherently wrong that we measure our progress by the numbers. The problem comes when numbers are the *only* thing we measure, and so become our ultimate marker of success.

You may be asking: "If success by the numbers isn't necessarily success, what is?"

Here's how I would answer that question: *Success, according to Scripture, is becoming the person God calls you to become, and doing what God calls you to do–in his way, and according to his timetable.* What this means is that it is possible for a ministry or organization to be growing numerically and yet actually failing. And that your ministry and numbers may be declining and yet actually be succeeding!

All numerical markers—increased attendance, bigger and better programs, a larger budget—must take a backseat to listening to Jesus. Jesus calls us to abide and abound in him (John 15:1–8). What this abiding and abounding looks like will differ depending on our unique leadership callings. A vocational pastor, a non-profit leader, and a businessperson in the marketplace will each bear a different kind and quality of fruit.

Perhaps one of the best pictures of success in the Bible is John the Baptist.

John was born into a highly respected family. His father, Zechariah, was a Levite priest with significant education and social standing in the community. It was expected that his eldest son, John, would follow in his footsteps. But he didn't.

Instead John moved to the desert to be with God. A few scholars believe John may have joined the Qumran community, a monastic sect of Jewish believers eagerly anticipating the Messiah's coming. We cannot know for sure.[23]

As it happened, John's ministry lasted less than two years. And yet, Jesus said of him, "Of all who have ever lived, none is greater than John the Baptist" (Matthew 11:11 NLT).

We do not know the specifics, but we do know John practiced being with God for years before launching his public ministry. Even while terrible world events swirled around him, John sunk his roots deeply into God. Rather than rushing in to address every need, John waited on God. In allowing the Word of God to penetrate the core of his being, *he became the message that he ultimately preached.*

Instead of moving to the urban center of Jerusalem to start his ministry, John began his work in the wilderness—a place that required people to travel long distances to get to him. He ate and dressed oddly, appearing rough, crude, almost fanatical. Nonetheless, the Jewish historian, Josephus, records that thousands flocked to see and hear him.

What is perhaps most striking about John the Baptist is his complete freedom from performing or impressing people. He did nothing to gain approval or to avoid disapproval. The religious leaders from Jerusalem, for example, were the most powerful people among first-century Jews. Yet, John did not preach to attract their attention or recognition. Instead, he preached *to* them, calling them to repentance. Not only was he completely free from wondering if they were impressed, he was also completely free from worrying about alienating them.

The religious leaders had advanced educations. John did not.

The religious leaders had wealth and status. John did not.

The religious leaders were powerful in the world's eyes. John was not.

None of this mattered to John.

We tend to show deference to those the world considers important. Our insecurities are often revealed in those moments. But John didn't adjust his message to avoid offending those in power. The fact that the religious leaders prayed five times a day, memorized large portions of Scripture, and fasted twice a week didn't keep John from calling them a brood of snakes (Luke 3:7). He had no problem stating the truth—that their relationship with God was superficial and that they were more concerned with accruing power and position than they were for the things of God.

Without apology, John summoned them, along with the rest of

God's people, to the humbling waters of baptism—a rite reserved for the conversion of pagan Gentiles, contaminated outsiders who needed a washing!

John was clear about who he was (his true self in God), and about who he was not (a false self). Without hesitation he stated his identity:

- I am not the Messiah (John 1:20).
- I am not Elijah. I am not the Prophet (John 1:21).
- I am a voice in the wilderness, preparing the way for the Lord (John 1:23).
- I baptize with water, but the Messiah is coming, and I am not worthy to untie the straps of his sandals (John 1:27).

As a result, John had an authority and commanding presence the people of Israel had not seen in hundreds of years. At the same time, he experienced a steady and then steep numerical decline in his ministry. And at that moment, he affirmed to his followers, "A person can receive only what is given them from heaven" (John 3:27). That, for John, was success.

It's hard to see how John would be considered successful in most Christian leadership circles today. (But neither would the prophets Jeremiah, Amos, Isaiah, Habakkuk, or even Jesus!) And yet, the Bible upholds him as a model and makes it clear that God approved his ministry.

When we define success wrongly, it means our best energies will be invested in things such as cutting-edge weekend services, cultivating our brand, and preparing captivating messages. Little is left over for discipleship—our own or that of others—especially when it produces what appears to be such a small and slow return.

With the little time left to invest in the messy work of discipleship, we do the next best thing. We standardize discipleship and make it scalable. Our approach resembles more of a conveyor belt in a manufacturing plant than the kind of relational discipleship Jesus modeled for us. We like standardization. Jesus preferred customization.

These two approaches to discipleship are contrasted in the illustration on the next page.

While Jesus did teach large groups, he knew that one size did not fit all when it came to discipleship. He chose just twelve individuals from the multitudes and customized their training and discipleship to meet their unique needs. And he did so over a period of time. Three years, to be exact. He knew that discipleship cannot be rushed.

CREATING A CHURCH CULTURE
THAT DEEPLY CHANGES LIVES

Let's circle back to the question posed at the beginning of the chapter: *What are the beneath-the-surface failures that undermine deep discipleship and keep people from becoming spiritually mature?* We have looked closely at four failures that we must address in order to move forward:

- Failure 1: We tolerate emotional immaturity.
- Failure 2: We choose to do for God rather than be with God.
- Failure 3: We ignore the treasures of church history.
- Failure 4: We define success wrongly.

We must address these failures in our own lives first, then in our equipping of others, and finally, in creating healthy, biblical communites that provide a context for serious discipleship. To do so effectively, we need a transformative discipleship pathway.

Notice the progression. Most people begin their discipleship journey as attenders who participate in a church or community. If they are seekers, often there is a seeker-targeted course or other one-on-one opportunities to explore faith in Jesus. The long-term goal is to help our people experience deep change within the context of community life so they can progress to the final circle on the right—to multiply by making disciples, thus impacting the world as Jesus commanded (Matthew 28:18–20).

Deep change is what Emotionally Healthy Discipleship (EHD) is all about. In Part 2, we will focus on the seven marks of a biblical discipleship that deeply transforms lives:

- Be Before You Do
- Follow the Crucified—not the "Americanized"—Jesus
- Embrace God's Gift of Limits
- Discover the Treasures Hidden in Grief and Loss
- Make Love the Measure of Spiritual Maturity
- Break the Power of the Past
- Lead out of Weakness and Vulnerability

It's important to keep in mind, however, that each of these marks fall within this larger biblical framework of community, including life-on-life discipling relationships, small groups, and serving.

In preparation for learning more about the seven marks, I invite you to take a personal assessment of your discipleship in the next chapter. This assessment has served tens of thousands of people from around the world by giving them a realistic picture of their current emotional and spiritual condition, and provided motivation to take this journey into what we call Emotionally Healthy Discipleship.

Chapter Two

The Emotionally Healthy
Discipleship Personal Assessment

What comes to mind when you think of an emotionally healthy disciple? How would you describe that person? While this book will expound on many different facets, the foundational definition of an emotionally healthy disciple is both simpler and more multifaceted than you might expect:

An emotionally healthy disciple slows down to be *with Jesus*, goes beneath the surface of their life to be deeply transformed *by Jesus*, and offers their life as a gift to the world *for Jesus*.

An emotionally healthy disciple refers to a person who rejects busyness and hurry in order to reorient their entire life around their personal relationship *with Jesus*, developing rhythms, setting limits, and following him wherever he leads. At the same time, they intentionally open the depths of their interior life—their history, their disorientations, their areas of brokenness, and their relationships—to be changed *by Jesus*. And they are deeply aware how everything they have and all they are is a gift. So they carry a profound awareness of stewarding their talents as a gift to bless the world *for Jesus*.

The following assessment is designed to help you get a picture of where you're at right now with your own spiritual and emotional maturity. It will help you get a sense of whether your discipleship has touched the emotional components of your life, and if so, how much. It will challenge you to consider whether you are an emotional infant, child, adolescent, or adult. Each of these stages of emotional maturity is described at the end of the chapter.

Even if some of the questions make you feel uneasy or uncomfortable, I invite you to answer with honesty and vulnerability. Be as open as possible before God, who loves you right where you are. Remember, the assessment will reveal nothing about you that is news to him. You may want to take a moment to pray, inviting God to guide your responses.

Next to each statement below through page 31, circle the number that best describes your response.

Mark 1. Be Before You Do

Not very true
Sometimes true
Mostly true
Very true

1. I spend sufficient time alone with God to sustain my work for God so that I live out of a cup that overflows (Mark 1:35; Luke 6:12). 1 2 3 4

2. It is easy for me to identify what I am feeling inside (Luke 19:41–44; John 11:33–35). 1 2 3 4

3. When I become anxious or feel like I have too much to do in too little time, I stop and slow down to be with God and myself as a way to recenter (Luke 4:42; Luke 10:38–42). 1 2 3 4

4. I set apart a twenty-four-hour period each week for Sabbath-keeping—to stop, to rest, to delight, and to contemplate God (Exodus 20:8–11). 1 2 3 4

5. People close to me would describe me as content, non-defensive, and free from the approval or disapproval of others (Philippians 4:11–12; John 5:44). 1 2 3 4

6. I regularly spend time in solitude and silence. This enables me to be still and undistracted in God's presence (Habakkuk 2:1–4; Psalm 46:10). 1 2 3 4

MARK 1 TOTAL _____

Not very true / Sometimes true / Mostly true / Very true

Mark 2. Follow the Crucified, Not the Americanized, Jesus

1. I have rejected the world's definition of success (e.g., bigger is better, be popular, attain earthly security) to become the person God has called me to become and to do what God has called me to do (John 4:34; Mark 14:35–39).   1 2 3 4

2. I rarely change the way I act so others will think highly of me or to assure a particular outcome (Matthew 6:1–2; Galatians 1:10).   1 2 3 4

3. I take a lot of time to carefully discern when my plans and ambitions are legitimately for the glory of God and when they cross the line into my own desire for greatness (Jeremiah 45:5; Mark 10:42–45).   1 2 3 4

4. Listening to Jesus and surrendering my will to his will is more important than any other project, program, or cause (Matthew 17:5; John 16:13).   1 2 3 4

5. People close to me would describe me as patient and calm during failures, disappointments, and setbacks (Isaiah 30:15; John 18:10–11).   1 2 3 4

MARK 2 TOTAL _____

Mark 3. Embrace God's Gift of Limits

1. I've never been accused of "trying to do it all" or of biting off more than I could chew (Matthew 4:1–11).   1 2 3 4

2. I am regularly able to say no to requests and opportunities rather than risk overextending myself (Mark 6:30–32).   1 2 3 4

3. I recognize the different situations where my unique, God-given personality can be either a help or a hindrance in responding appropriately (Psalm 139; Romans 12:3).   1 2 3 4

4. It's easy for me to distinguish the difference between when to help carry someone else's burden and when to let it go so they can carry their own burden (Galatians 6:2, 5).   1 2 3 4

5. I have a good sense of my emotional, relational, physical, and spiritual capacities, intentionally pulling back to rest and replenish (Mark 1:21–39).   1 2 3 4

6. Those close to me would say that I am good at balancing family, rest, work, and play in a biblical way (Exodus 20:8).   1 2 3 4

MARK 3 TOTAL _____

	Not very true	Sometimes true	Mostly true	Very true

Mark 4. Discover the Hidden Treasures Buried in Grief and Loss

1. I openly admit my losses and disappointments (Psalm 3, 5).   1 2 3 4

2. When I go through a disappointment or a loss, I reflect on how I'm feeling rather than pretend that nothing is wrong (2 Samuel 1:4, 17–27; Psalm 51:1–17).   1 2 3 4

3. I take time to grieve my losses as David and Jesus did (Psalm 69; Matthew 26:39; John 11:35; 12:27).   1 2 3 4

4. People who are in great pain and sorrow tend to seek me out because it's clear to them that I am in touch with the losses and sorrows in my own life (2 Corinthians 1:3–7).   1 2 3 4

5. I am able to cry and experience depression or sadness, explore the reasons behind it, and allow God to work in me through it (Psalm 42; Matthew 26:36–46).   1 2 3 4

MARK 4 TOTAL _____

Mark 5. Make Love the Measure of Spiritual Maturity

1. I am regularly able to enter into the experiences and feelings of other people, connecting deeply with them and taking time to imagine what it feels like to live in their shoes (John 1:1–14; 2 Corinthians 8:9; Philippians 2:3–5).   1 2 3 4

2. People close to me would describe me as a responsive listener (Proverbs 10:19; 29:11; James 1:19).   1 2 3 4

3. When I confront someone who has hurt or wronged me, I speak more in the first person ("I" and "me") about how I am feeling rather than speak in blaming tones ("you" or "they") about what was done (Proverbs 25:11; Ephesians 4:29–32).   1 2 3 4

4. I have little interest in making snap judgments about other people (Matthew 7:1–5).   1 2 3 4

5. People would describe me as someone who makes "loving well" my number one aim (John 13:34–35; 1 Corinthians 13).   1 2 3 4

MARK 5 TOTAL _____

Not very true
Sometimes true
Mostly true
Very true

Mark 6. Break the Power of the Past

1. I resolve conflict in a clear, direct, and respectful way, avoiding unhealthy behaviors I may have learned growing up in my family, such as painful putdowns, avoidance, escalating tensions, or going to a third party rather than to the person directly (Matthew 18:15–18).   1 2 3 4

2. I am intentional at working through the impact of significant "earthquake" events from the past that have shaped my present, such as the death of a family member, an unexpected pregnancy, divorce, addiction, or financial disaster (Genesis 50:20; Psalm 51).   1 2 3 4

3. I am able to thank God for all my past experiences, seeing how he has used them to uniquely shape me into who I am (Genesis 50:20; Romans 8:28–30).   1 2 3 4

4. I can see how certain "generational sins" have been passed down to me through my family history, including character flaws, lies, secrets, ways of coping with pain, and unhealthy tendencies in relating to others (Exodus 20:5; cf. Genesis 20:2; 26:7; 27:19; 37:1–33).   1 2 3 4

5. I don't need approval from others to feel good about myself (Proverbs 29:25; Galatians 1:10).   1 2 3 4

6. I take responsibility and ownership for my past rather than blame others (John 5:5–7).   1 2 3 4

MARK 6 TOTAL _____

Mark 7. Lead out of Weakness and Vulnerability

1. I often admit when I'm wrong, readily asking forgiveness from others (Matthew 5:23–24).   1 2 3 4

2. I am able to speak freely about my weaknesses, failures, and mistakes (2 Corinthians 12:7–12).   1 2 3 4

3. Others would readily describe me as approachable, gentle, open, and transparent (Galatians 5:22–23; 1 Corinthians 13:1–6).   1 2 3 4

4. Those close to me would say that I am not easily offended or hurt (Matthew 5:39–42; 1 Corinthians 13:5).   1 2 3 4

30

		Not very true	Sometimes true	Mostly true	Very true

5. I am consistently open to hearing and applying constructive criticism and feedback that others might have for me (Proverbs 10:17; 17:10; 25:12).   1 2 3 4

6. I am rarely judgmental or critical of others (Matthew 7:1–5).   1 2 3 4

7. Others would say that I am slow to speak, quick to listen, and good at seeing things from their perspective (James 1:19–20).   1 2 3 4

MARK 7 TOTAL _____

TALLY YOUR ASSESSMENT RESULTS

For each group of questions:

- Add your responses to get the total for that group.
- Transfer your totals to the the right column of the chart on page 32.
- Plot your answers and connect the dots to create a graph on the bottom portion of page 32, following the sample at the top of the same page.
- Read the descriptions on pages 33–34 to learn more about your level of emotional health in each area. What patterns do you discern?

SAMPLE

Marks of Emotionally Healthy Discipleship	Totals
Mark 1. Be Before You Do	20 / 24
Mark 2. Follow the Crucified, Not the Americanized, Jesus	9 / 20
Mark 3. Receive God's Gift of Limits	10 / 24
Mark 4. Discover the Treasures Buried in Grief and Loss	13 / 20
Mark 5. Make Love the Measure of Spiritual Maturity	16 / 20
Mark 6. Break the Power of the Past	14 / 24
Mark 7. Lead out of Weakness and Vulnerability	21 / 28

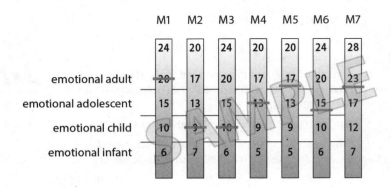

	M1	M2	M3	M4	M5	M6	M7
	24	20	24	20	20	24	28
emotional adult	20	17	20	17	17	20	23
emotional adolescent	15	13	15	13	13	15	17
emotional child	10	9	10	9	9	10	12
emotional infant	6	7	6	5	5	6	7

Marks of Emotionally Healthy Discipleship	**Totals**
Mark 1. Be Before You Do	___/ 24
Mark 2. Follow the Crucified, Not the Americanized, Jesus	___/ 20
Mark 3. Receive God's Gift of Limits	___/ 24
Mark 4. Discover the Treasures Buried in Grief and Loss	___/ 20
Mark 5. Make Love the Measure of Spiritual Maturity	___/ 20
Mark 6. Break the Power of the Past	___/ 24
Mark 7. Lead out of Weakness and Vulnerability	___/ 28

	M1	M2	M3	M4	M5	M6	M7
	24	20	24	20	20	24	28
emotional adult	20	17	20	17	17	20	23
emotional adolescent	15	13	15	13	13	15	17
emotional child	10	9	10	9	9	10	12
emotional infant	6	7	6	5	5	6	7

UNDERSTANDING YOUR ASSESSMENT: LEVELS OF EMOTIONAL MATURITY

Being an emotionally healthy disciple is not an all-or-nothing condition; it operates on a continuum that ranges from mild to severe, and may change from one season of life and ministry to the next. As you read through the descriptions below, what stands out to you? Wherever you find yourself, the good news is that you can make progress and become an increasingly more mature disciple. So even if your current state of discipleship is sobering, don't be discouraged. If someone like me can learn and grow through all the failures and mistakes I've made, it is possible for anyone to make progress.

Here are some observations to help you better understand your assessment results.

Emotional infant. I look for other people to take care of me emotionally and spiritually. I often have difficulty in describing and experiencing my feelings in healthy ways and rarely enter the emotional world of others. I am consistently driven by a need for instant gratification, often using others as objects to meet my needs. People sometimes perceive me as inconsiderate and insensitive. I am uncomfortable with silence or being alone. When trials, hardships, or difficulties come, I want to quit God and the Christian life. I sometimes experience God at church and when I am with other Christians, but rarely when I am at work or home.

Emotional child. When life is going my way, I am content. However, as soon as disappointment or stress enter the picture, I quickly unravel inside. I often take things personally, interpreting disagreements or criticism as a personal offense. When I don't get my way, I often complain, withdraw, manipulate, drag my feet, become sarcastic, or take revenge. I often end up living off the spirituality of other people because I am so overloaded and distracted. My prayer life is primarily talking to God, telling him what to do and how to fix my problems. Prayer is more a duty than a delight.

Emotional adolescent. I don't like it when others question me. I often make quick judgments and interpretations of people's behavior. I withhold forgiveness from those who sin against me, avoiding or cutting them off when they do something to hurt me. I subconsciously keep records on the love I give out. I have trouble really listening to another person's pain, disappointments, or needs without becoming preoccupied with myself. I sometimes find myself too busy to spend adequate time nourishing my spiritual life. I attend church and serve others but enjoy few delights in Christ. My Christian life is still primarily about doing, not being with him. Prayer continues to be mostly me talking with little silence, solitude, or listening to God.

Emotional adult. I respect and love others without having to change them or becoming judgmental. I value people for who they are, not for what they can give me or how they behave. I take responsibility for my own thoughts, feelings, goals, and actions. I can state my own beliefs and values to those who disagree with me—without becoming adversarial. I am able to accurately self-assess my limits, strengths, and weaknesses. I am deeply convinced that I am absolutely loved by Christ and do not look to others to tell me I'm okay. I am able to integrate *doing* for God and *being* with him (Mary and Martha). My Christian life has moved beyond simply serving Christ to loving him and enjoying communion with him.

Part Two

The Seven Marks of Healthy Discipleship

Chapter Three

Be Before You Do

T oo many followers of Jesus are chronically overextended and
doing more for Jesus than their inner life with him can sustain.
They have too much to do in too little time and say a default yes to
requests and opportunities without carefully discerning God's will.
Overloaded and depleted constitute "normal" for their lives.

The notion of a slowed-down spirituality, or slowed-down discipleship in which their *doing for* Jesus flows out of their *being with* Jesus, is
a foreign concept. But what does this look like in everyday life? What's
the difference between a *doing-for* leader and a *being-with* leader?
Perhaps the best way to describe the difference is to invite you into two
versions of a typical morning for a leader named Carlos.

CARLOS: THE *DOING* LEADER

Carlos wakes up at 6:30 a.m. to shower, dress, and spend a few quick
minutes with God in prayer and Scripture before waking up his two
sons, ages ten and seven, for school. He had missed dinner last night
with his family in order to meet with the treasurer about aligning next
year's budget to their new strategic plan. Then his evening training
session for small group leaders finished an hour late. By the time he got
home, everyone was already in bed.

He's sensitive to the fact that it was probably a stressful evening for
his wife, Sophia. Cooking and cleaning up dinner, supervising homework, and getting the two boys to bed is a lot to manage even when
they are both home.

Feeling guilty, Carlos puts his best energy into carrying the parenting load this morning. "I'm sure Sophia will appreciate that," he assures himself. "And maybe it will make up for getting home late last night . . . hopefully."

However, the atmosphere at the breakfast table is tense. Sophia is clearly annoyed. Carlos avoids eye contact. He finds tension and conflict between them overwhelming. "The boys need to leave for school soon anyway," he thinks to himself. "I'll call her at lunch and let her know she's in my thoughts and prayers."

Fortunately for Carlos, Sophia teaches first grade at their sons' school, so the three of them leave the house together shortly after breakfast. Once they leave, Carlos hurriedly gathers up his laptop and some files for the nine o'clock meeting with his team.

"Oh, Lord, please let the traffic be light today," he prays as he walks out the door.

Once in the car, Carlos scribbles some last-minute notes for the meeting on the back of one of the file folders. Although he'd drafted an agenda the day before, the twenty-minute commute to the church always offers space for new ideas to percolate. He sets the file folders on the passenger seat in case he has a chance to make additional adjustments to the agenda at long traffic lights.

Carlos likes to arrive first to the meeting, but traffic is slightly heavier than usual. He decides to drive more aggressively. "Fifteen miles an hour over the limit is acceptable," he rationalizes. But just in case, he keeps a lookout for police cars.

When he pulls into the parking lot, his phone rings. It's the church administrator reminding him that his report for the board meeting is due at four this afternoon.

"I'm on it!" he exclaims confidently. He's scheduled time later in the day to write the report. "It won't take long," he thinks, "I know what I need to say. I just need to organize my thoughts and type them out."

Before getting out of the car, he responds to a text message from his executive assistant and takes a quick look at his social media accounts. He gives in to the temptation to interact with those who've commented on his recent post for fear of alienating any of his followers.

Carlos arrives at the meeting at 8:58 a.m. feeling harried but smiling, warmly welcoming his team into the room. He asks Sarah to open in prayer. Then they begin discussing the meeting agenda items.

Sounds like a pretty normal morning, right? But there is another way.

CARLOS: THE *BEING* LEADER

Carlos wakes up at 6:30 to shower, dress, and spend twenty minutes with God before waking up his two sons, ages ten and seven, for school. Instead of using his quiet time to read through four chapters of Scripture (he is following a plan to read the Bible in a year), he starts with five minutes for silence and stillness before God. He feels a low-level anxiety in his body, having arrived home late last night and anticipating a full day of meetings ahead. He breathes in and out deeply, inviting God's love to fill him. He surrenders his will to God's will.

He takes several minutes to read through Psalm 130, prayerfully meditating on different phrases. He also offers each meeting of his day to God, one at a time, asking for God's wisdom and leadership.

He closes his eyes and takes a deep breath with five minutes remaining. Something is bothering him about the leadership training meeting that ended an hour late last night. He opens his journal and makes the following notations: "Leadership training meeting—I felt drained and depressed afterward. Unsure why. Did we have to go that extra hour?" As he gets up from his chair, he makes a commitment to journal about this again tomorrow. "What might God be saying to me through this?"

He glances again at the agenda for his nine o'clock team meeting. He makes two adjustments—to start with silence (as he needs it himself), and to get feedback on the previous night's training meeting. He also thanks God that his first meeting tomorrow is not till lunchtime, and that Friday is their family Sabbath.

Since both Carlos and Sophia work full time and are raising two sons, they have a weekly planning meeting on Sunday evenings along with regular check-ins as needed. Because of that, Carlos had rescheduled his budgeting meeting with the treasurer to a different time so he could be home for dinner with his family.

Yet, Carlos feels some tension at the breakfast table. He becomes aware of his own anxiety, as well as his desire to run from conflict. He wonders if Sophia is annoyed with him about getting home late last night.

Carlos establishes eye contact with Sophia.

"How are you?" he asks. "Is everything okay?"

"No, it's not," she replies. "I really wish you had called me last night when you realized the meeting was going late. It affected me badly because I had a painful phone call from Maya in my small group. She told me she's leaving our group, but she wouldn't say why . . . and it's really bothering me."

Carlos feels his body tense up. Part of him wants to run away from their conversation or justify why it would have been so awkward to call her, but he prays a quick prayer, "Lord help me!"

When Sophia turns away to do the dishes, Carlos moves toward her and says, "Tell me more, Sophia. What happened?"

She shares for another five minutes, opening up about why the phone call from Maya was so upsetting.

"Will you please forgive me for not calling you last night?" Carlos asks. "It was insensitive on my part."

Sophia nods and smiles.

"This is really important," Carlos says, "and I want to hear more, but we both have to leave in a few minutes. Can we talk later, after you get out of school this afternoon or after dinner—without distractions?"

"That would be nice," she replies. They agree on a time.

Carlos hugs Sophia before gathering his laptop and a couple of files, and then walks to his car to drive to church. He knows he will arrive in plenty of time, even if there's traffic. He drives the speed limit and prays for Sophia. He's already finalized an agenda, so there is no need to take notes at stoplights for his nine o'clock. team meeting.

When Carlos pulls into the parking lot, his phone rings. It's the church administrator reminding him that his report for the board meeting is due at four this afternoon.

"No problem," Carlos says, "I'll have it to you by noon." He has already written multiple drafts and simply wants to read it through one more time after his morning team meeting.

Once he parks, he thinks about checking social media and text messages, but decides not to. He knows that kind of multitasking distracts him from being present to his team and from knowing what God might want to do at their meeting.

Carlos steps into the meeting room at 8:58 and welcomes everyone as they wander into the team meeting. He's excited about beginning with a time of silence and a rereading of Psalm 130 from his devotional time earlier, and also hearing his team's perspectives on last night's training meeting.

Every aspect of Carlos's day is different because of his commitment to *being before doing*.

WHAT DOES IT MEAN TO
BE BEFORE YOU DO?

A person who practices *being before doing* operates from a place of emotional and spiritual fullness, deeply aware of themselves, others, and God. As a result, their *being with* God is sufficient to sustain their *doing for* God.

Healthy Christian disciples and leaders are those who consistently live from this emotional and spiritual fullness, and it impacts every aspect of their lives. *Emotional fullness* is manifested primarily by a high level of awareness—of their feelings, their weaknesses and limits, how their past impacts their present, and how others experience them. They have the capacity to enter into the feelings and perspectives of others. And they carry these maturities with them into everything they do.

Spiritual fullness reveals itself in a healthy balance between their *being with* God and their *doing for* God. They are careful not to engage in more activities than their spiritual, physical, and emotional reserves can sustain. They receive *from* God more than they do *for* him. They enjoy the Jesus they share with others. They establish regular and sustainable rhythms that make it possible to handle the demands and pressures of leadership. Their cup with God is full, not empty, because they are consistently receiving the love they offer to others. And when their lives begin to feel depleted, they have the ability to pivot and adjust their schedules.

They recognize their presence—with God, themselves, and others—is their greatest gift and contribution to those they lead. Because of this, they carry an unrelenting commitment to not allow their *doing* to exceed their *being*.

Mary and Martha Revisited

In chapter 1, we looked briefly at the *doing-for versus being-with* dynamic through the story of Mary and Martha (Luke 10:38–42). Martha is actively serving Jesus, but the pressures and demands of her work distract her from him. She is scattered and uncentered, irritable and anxious. While her hospitality is to be commended, her *being with* Jesus is not sufficient to sustain her *doing for* Jesus. Her spiritual life is imbalanced. Mary, on the other hand, sits at the feet of Jesus, listening to him. She knows how to prioritize *being with* Jesus over *doing for* Jesus. Note the contrast in the two diagrams here:

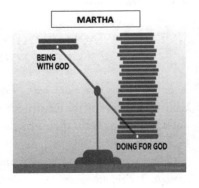

Jesus makes it clear that Mary has chosen what is better—sitting at his feet and listening to him— and it will not be taken from her (Luke 10:42).

The story of Mary and Martha demonstrates a vitally important truth: the active life in the world for God can only properly flow from a deep inner life with God. When we integrate our *doing-for* and our *being-with*, our lives have a beauty, a harmony, and a clarity

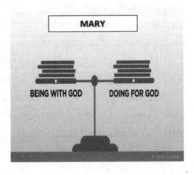

that makes the spiritual life both full and joyful.[1] When we have sufficiently slowed down to *be with* God, our activity for God is marked by a deep, loving communion with God. That's when Christ's life, more often than not, is able to flow through us to others. Which means it is naturally reflected in the way we make disciples and build healthy communities.

Jesus and the Early Church: *Doing for* God Out of a Deep *Being with* God

Prioritizing *being-with* over *doing-for* has deep roots in the New Testament and in early church history. Here are just a few examples.

Jesus. Before launching his public ministry of doing, Jesus spent almost thirty years in hiddenness and being, deeply establishing his identity and oneness with the Father. Once he launched his ministry, Jesus intentionally moved back and forth between *doing* active ministry and *being* alone with the Father (Luke 5:15–16).

When Jesus selected the Twelve to be his inner circle, he followed the same pattern, requiring that they *be with* him before doing active ministry for him: "He appointed twelve that they might *be with him* and that he might send them out to preach and to have authority to drive out demons" (Mark 3:14–15, emphasis added).

The Twelve. After Jesus's death and resurrection, the Twelve then carry on in this pattern of *being before doing* as they lead the early church. Giving their attention to prayer and ministry of the Word took precedence over all else (Acts 6:2–4). Even when the church experienced explosive growth, they refused to allow the incessant demands and problems of ministry to compromise their grounding in being with Jesus.

The early church. In the first three hundred years of the church, leaders developed a "catechumenate," a serious discipleship training process.[2] Why? The Roman Empire, at different times and in different regions, unleashed severe persecutions against believers. Christians who denied the faith rather than be martyred (and were subsequently known as the "lapsed") created a serious problem when some wanted to return to the community after the persecution subsided.[3] The early church realized that simply getting people *to do* Christian behaviors—attending worship, evangelizing, and participating in fellowship—would not be enough for people to stand firm in Jesus amidst such pressure. So they established a clear pathway to help people grow in their *being-with* Jesus so they could persevere in their witness and life *for-Jesus*.

> **Theologians from the early church into the Middle Ages.** From the second to the seventh centuries, most of the eight greatest pastors and leaders (referred to as Doctors of the Church)—Athanasius, Gregory of Nazianzus, Basil the Great, Ambrose, Jerome, John Chrysostom, Augustine, Gregory the Great—were first monks anchored in a life of prayer and *being with* God.[4] Their service flowed out from that abundance and experience with Jesus.

Disciple Making in Our Churches

When I came to faith in Jesus, I was taught to do a lot of things—how to pray, read Scripture, share the gospel, discover and use my spiritual gifts, lead a small group—the list goes on. This list expanded when I became a leader and had to learn how to do more things—such as delegate, cast vision, and teach effectively. However, one practice that never made it to our list of necessary discipling skills was how to lead out of our being. We emphasized doing so strongly that teaching people to be with Jesus, and themselves, was mostly lost in the process.

We did emphasize the call "to follow my example as I follow the example of Christ" (1 Corinthians 11:1), but that revolved primarily around doing particular activities and remaining faithful. I spent years, literally, developing training to teach people how to do things for Jesus. We assumed their being would somehow be taken care of in the process.

It was a traditional discipleship model that was measurable, predictable, and scalable. We could train almost anyone to do it.

Emotionally healthy discipleship, however, emphasizes *being* before *doing* in order to get beneath the surface of people's lives. See the contrast with traditional discipleship below.

TRADITIONAL DISCIPLESHIP	EMOTIONALLY HEALTHY DISCIPLESHIP
1. I do. You watch. We talk.	1. I be. You watch. We talk.
2. I do. You help. We talk.	2. I be. You be. We talk.
3. You do. I help. We talk.	3. I do out of my being. You watch. We talk.
4. You do. I watch. We talk.	4. You do out of your being. I watch. We talk.
5. You do. Someone else watches.	5. You be. Someone else watches.

A leadership culture committed to *being before doing* slows down the discipleship process and radically shifts priorities. The conversations are different. So are the questions we ask. We become more reflective and now regularly ask ourselves, "Do I really want people to imitate the way I am living? In what areas of my life am I speaking of things I am not living?"

These three statements summarize this *be-before-you-do* approach to ministry:

1. You cannot give what you do not possess.
2. What you do is important, but who you are is even more important.
3. The state you are in is the state you give to others.

They're easy to preach and teach, but challenging to live out.

WHY *BEING BEFORE DOING* IS SUCH A CHALLENGE TODAY

To be before you do is as revolutionary today as it was when Jesus gathered the Twelve 2,000 years ago, though perhaps for different reasons. The core challenge that makes *being before doing* so difficult is that it forces us to come face-to-face with our false self. The false self is not a bad or deceitful self so much as a construct of externals—everything from appearance and education to talents and success—that we use to both protect ourselves and to bolster our sense of self-worth.[5] Here's a snapshot of what the false self might look like in the context of ministry.

Craig is a young, gifted preacher and pastor. Raised in a Christian family, he was always encouraged to be all that God called him to be. The motto of his family was, "Good is the enemy of the best." So Craig worked hard to excel at everything from athletics to academics to church.

After sensing God's call to vocational leadership and attending seminary, Craig planted a church. The church thrived. I met him three years into his fast-growing church plant. After a few weeks of being in *The Emotionally Healthy Spirituality Course* with Geri and me, a light went on for Craig. Here is what he said:

> When I walk into a room, my subconscious question is, *What do these people need me to be so we can relate together?* It sounds selfless, but I don't think it is; rather, it's my attempt to be and do whatever the person before me needs. I'm terrified that if I am simply myself, it will not be enough to foster connection and friendship. I'm terrified of rejection. So, I choose certain connection over possible rejection. I immediately and subconsciously look to adapt myself, my behavior, and my speech, to best suit the needs of the room.
>
> That means I basically spend my entire day wearing different masks. Not malicious or malevolent masks, but masks all the same. But when I slow down and spend time in solitude before God, before I can subconsciously ask, *Who does God need me to be so we can relate?* God asks, "Where are you, my son?"
>
> I have no idea how to answer because I don't know where I am, or who I am, or how I am—other than tired. I've spent so much time wearing masks for others (my doing) that I've forgotten what my real face actually looks like (my being).

Craig's self-confrontation, while painful, launched him on a journey into truth. He began the process of paying attention to his emotions, especially the more difficult ones such as anger, sadness, and fear. He has become profoundly aware of his tendency to pretend to be someone on the outside that he is not on the inside—the very definition of a false self. The fruit of this has been revolutionary—personally, as well as in his marriage and his leadership.

Scripture challenges us to shed the "old self" or false self in order to live authentically in our "new self" or true self (Ephesians 4:22, 24). The question then becomes, how do we know if we're living out of a false self? At times, our false self has become such a part of who we are that we don't even realize it. However, the external behaviors of the false self are easier to spot—self-protection, possessiveness, manipulation, self-promotion, and a need to distinguish ourselves from others. When we add a religious layer to this false self, the challenge of dismantling it becomes even more difficult.[6]

So, what does it take to identify our false self? Use this brief assessment as a starting point.

Assessing the False Self

Use the list of statements that follow to get an idea of where you're at right now when it comes to living out of your false self. Next to each statement, circle the number that best describes your response. Use the following scale:

Not very true / Sometimes true / Mostly true / Very true

1.	I compare myself a lot to other people.	1 2 3 4
2.	I often say yes when I prefer to say no.	1 2 3 4
3.	I often don't speak up to avoid the disapproval of others.	1 2 3 4
4.	People close to me would describe me as defensive and easily offended.	1 2 3 4
5.	I have a hard time laughing at my shortcomings and failures.	1 2 3 4
6.	I avoid looking weak or foolish in social situations.	1 2 3 4
7.	I am not always the person I appear to be.	1 2 3 4
8.	I struggle with taking risks because I could fail or look foolish.	1 2 3 4
9.	My sense of worth/well-being comes from what I have (possessions), what I do (accomplishments), or what others think of me (popularity).	1 2 3 4
10.	I often act like a different person when in different situations and with different people.	1 2 3 4

Here are a few observations to help you reflect on your responses.

If you scored mostly threes and fours, you have a strong attachment with your false self. Most likely, this may have been a difficult, even scary, assessment for you. If so, don't worry. Just taking this short assessment was a great first step. Ask yourself, "What invitation might God be offering me through this new awareness?"

If you scored mostly twos and threes, you have likely already begun to dismantle your false self and God is inviting you to the next level of awareness and growth. Your challenge now will be to truly get beneath the surface of your interior life.

If you scored mostly ones and twos, you likely have a healthy awareness of your true self and notice when you are slipping into a false self. That is wonderful. You can expect new levels of discovery as you continue through the seven marks of Emotionally Healthy Discipleship.

The true self is the exact opposite of the false self. David Benner, a Christian writer and psychologist, describes it as "your total self as you were created by God . . . the unique face of God that has been set aside from eternity for you."[7] God invites us to remove the false layers we wear so that the "seeds of true self" he has planted inside of us can emerge. While following this path may appear impossible, the God of the universe has made his home in us (John 14:23) and given us the very glory he gave Jesus (John 17:21–23). As we open ourselves to the Holy Spirit, we discover God does in us what we cannot do for ourselves.

The question then, is how do we break free from our fears of confronting our false self? How do we integrate a *being-with* Jesus and a *doing-for* him in such a way that our spiritual lives are characterized by fullness, courage, and peace—not emptiness, discouragement, and anxiety?

You might be wondering something like this: "Pete, am I supposed to sit around and pray all day? Do you want me to quit my job along with the responsibilities I'm carrying in the ministry?"

Well, I'm so glad you asked.

FOUR WAYS TO *BE WITH* GOD
BEFORE *DOING FOR* GOD

The principle and practice of *being with* God before *doing for* God is as ancient as Scripture itself, and much has been written about it throughout the two-thousand-year history of the church. In light of that, my twenty-six years of studying and practicing this is limited. Nonetheless, I have been able to discover a few golden nuggets from this inexhaustible treasure, four of which have made significant contributions to my understanding and experience of how to enter into this new way of living. In order to *be with* God before *doing for* God, we need to: make a radical decision, feel our feelings, integrate silence, and commune with Jesus throughout the day.

I pray each golden nugget will motivate and encourage you to take your next steps to reorder your life and to say a daily no to the relentless pressure around you to be a "human doing" rather than a "human being."

1. Make a Radical Decision

Shortly after I first learned about *being before doing*, I read about the Desert Fathers of the third to the fifth centuries and immediately recognized a parallel between the challenges they faced and those we face today, both personally and in ministry. Like us, the Desert Fathers lived at a time when the church had grown shallow and indistinct from the prevailing culture.

In response, they did something radical and extraordinary by fleeing to the deserts of Egypt to *be with* God. It was a movement that started in AD 270, when a twenty-year-old named Anthony went to live alone with God in the desert. Christian men and women followed suit in large numbers, leaving their cities and villages on the Nile Delta to live a holy life by separating themselves from the worldly culture that had infiltrated much of the church.

> **4 WAYS TO *BE WITH* GOD BEFORE *DOING FOR* GOD**
>
> 1. **Make a radical decision.**
> 2. Feel your feelings.
> 3. Integrate silence.
> 4. Commune with Jesus throughout the day.

They understood themselves to be following the ancient path of Moses, Elijah, and John the Baptist, each of whom had spent much time alone in the desert with God. Over time, they gathered in communities and became known as the Desert Fathers and Mothers.[8]

Everyone from ordinary people to emperors then began to travel to the desert to meet with them for guidance and wisdom. With their deep knowledge of God and the human heart, they were, in a sense, the psychologists and spiritual directors of their day. Eventually, their wisdom and insights, known as the "Sayings of the Desert Fathers and Mothers," were written down. The following are two of those sayings about a man named Arsenius, who provides a model for us of the radical decision I believe each of us must make in order to *be with* God before *doing for* God.

Arsenius was born in Rome in AD 350 and grew up in a wealthy and respected Christian family. As a highly educated Roman senator, he was chosen by Emperor Theodosius the Great to be a tutor for his children. However, after eleven years of living a lavish life in the palace, Arsenius longed for something different. When praying for guidance, Arsenius said, "Lord, show me the way to be saved." In response, he heard a voice say, "Arsenius, flee from people and you shall be saved."[9]

Arsenius did just that. He fled the palace and moved to the deserts of Egypt. Having withdrawn to the solitary life, he prayed the same prayer again and heard a voice saying to him, "Arsenius, flee, be silent, pray always, for these are the source of sinlessness."[10] Once again, Arsenius did just that. That was his radical decision.

If you'll allow me to once more guess what you might be thinking, it might be something like this: "Pete, I don't see the connection. Do you expect all of us to move to a literal desert?" The answer, of course, is no. *But the drastic nature of the decision we must make is similar in that it requires making a clean and total break from our present habits and rhythms.*

The radical decision is to end our addiction, not to drugs or alcohol, but to tasks and *doing.* We must flee from a life of overcommitment and hurry in order to learn how to *be before we do.* This decision is grounded in a deep inner resolve in which we affirm: "I cannot *not* do this. I'd rather die than *not* go on this journey—regardless of the cost."

Make no mistake about it: this decision is truly as radical as the decision Arsenius made.

Before Carlos started his day, he had made a firm, no-turning-back decision to commit himself, without reserve, to move from being a *doing* leader to a *being* leader. As a *doing* leader in the first scenario, Carlos was not reflective, but rushed, with too much to do in too little time. This was reflected in everything from his rigid approach to his morning devotions to his avoidance of conflict and skimming in his preparation for his team meeting.

The Carlos we see as a *being* leader, however, is almost unrecognizable from the *doing-centered* Carlos. He is measured, thoughtful, present, and connected to himself, to God, and to others. His inner life reflects the peace of God as he moves through his day. He has boundaries and limits that flow from a centered place where he can see God's priorities for him as his morning unfolds.

2. Feel Your Feelings

My friend Dave is a man of few words. He is a gifted leader who has led thousands of children and hundreds of parents in his career as a children's ministry director. For most of his life, he struggled to feel his feelings and share them with others. He also found it difficult to express affection or resolve conflicts maturely.

> **4 WAYS TO *BE WITH* GOD BEFORE *DOING FOR* GOD**
> 1. Make a radical decision.
> 2. **Feel your feelings.**
> 3. Integrate silence.
> 4. Commune with Jesus throughout the day.

But it wasn't until tragedy struck that the limits of Dave's discipleship became obvious. Dave's thirty-nine-year-old aunt was in the World Trade Center when hijackers flew two airliners into the buildings on 9/11. Tragically, she died, leaving behind two young children. While most of Dave's extended family were Christians, they didn't have an emotional or biblical framework to help them process such a shattering event.

When he shared the story with me, he lamented, "They never found her body. And we never talked about 9/11 after her funeral. In fact, even when they found a part of her DNA a few years later, we were overwhelmed again—in a sense, retraumatized. But since we didn't do feelings, there was nowhere to go with it."

There was a long pause. He stared at the floor.

"We were sad . . . I was sad, but outside the moment, I never grieved it."

Then, slowly, as if he were whispering it to himself, he said, "I didn't know how . . . We didn't know how. It was just expected that we suck it up and keep going."

What is particularly alarming about this is that Dave grew up in a Christian home and gave his life to Christ as an eight-year-old. His father was the church treasurer, and if the church doors were open, the family was there.

It wasn't until several years later that Dave finally had a break-through when he participated in a nine-month, intensive small group Geri and I led. Eventually, he was able to talk about letting himself feel "stuff I never did before," such as sadness and grief. That's when things began to change for Dave.

"Instead of putting on a show and wowing people, I started listening to my kids and wanting to just be with them," he said. "Practicing Sabbath and silence became a big part of my life. All of my relationships actually changed."

He describes the nine months in our basement group as torture and life-changing at the same time. Why? He came alive.

Like Dave, I too was taught not to do feelings, especially anger, sadness, and fear.

The focus of my spiritual life was also upward and outward—to grow our church, reach people for Christ, release others for ministry, learn how to be a better leader, and so on. But I did not realize that a relationship with Christ required listening to my feelings before God. As a Christian leader, I was more equipped to arrange organizational charts, solve problems, and *do* things than I was to take that difficult journey inward.

So I didn't.

I rarely looked at the inner chaos that was my thoughts and feelings. The very thought of going down that road of introspection, or self-reflection, was frightening. I feared a dam to my interior life might break open and drown me and the ministry I had built. What good would it be to look at my worst thoughts, envious desires, and inner rages? I sincerely believed it was more godly to suppress them and set my mind on things above (Colossians 3:2).

My spirituality was too heavenly minded.

In contrast, all the Desert Fathers and Mothers, including Arsenius, were actually very earthly minded.[11] They required coming to terms with our struggles and shadows—those untamed emotions, less-than-pure motives, and thoughts that shape our behaviors.[12] They understood that a necessary condition for growing into a mature disciple is having the courage to meet the unvarnished truth about ourselves head on instead of running from it.

Evagrius of Pontus, another Desert Father, summarized it best, "You want to know God? First know yourself."[13] *In other words, the pathway to God inevitably passes through self-knowledge.*

It is fascinating that we observe people doing this throughout Scripture, but we somehow don't imagine it applies to us. From Job's ranting before God and Jeremiah's depression, to Moses's anguish in the wilderness and David's raw emotions in the Psalms, all these expressed their emotions with unashamed freedom.[14]

Once I begin to be aware of what I am doing, how I am feeling, and how it is impacting others, I ask myself the difficult "why" questions. For example:

- *Why am I always in a hurry?*
- *Why am I so impatient?*
- *What is that anxiety all about?*
- *Why am I so angry, and why did I get so defensive when Jane told me she was thinking about leaving our church?*
- *Why do I avoid conflicts?*

When I first began to allow myself to feel my feelings, my emotions were so underdeveloped that I did "feeling workouts" for over two years.[15] As part of my time alone with Jesus each morning, I wrote in my journal what I had felt the day before. And I was rigorously honest. *Why did I feel so uncomfortable in that conversation yesterday? Why was I so angry that he never asked for my perspective but simply judged mine?*

I soon discovered the truth that when we're not in touch with what is going on inside us, we are not in reality but in illusion or denial. And when we are not in reality, we are not in spirituality, because the authentic spiritual life is not an escape from reality but an absolute commitment to it.

Sadly, our failure to recognize what is going on in our interior worlds causes us to miss many gifts from God. We're not open to God speaking through feelings such as sadness, depression, anger, an unhappy spouse, or a life that periodically spins out of control. Our paradigm includes God speaking through Scripture, prayer, sermons, a prophetic word, and sometimes circumstances—but surely not our emotions!

This slowing down to feel is essential if we are to *be before we do*. It requires that we decide what practices (such as journaling) might help us come alive to our feelings, and then integrate those feelings into our discernment of God's will.

3. Integrate Silence

If we are going to *do for* God out of our *being with* God, we must practice silence and stillness in order to nurture our relationship with him. In fact, without the practice of intentional silence before the Lord, it is almost impossible to mature into spiritual adulthood with a *doing-for* God that is sustained by a *being-with* God. Why? Because we are so full of distractions, worries, and plans that our inner world is jam-packed, allowing limited room for God to fill us.

> **4 WAYS TO *BE WITH* GOD BEFORE *DOING FOR* GOD**
>
> 1. Make a radical decision.
> 2. Feel your feelings.
> 3. **Integrate silence.**
> 4. Commune with Jesus throughout the day.

Let me say this as clearly as possible: *Integrating silence and stillness utterly transforms the way we follow Jesus and the way we lead.* Here are a few reasons why.

In silence we let go, surrendering our will to God's will. At the core of God's words to Arsenius, and to us, is the invitation to surrender control of our lives—to practice letting go, moment by moment, of the illusion that we are the center of the universe. In prayer, we surrender our desire for control, approval, and security.

Once I began to practice silence, I realized most of my petitions to

God were coming from a place of fear and loss of control. I had so many things I wanted God to do for me that the joy of communion with him was often lost.

A pastor asked me recently, "Pete, as leaders we have a responsibility to intercede for those we lead. It seems to me this emphasis on silence will hurt this gift we give our people." I answered, "Silence will actually change the way you intercede! So many of our prayers for the people around us come out of our self-will. In practicing silence, we let go of our willfulness and clutching. Our approach to prayer changes from focusing on getting God to do what we want, to positioning ourselves so that we want what God wants."

Fewer things in life are more difficult than accepting what God wants us to do. And at the same time, nothing is more wonderful. In my own practice of silence, I sometimes imagine myself on a river that is God's love. Rather than resisting surrender and trying to swim upstream against the current, I say yes to the flow of God's love, allowing him to carry me where he wills.

In silence we let go of our agendas, allowing communion with God to become the core of our lives. We come to God in prayer not to get something from him, such as a word of encouragement or guidance, but simply *to be with* him. Being silent in God's presence *is* prayer.

Silence slows us down enough to receive God's love without distractions. We realize our very existence as human beings is an expression of God's generosity and love flowing to us. Now we have space to receive that love and allow it to saturate every aspect of our being, one level at a time.

In silence we let go, allowing God to deeply transform us. Thomas Keating compares God's work in us to that of archaeologists who excavate the soil, level by level, to unearth buried structures and treasures. The Holy Spirit is like a divine archaeologist digging through the layers of our lives.

The Spirit searches through our whole life history, layer by layer, seeking the bedrock of our earliest emotional life. In the process, the Spirit separates the essential from the nonessential, the junk from the treasures. Here is how Keating describes what this experience is like:

> Hence, as we progress toward the center where God actually is waiting for us, we are naturally going to feel that we are getting worse. This

warns us that the spiritual journey is not a success story or a career move. It is rather a series of humiliations of the false self.[16]

Sooner or later, every true spiritual journey brings us face-to-face with the hardest realities in our lives, the monsters within, our shadows and strongholds, our willfulness, our inner demons. It is essential we allow God access to those dynamics that are sometimes beyond our awareness or else we will inevitably project them outward on to other people.[17]

In silence we let go, opening ourselves to hear God speak. Imagine having a relationship with a person and all they do is speak. Words. Words. Words. Requests. Requests. Requests. This is a one-way relationship. However, when we integrate intentional silence into our prayer life, we enter into a two-way relationship, one that allows us to abide with God, be held by God, and listen to God. If we stay with silence—be it for two minutes, five minutes, twenty minutes, or more each day—it revolutionizes our relationship with God in Christ.[18]

While listening for a message is not the primary goal of spending time with God in silence, I often find God nudging me toward better choices, inviting me to let go of anxiety, or speaking to me about a blindspot in a particular area of my life. I never cease to be amazed at how much God wants to say when I turn away from the external and internal noise around me.

4. Commune with Jesus throughout the Day

A central theme of the monastic life is that each of us needs to go alone to our cell (a simple hut or room), sit before God in silence, and persevere in his presence. It is a space set apart to meet with him. However, the goal of spending time alone is not just to devote that time to prayer, but to become a person who prays always. A person who prays always has a continual and easy familiarity with God's presence at all times—while working, playing, cooking, leading a meeting, driving, visiting friends, as well as during worship, prayer, and Bible study. In other words, the goal is to be continually conscious of God, remembering him, abiding in him, all through every waking hour.

Until I spent time with monks on retreats, I never understood how it was possible to "pray without ceasing" (1 Thessalonians 5:17 KJV).

My prayer life and leadership, up to that time, was compartmentalized, divided into sacred and secular compartments. I had time for devotions, Bible study, and prayer, but I easily spent large portions of the day without remembering or communing with God. That all changed when I realized that the goal of the Christian life was to abide in Jesus all day, remaining in communion with him in everything.

The great problem, however, was that my *doing-for* Jesus often got beyond my *being-with* or abiding in Jesus. One triggering event or conversation was all I needed to be derailed. So I identified ten indicators to help me recognize when I have moved away from a centered place with him. Then, if at all possible, I stop, take a few deep breaths, and retreat for a bit of silence to get back on track.

> **4 WAYS TO *BE WITH* GOD BEFORE *DOING FOR* GOD**
> 1. Make a radical decision.
> 2. Feel your feelings.
> 3. Integrate silence.
> 4. **Commune with Jesus throughout the day.**

I trust some of these indicators will serve you, but I encourage you to identify and add others that fit your particular circumstances and vulnerabilities.

I Know My Doing Exceeds My Being When . . .

_____ I can't shake the pressure I feel from having too much to do in too little time.

_____ I am ignoring the stress, anxiety, and tightness of my body.[19]

_____ I am concerned with what others think.

_____ I am often fearful about the future.

_____ I am always rushing.

_____ I am defensive and easily offended.

_____ I am preoccupied and distracted.

_____ I fire off quick opinions and judgments.

_____ I feel unenthusiastic about or threatened by the success of others.

_____ I spend more time talking than listening.

So, to wrap things up, we covered four ways to *be with* God before *doing for* God: make a radical decision, feel your feelings, integrate silence, and commune with Jesus throughout the day. And we barely scratched the surface!

As you begin to consider what *being before doing* might mean for you, I invite you to follow through on at least one of these as a first step. These pathways will serve you well on your journey. Most importantly, stay with Jesus, listening to him as he directs you in the pace and specifics in how to make this significant and challenging transition in your spiritual life.

CREATE A CONTAINER
TO BE BEFORE YOU DO

It takes creativity and perseverance as well as trial and error to make the transition from merely practicing spiritual disciplines to actually *being with* God as the source of your *doing for* him. Anyone who's tried to do this quickly realizes that it requires serious thought and advance planning.

To be before you do is a rich and beautiful way to live, but we have to be willing to create a protective container—the boundaries—that make it possible. Here are some guidelines to consider as you begin to create your own container.

Adjust your job description and supervision. For the first ten years of this journey, I made *being with God* the first priority in my job description. It read something like this: *To grow and mature as a disciple of Jesus, leading others out of a deep inner life with Jesus. To be* became my first work. Eventually, this requirement was added to the the job descriptions of others on our staff. We also built into the culture, over time, a question that was used in supervision and mentoring contexts: "How is it going with balancing your *doing* and your *being*? How are you doing your rhythms in this season?"

Practice Sabbath delight. We stop and rest on Sabbath for a twenty-four-hour period because God is on the throne, assuring us the world will not fall apart if we stop working. God is taking care of the universe and manages quite well without us having to run things.

When we sleep, he is working. While Jesus is our Sabbath rest and we are headed for an eternal Sabbath when we see him face to face, keeping Sabbath here on earth is a core spiritual practice to help us mature in Christ. Just as it is with any other spiritual discipline, such as reading the Bible, prayer, fellowship, and worship, Sabbath does not save us. But if we are not implenting these core practices, it is unlikely we are growing much spiritually. Sabbath is one of God's good gifts to us that we are to receive as an essential delivery mechanism of his love.[20]

Discover the rhythms of the Daily Office. The term Daily Office (also called fixed-hour prayer) has a rich biblical history going back to David, who practiced set times of prayer seven times a day (Psalm 119:164); Daniel, who prayed three times a day (Daniel 6:10); and devout Jews in Jesus's day, who prayed three times a day. The purpose of the Daily Office is create a rhythm that enables us to stop at set times in order to be present with God during all of our active hours.

Stopping three to four times a day *to be with* God has utterly transformed my spiritual life since I integrated this practice nearly twenty years ago. It has anchored me to be aware of Jesus's presence in my *doing-for him* like few other practices.[21]

Craft a Rule of Life. A Rule of Life, very simply, is an intentional, conscious plan to keep God as the center of everything we do. It includes our unique combination of spiritual practices that provide structure and direction for us to pay attention to and remember God in everything we do. It is a powerful tool dating back to the Desert Fathers and Mothers in the third to fifth centuries, and enables us to regulate our entire lives in such a way that we prefer the love of Jesus above all things.[22]

Learn from trusted companions who are ahead of you. Along with a commitment to a local community of believers, we need mature companions for each stage of our journey—be it in the form of a small group, spiritual director, mentors, or professional counselors equipped to help us navigate transitions. They are able to provide resources along with support for the questions you will have. Without mature companions, we can easily get stuck or fall into the trap of going down paths that are not very helpful for the stage of the journey in which we find ourselves.

Experiment and make adjustments. As you integrate new practices to slow down in order to balance *your doing* with *your being*, expect to encounter challenges and disruptions. After several weeks, make needed adjustments. I promise you, it gets easier as you go. After about six months, you should have a good idea of the core practices that work best for you. Always remember: God has made each of us different. Your combination of *doing* and *being* will be different from mine. God has crafted each of our personalities, temperaments, life situations, passions, and callings in a unique way.

BE PATIENT WITH YOURSELF

The choice *to be before you do* is a radical one, both within and beyond the church. You will likely find yourself fighting against a powerful current that appears, at least on the surface, impossible to resist. You will encounter resistance. But the greatest opposition you encounter will no doubt come from within yourself! That certainly has been the case for me.

So I encourage you to begin humbly, seeking God's guidance in prayer. And be patient with yourself. Learn to wait on God, anchoring yourself in his love as you begin taking the difficult steps *to be* before *you do.* Anytime you choose to die to self for love of Christ, resurrection will be a certainty. Based on personal experience, I can promise that you will be reborn into a new place of maturity in Christ and discover God is eager to lead you to new, greener pastures.

Chapter Four

Follow the Crucified, Not the Americanized, Jesus

The relationship of the church to the broader culture has been a challenging issue since Jesus began his ministry.[1] Today, Western culture dominates our landscape. And because the United States exerts an enormous amount of influence—through economic and political power, movies and music, technology, and communications—we have influenced Western culture, and the rest of the world, disproportionally.

To "Americanize" something is "to cause to acquire or conform to American characteristics" or "to bring something under the political, cultural, or commercial influence of the United States."[2] Within the church, to Americanize Jesus is to follow him because he makes my life better and more enjoyable. Even if you are from a country outside of the United States, traces of this Americanized Jesus can be found in churches around the world—from Africa to Asia to Europe to Latin America to the Mideast to Australia and New Zealand.

The challenge is that most of us are so immersed in Western culture, if not American culture, that it's hard for us to recognize how Americanized our view of Jesus really is. What makes it particularly difficult to identify is that it looks so good, feels so good, and does so much good. Or so we think.

So, what does following an Americanized Jesus look like? It's subtle, so we'll begin by looking at what an ancient version of feel-good discipleship looked like in the life of Peter.

CAN YOU FOLLOW JESUS WITHOUT EMBRACING THE CROSS?

It wasn't until Jesus was at least halfway through his ministry that he clearly explained to his disciples the centrality of the cross to his life and mission. Scripture records Peter's horrified reaction:

> Peter took him aside and began to rebuke him. "Never, Lord!" he said. "This shall never happen to you!"
>
> Jesus turned and said to Peter, "Get behind me, Satan! You are a stumbling block to me; you do not have in mind the concerns of God, but merely human concerns." (Matthew 16:22–23)

At this point, Peter understands only half the gospel. Like so many of us, he is *Christ-centered* but not *cross-centered*.[3] Peter has a high view of Jesus as the Messiah. He is captivated by him as the miracle working, triumphant Savior. Peter truly wants to follow Jesus—in fact, he's left everything to follow him. But he wants to follow a Jesus who avoids, not embraces, the cross.

Peter holds fixed, culturally informed ideas of how God's work in the world should unfold—and those ideas make no provisions for Jesus being killed. Nonetheless, Jesus wants to take Peter on a deeper spiritual journey, even though everything in Peter resists the suffering and pain this involves.

Peter is not curious. He does not ask Jesus questions in order to learn something new. He simply becomes agitated and defiant.

So Peter moves *in front of* Jesus, ordering him not to talk so foolishly. Up to this point, following Jesus has given Peter a greater, not a lesser, sense of power, control, and influence. He now understands that is about to change. So he rebukes Jesus, telling him what to do.

Jesus's reaction is visceral and swift; he says to Peter, "Get behind me, Satan!" He then shocks the disciples even more when he says, "Whoever wants to be my disciple must deny themselves and take up their cross and follow me" (Matthew 16:24). Not only is Jesus clear that his death on the cross is necessary to make atonement for our sin, he calls every disciple to embrace a way of life informed by the crucifixion.

Jesus reframes the nature of reality for the Twelve, summarizing it in his statement, "What people value highly is detestable in God's sight" (Luke 16:15). "Detestable" is an extremely strong word to describe how God feels about the things we tend to value. He knows that our understanding of his ways is not only too small and too shallow, but also wrongheaded and upside down.

The question then becomes, "What does it mean for us to follow the crucified Jesus in our context?"

Remember, the Americanization of discipleship is often subtle, so let's consider two sets of snapshots that demonstrate the difference between a Christ-centered discipleship that avoids the cross and a cross-centered discipleship that embraces it.

Madison, Alex, and Joan: Leaders Avoiding the Cross

Madison is a volunteer member of the leadership team that oversees the small group ministry in her church. Married with three small children, Madison loves participating in the ministry's monthly planning meetings and also leading her own small group. While Madison and her husband, Brad, are known in the church for being exemplary believers, their marriage has experienced unresolved tensions over the last year. Their youngest son's behavioral problems at school have only compounded that stress. But Madison is reluctant to share about these struggles with others. She wants people to know that Jesus really does make our lives better.

Alex, a thirty-seven-year-old lead pastor, is articulate and an effective communicator. His insightful messages have increased his popularity both within and beyond the church. Alex now finds himself responding to emails from people around the world and fielding questions from other pastors in his city. While he loves the attention, it has also made the day-to-day, detailed work of running a church more burdensome than in the past. He is grateful the board has been willing to provide pastoral care for his key volunteers so he can devote more time to improving his craft as a preacher/teacher. He believes the "good life from God" he enjoys comes to all who follow Jesus.

Joan is an associate pastor at her church. However, her road to this role has been anything but smooth. Being a female pastor, for Joan, has meant she has often been the only woman in the room at leadership gatherings, or been the first woman to hold various ministry leadership positions—and she feels the pressure of both. When she was hired, the two-hundred-member church had already been declining for years. But her experience in turning around her previous church had been a significant factor in the board's decision to hire her at this church. When a long-term member recently commented that the church still seemed to be declining, Joan felt hurt, interpreting it as a sign of no confidence in her. She feels great pressure to get the church moving and rarely takes a day off. Her husband wonders when things will lighten up for Joan. So does she.

There is no question that Madison, Alex, and Joan all love Jesus. In fact, their whole lives revolve around Jesus and his work. But being cross-centered would significantly change the way they lead. It's one thing to affirm that Jesus died for our sins and rose from the dead, but it's another to lead out of a discipleship deeply informed by the crucified Jesus, and by the reality that the cross is not only the most important event in world history, but also the lens through which we follow him.

What might it look like for Madison, Alex, and Joan to "get" the crucified part of following Jesus? Let's take a look at another set of snapshots, this time through the lens of cross-centered discipleship.

Madison, Alex, and Joan: Leaders Embracing the Cross

Madison. Instead of hiding her problems from others in an effort to be a good role model, Madison openly shares the pain and struggles she's experiencing in her marriage and parenting. The way of the cross for her is honesty, vulnerability, and humility, and she is willing to share that she too is a wounded healer.

Alex. Alex still works hard on his messages, but he lets go of his need to be a popular communicator and to create "wow" moments in his messages. The way of the cross for him is to reprioritize his time around the ordinary, day-to-day pastoring and leading of his people in the church rather than trying to build a larger platform that will garner even more applause for his gifts. He also needs to remember that the "good life from God" described in Scripture also includes suffering, setbacks, and the crucifixion of his pride.

Joan. Instead of taking on the entire burden of turning around the church, Joan encourages the lead pastor and the church board to enter a discernment process about what God's plans for the church might be. The way of the cross for her is to surrender her need to be seen as a success. Maybe she needs to allow that the best thing might actually be for the church to merge with another church, or even to close its doors, in order to receive the new thing God may want to do in all their lives.

I suspect that all three leaders might shrink back from these alternative responses to their circumstances, at least at first. I know that shrinking back was initially my response as God transitioned me slowly from a Christ-centered to a cross-centered lens to see how to live and follow him.

WORLDLY DISCIPLESHIP VERSUS JESUS'S DISCIPLESHIP

The question then becomes, what does it mean for us to be cross-centered—to follow the crucified Jesus in our context and moment in history?[4] The best way to get at an answer to this is to better understand the contrast between what Jesus taught and modeled about discipleship and what the religious leaders of his day taught and modeled.[5] In other words, to make a distinction between the world's discipleship and Jesus's discipleship. It comes down to four key differences:

The World's Discipleship	Jesus' Discipleship
Be popular.	Reject popularity. *(Be popular with me.)*
Be great.	Reject "greatness-ism." *(Be great with me.)*
Be successful.	Reject "success-ism." *(Be a success with me.)*
Avoid suffering and failure.	Embrace suffering and failure. *(Be faithful to me.)*

As we shall see, these four sets of characteristics overlap and interpret one another, yet they also merit separate treatment. In fact, each of the four descriptions of the world's discipleship are powerfully and deeply ingrained in the church. Just as Jesus taught the Twelve, we too must reject them categorically, not only because they are illusory and temporary, but because they damage us and the people we lead.

Let's begin with the first great challenge of popularity, which is a preoccupation with what others think.

1. Be Popular versus Reject Popularity

I vividly remember a conversation I had with a pastor of a large, prominent church when I was still in the early years of my ministry. I had just finished telling him about our commitment to racial reconciliation and to working among the poor. With a big grin on his face, he encouraged me to shift my focus to building a big church just as he had. "Pete, you don't get it," he said matter-of-factly. "When I walk into a room with a group of pastors, it's like the Red Sea parts. Why? Because of the size of our church. If you want people to listen to what you have to say, you'll need numbers behind you."

> **WORLD'S DISCIPLESHIP VERSUS JESUS'S DISCIPLESHIP**
>
> 1. Be popular versus reject popularity.
> 2. Be great versus reject great-ism.
> 3. Be successful versus reject success-ism.
> 4. Avoid suffering and failure versus embrace suffering and failure.

I thought, *This pastor is a godly fellow. Many people have come to Christ in his church. I've learned a lot from him.*

But I left feeling confused.

A few years later, I had coffee with another well-known pastor of an even larger church who encouraged me to open up an office in Manhattan, near the corridors of political and financial power. "Pete, you can't make an impact in Queens," he said. "The only way people in this city will know who you are is if you become a player on the large political platforms."

Again, I left feeling confused.

I left both conversations confused because both of these men were making a significant impact on our city and were trying to help me. Yet, I knew something about their counsel wasn't quite right, at least for me.

A common definition of popular is "to be liked, enjoyed, or admired by many people."[6] Who doesn't want to be popular? The problem is that it leads us to do and say things to impress other people, and to make decisions that we might not otherwise make.

It has taken me decades to grasp the enormous power of the temptation to be popular. In fact, it was one of the three temptations the devil used in an attempt to drive a wedge between Jesus and the Father. Satan, quoting Scripture, invited Jesus to throw himself down from the highest spot of the temple so people might believe in him (Matthew 4:5–6). At this point, Jesus was not popular. He was, in effect, invisible to them—just another face in the crowd. But Jesus refused to perform for recognition and left the pinnacle of the temple alone and unrecognized.

When the religious authorities, who were unimpressed with Jesus, asked for a sign, Jesus refused to do a miracle on demand (Matthew 16:1–4). In fact, Jesus always seemed to do his miracles as inconspicuously as possible. The loaves and fishes, for example, were not multiplied through an explosive thunderclap but almost invisibly, through the hands of the Twelve, until more than five thousand were fed. Jesus refused to act in ways to be admired or liked.

The desire to be popular was so deeply ingrained in the secular and religious cultures of the first century that Jesus publicly called out the Pharisees and teachers of the law, saying, "Everything they do is done for people to see" (Matthew 23:5). Jesus's disciples, on the other hand, were to utterly reject a showy spirituality to impress other people—whether it be in the way they gave, prayed, fasted, or offered any other service to God.[7]

Let me say this as clearly as possible: *Jesus denounced any activity that had traces of seeking the approval or admiration of others.* We are to give up all acting and every quest to be noticed by someone else, whether it be by building a larger or more unique ministry, accumulating more money or possessions, or advancing up a career ladder.

Jesus knew the weaknesses of the human heart; he knew that the desire to impress others would be a constant temptation. He said to the religious leaders, "How can you believe since you accept glory from one another but do not seek the glory that comes from the only God?"

(John 5:44). He knew the desire for popularity had poisoned their faith and their leadership. He also knew it had the potential to poison the discipleship of his followers as well.

We might like to think that we've advanced beyond the popularity concerns held by the religious leaders in Jesus's day. But most of us place a higher premium on what other people think than we realize. If you doubt that, consider if you've ever had any thoughts such as these:

> *How am I coming off as I preach this message and use this illustration?*
> *If I talk with that person about how they hurt me, will they see*
>   *me differently?*
> *If I share my hopes and dreams, will they think I'm selfish?*
> *Will my supervisor treat me differently if I share my struggles?*
> *How many likes or followers might I pick up if I post this on*
>   *social media?*

Often, our longing to be noticed and esteemed by others is so deep and unconscious that it can be difficult to recognize it for what it is. And yet, it surfaces in subtle but recognizable ways. For example, saying yes when we would rather say no, refusing to speak up because we don't want to "rock the boat," or remaining silent about our preferences and desires out of fear of what others might think.[8]

In my early ministry years, my desire to impress others led me to make decisions far outside of God's plan and timetable for our church. When other ministries seemed to grow quickly, I didn't want to be perceived as a failure, so I started ministries, and even churches, before we were ready. And because those new initiatives needed leaders, I released people into significant ministry roles prematurely. (I trust you can imagine what happened as a result.)

When God was seeking to mature me and our church through tests and trials, I was more concerned with how other pastors or leaders might view the slow, messy path we were on. Sadly, I allowed that self-imposed pressure to rob me, our family, and our church leadership of the many joys God had in store for us.

Another consequence of my need to impress others was that I inadvertently lied a lot. Like most people, I lied before I committed my life to Christ at age nineteen. What is more alarming, however, is how much lying I continued to do. I lied first and foremost to myself, then to others, and even to God in order to be a "good witness" as a young leader. I pretended things were okay when they were not. In order to keep the peace—even if it was a false peace—I was dishonest in difficult conversations.

When we did our annual review of key volunteer and paid positions in the church, I withheld honest feedback when there were improvements to be made. Why? I couldn't bear people not being "okay" with me. And if someone needed to be let go from a position, I was overly concerned about how that might reflect poorly on me. As a result, I often said nothing about legitimate concerns, finding it easier to spin a few facts rather than risk losing relationships.

The problem was that I wasn't truly free. Freedom comes when we no longer need to be somebody special in other people's eyes. *We are to be content to be popular with him alone.*

It is important to note that Jesus doesn't criticize the fundamental human desire to be popular, but he does redirect it. He wants us to shift our desire from focusing on people to focusing on the Father. At the end of our earthly journey, he wants to be able to say to each of us, "Well done, good and faithful servant" (Matthew 25:21). This is the only affirmation that will ever truly satisfy our desire for recognition. The longing to be popular—to be loved, enjoyed, and accepted—is God-given, but it is also unquenchable this side of heaven. Jesus wants us to know that God alone is the only deeply satisfying source of recognition. He knows that if the praise and notice of the whole world were given to us, we would still say, "It is too little."[9]

Thus, rejecting earthly popularity is essential for following the crucified Jesus and engaging in deeply transformative discipleship with him. But we also need to do the same thing with the world's idea of greatness.

2. Be Great versus Reject Greatness-ism

Every culture and field of human endeavor has its ways of honoring those who attain greatness. We award the Nobel Prize to recognize academic, cultural, or scientific achievements. There are Oscars and

Tonys for outstanding performance in film and on stage. We award medals to Olympic athletes, and trophies to World Cup and Super Bowl champions. We erect monuments, create days of remembrance, and even canonize those who do great things for humanity.

We also create definitions of greatness out of our unique cultures and families of origin. For example, since both my mother's and father's parents emigrated to the United States from Italy, they grew up with a drive to succeed that so often characterizes immigrant families. They then passed that drive on to my three siblings and me. Their greatness goals for each of us included graduating college, making a lot of money, and moving up the social class ladder. (My mom, on hearing that I was going to be a pastor, mumbled, "Well, don't be a loser. At least be like Billy Graham!")

> **WORLD'S DISCIPLESHIP VERSUS JESUS'S DISCIPLESHIP**
>
> 1. Be popular versus reject popularity.
> 2. **Be great versus reject greatness-ism.**
> 3. Be successful versus reject success-ism.
> 4. Avoid suffering and failure versus embrace suffering and failure.

Greatness in any given family or culture might include earning straight As in school, graduating from a prestigious university, becoming a lawyer or medical doctor, getting married and having children, becoming a pastor or vocational Christian worker. The list goes on.

That same dynamic plays out, often unconsciously, in ministry. Our desires for greatness might sound like this:

I want to build a great church with one-, two-, or even five-hundred people attending our services.

I want to build a great ministry that effectively reaches young people.

I want to lead a great small group that grows quickly.

I want to be a great board member who offers wisdom and direction to the ministry.

I want to be a great prayer team member who helps release God's power in people.

I want to be a great teacher of God's Word.

I want to be a great financial giver to ministries.

As a visionary who routinely eats three new ideas for breakfast, I love dreaming about great things our ministry could do for God. The danger is, again, the audience. For whom am I seeking to be great? What is the deeper, often unconscious, motive behind my visions and dreams?

Jesus does call us to greatness, but it is utterly different than the world's definition of greatness, which he condemns. The cultural-ized view of greatness most of us experience is what might be called "greatness-ism." As theologian Frederick Dale Bruner describes it, greatness-ism is "a major social-spiritual disease and a principal source of false faith."[10] Greatness-ism is what led the Pharisees and teachers of the law to view themselves as a cut above everyone else. Their knowl-edge of Scripture and their legalistic zeal earned them perks, such as the "first" or best seats in the synagogue, honorary titles, and distinctive clothing that set them apart from others. Their greatness-ism, however, contrasted with the life and ministry of Jesus that was anything but great by the religious and cultural standards of that day.

Jesus's beginnings were not great. He was born in a manger in a small village to a poor family. He had to flee as a fugitive and refugee to Egypt. He grew up in a small town called Nazareth that was considered "nowheres-ville." Unlike other prominent rabbis of the day, he did not study at any of the established rabbinical schools in Jerusalem.

Jesus's disciples were not great. His chosen staff and leadership team were Galileans and mostly blue-collar, uneducated fishermen. They were not impressive people of great influence or intellect. And they surely weren't setting the world on fire during their three years with Jesus.

Jesus's ministry was not great. Jesus seemed to run more of an ambulance ministry, driving around and picking up the crushed vic-tims of oppression, rather than working to overthrow the evil political, military, and economic structures of his day. Jesus's miracles happened mostly in the backwoods of Galilee, not in strategic places such as Jerusalem or Rome. The Pharisees and Sadducees, along with Herod and the Roman Empire, all remained in power. Jesus's command to his followers to love their enemies, in the context of the cruel oppression of the Romans, seemed a weak and ineffective strategy for social change.

Jesus's impact was not great. The small towns in which Jesus concentrated his ministry and miracles—such as Capernaum, Bethsaida, Chorazin, and even his hometown of Nazareth—rejected him. He didn't even seem to have the ability to convince Judas, his treasurer and one of the Twelve, to stick with him when things grew difficult. Even John the Baptist doubted him as he sat in prison: "Are you the one who is to come, or should we expect someone else?" (Matthew 11:3).

Jesus knew that, just as he had renounced greatness-ism when tempted by Satan, we too must make the same decision to categorically reject greatness-ism for the deadly threat it is. In fact, Jesus calls us to give up the whole idea of greatness and status completely—even in spiritual matters. So, in the same way we are to be popular with God, we are to be great with him as well, looking for his affirmation alone: "Well done, good and faithful servant!" (Matthew 25:21).

The pathway Jesus calls us to walk is an intentional move away from greatness-ism to being little or lowly. Jesus said, "Whoever takes the lowly position of this child is the greatest in the kingdom of heaven" (Matthew 18:4). Such lowliness is not abasement, self-deprecation, or a martyr complex. Instead, it is a humility that expresses itself in a willingness to be curious, open, flexible, and teachable—regardless of the title or position we hold. In other words, we do not always need to be in charge. In conversations, we don't engage in impression management to cover our weaknesses in the hope that people will think we are somebody. Nor do we limit the kinds of people from whom we can learn or by whom we can be led.

We choose to practice humility and servanthood by actually *being with* those who tend to be marginalized by the wider culture—the unattractive, the socially nonstrategic, the elderly, the mentally or physically handicapped, the prisoner, the battered, the poor. We join Jesus in being impressed by, and in awe of, people the world considers unimpressive. Like the apostle Paul, we are to internalize how the cross of Christ has put to death the old world of distinctions, divisions, and hierarchies. As a result, we "regard no one from a worldly point of view" (2 Corinthians 5:16).[11]

In following the crucified Jesus, we shift our focus from our great plans for God to the largely hidden work of doing small deeds of service for others. Toward this end, I regularly ask myself two questions:

- When are my plans and ambitions legitimately for the glory of God, and when do they cross the line into my own desire for greatness?
- What opportunities has God placed before me to be lowly with the lowly, to be little with the little?

The first question slows me down to ensure I am not making plans without God or rebelling against his limits. The second reminds me that it is crucial I be with the lowly, the poor, and those whom the world ignores—because it is through them that I meet Jesus (see Matthew 25:31–46).

This redefinition of greatness by Jesus leads us to the third core aspect of his reframing of reality for us as disciples—the rejection of worldly success.

3. Be Successful versus Reject Success-ism

Who doesn't want to be a success? We look up to and admire successful people. We pay extra attention to them. Being a success may truly be the world's most universal religion, one called *success-ism*. For this reason, we need to see success-ism for what it is—a counterfeit faith that has the power to separate us from Jesus.[12]

Remember, we live in a larger culture that believes bigger is *always* better—bigger profits, bigger influence, bigger impact. And the church more or less believes the same thing. We measure success by the numbers, and bigger is always the goal. If our

> **WORLD'S DISCIPLESHIP VERSUS JESUS'S DISCIPLESHIP**
>
> 1. Be popular versus reject popularity.
> 2. Be great versus reject great-ism.
> 3. **Be successful versus reject success-ism.**
> 4. Avoid suffering and failure versus embrace suffering and failure.

numbers are increasing, we feel great and consider our efforts a success. If they are not, we feel despondent and consider our efforts a failure. Which is why it is essential that we define success rightly. According to Jesus, success is becoming the person God calls you to become, and doing what God calls you to do—in his way, and according to his timetable.

This is so important that I ask that you read that sentence one more time. Slowly. *Success is becoming the person God calls you to become, and doing what God calls you to do—in his way, and according to his timetable.*

The apostle Peter went down swinging as Jesus led him, step by step, into a rejection of worldly success. Peter, like most leaders, wanted to change the world through Jesus. But the culture of success-ism was so deeply embedded in him that he resisted Jesus on this at every turn.

Peter simply could not reconcile his understanding of success with the crucifixion—with failures, rejections, and defeats; with mustard seeds and a few loaves and fishes. Despite three years of being with Jesus, he remained so infected with success-ism that, at Jesus's arrest, he could justify resorting to violence to protect it. With success as a supreme value, he didn't think twice about drawing a sword and cutting off the ear of the high priest's servant (Matthew 26:51).

We are not unlike the apostle Peter. Our success-ism drives us to make misguided decisions and to treat people in ways antithetical to the heart of Jesus.

At least 90 percent of pastors and leaders I speak with, young and old alike, experience an ironic consequence of success-ism. They feel like failures. Underperformers. Subpar representatives of Jesus.

"It's never enough," an associate pastor named Fran lamented to me. "I'm working six days a week and I still can't keep up. My husband complains and my two middle-school boys know I'm constantly distracted when I'm home. But what can I do? There just isn't enough time."

I know this ever-gnawing ache of the soul only too well, along with its crushing weight. In my early years of pastoring, it wasn't until I began the journey of emotionally healthy discipleship that the ache dissipated and the heavy weight began to lift.

What makes this so challenging when we begin serving and leading is that our relationship *with* God gets so wed to our work *for* God that the two become almost indistinguishable. When who we are—our identity as a loved daughter or son of God—becomes inseparable from our leadership role, we are especially vulnerable to one of the most subtle and treacherous temptations from the Evil One: to equate our worth with our success in ministry and leadership.

Few of us appreciate that the final temptation Satan posed to Jesus in the desert revolved around success (Matthew 4:8–9). Satan offers him immediate success in saving the world. Every person in the world would bow to him as Savior. And this could be accomplished without the agony of the crucifixion. Jesus could eliminate everything he knows is coming—a downward journey into failure and defeat. All he has to do is violate the Father's gift of limits (more about this in Chapter 5, "God's Gift of Limits").

Had Jesus succumbed to the temptation, he might have "succeeded" in getting the ministry work done, but he would have utterly failed by God's definition of success. He would *not* have done God's work, in God's way, according to God's timetable.

Theologian Frederick Dale Bruner aptly summarizes the real threat behind the success-ism temptation: "We will sometimes do absolutely anything to keep our work from failing. But the moment we do *absolutely anything* to keep our work for God from failing, we have made our work God, and perhaps without realizing it, we have worshipped Satan."[13]

For this reason, we must expose and reject the success-ism that so permeates our churches today and leads so often to a compromise in our integrity.[14] Remember, not every opportunity to expand the work of God is actually an invitation from God.

This unhealthy striving for worldly success also leads us to be even more resistant to another essential component of Jesus's discipleship—the unique way we are to approach suffering and failure.

4. Avoid Suffering and Failure versus Embrace Suffering and Failure

Contemporary churches immersed in Western culture have much in common with the Corinthian church of the first century. Being the wealthiest city in Greece and one of the biggest cities in the Roman Empire, Corinth was the New York City, Los Angeles, and Las Vegas of the ancient world.[15] People from around the world came to Corinth to "make it" there. The church was zealous, brilliant, and gifted but also beset with a wide assortment of problems—divisions, arrogance, poor treatment of weaker members, dangerous accommodations to culture, and a confused sexuality for singles and marrieds.

As Paul begins to address their questions and problems, he reminds them, "For I resolved to know nothing while I was with you except Jesus Christ and him crucified" (1 Corinthians 2:2). This is the lens through which Paul views leadership, relationships, discernment, and the church. For example, he refused to boast in his visions and revelations from God as a source of his authority. He pointed those questioning his leadership to his weaknesses. As he wrote to another church, "May I never boast except in the cross of our Lord Jesus Christ, through which the world has been crucified to me, and I to the world" (Galatians 6:14).[16]

> **WORLD'S DISCIPLESHIP VERSUS JESUS'S DISCIPLESHIP**
>
> 1. Be popular versus reject popularity.
> 2. Be great versus reject great-ism.
> 3. Be successful versus reject success-ism.
> 4. **Avoid suffering and failure versus embrace suffering and failure.**

The Corinthians forgot, much as we do today, that they were called to a way of life that reveals the glory of Christ in weakness and suffering, not in the escape or denial of the painful realities around them.[17] The cross was a scandal for them and it remains a scandal for us today. In contemporary religious life, "our stock-in-trade is 'positive thinking,' with its partner, avoidance—blocking out difficult and painful issues."[18] This is the very opposite of a way of life where God's power is revealed in weakness.

What does it look like for us to embrace God's way of weakness? It means, for example, that:

- I am willing to look foolish, even like I'm failing, and can wait on God rather than manipulate people and plans for numerical growth in my ministry;
- I am willing to be a true peacemaker, as Jesus modeled, and deal with conflicts rather than sweep them under the rug—even though the ministry may look worse, at least in the short run;
- I am willing to limit my plans and activities so as not to skimp on self-care or my relationships with those closest to me. I refuse to "fake it till I make it";

- I'm willing to take time to grieve the losses around me and trust God to reveal the treasures he has for me in them, and to take the necessary time to be present to people as Jesus was—even if it makes me look weak to those around me;
- I'm willing to be honest about what is happening in the ministry, and not exaggerate—even though it may hinder people's excitement to give financially.

Is it any wonder Jesus did not stop reminding the Twelve, again and again, that God's way of salvation is slow and small, a mustard seed to demonstrate the power is always God's and not ours?

Imagine if Peter had not been broken by his humiliating failures but was leading the church after Pentecost from a place of smugness and unteachability.

Imagine if Paul, with all his gifting, drive, and intellect, had not had a "thorn in the flesh" that he could not remove or pray away.

Imagine if Moses had not spent forty years in exile in Midian after murdering an Egyptian, or had not experienced the humiliations of unjust accusations and rebellions against his leadership during his forty years in the desert.

Suffering and failure have always been God's means to transform us from willful to willing, from swimming upstream against the current of God's love to floating downstream, trusting in him to take care of us. It is also the primary way he teaches us to be patient.

Jesus's greatest miracle was the resurrection. But his second greatest miracle was something he did *not* do. Jesus models patience for us when he refuses to use his power to come down from the cross. The temptation came in hurled insults from those who passed by: "Save yourself! Come down from the cross, if you are the Son of God!" (Matthew 27:40). Yet what looked like a colossal failure turned out to be a great victory. The worst moment in history became the world's greatest moment.

And so it is with us, if we are patient. Jesus had a choice—to leave the cross or to stay on it. We face the same choice whenever we're in situations where everything in us wants to "save ourselves" instead.

What does it look like to save ourselves, to come down from a cross? In my own life, I come down from the cross when I don't want to look like a failure. I launch initiatives out of impatience, make hasty decisions without taking the time to seek wise counsel, and frantically overwork out of fear the ministry might decline or stagnate.[19]

Ask yourself:

- In what ways do I try to avoid the suffering and failure Jesus might be setting before me?
- Before whom do I most dread looking foolish? Name them.

And rest assured, God wants to show you that your worst moments of failures and defeats may actually be your greatest moments of success in terms of God doing a transformative work in and through you.

In asking you to make the necessary changes to follow the crucified, not the Americanized, Jesus, I am not asking you to add one more item to your already overloaded schedule. I am asking you to make a U-turn and rearrange your life around an entirely new way of serving and leading for Jesus. This is nothing short of a groundbreaking and culture-defying act of rebellion against much of Western Christianity.

TAKE YOUR FIRST STEPS TO FOLLOW THE CRUCIFIED JESUS

You may be wondering at this point, "You want me to reject popularity, greatness-ism, and success-ism, and embrace suffering and failure? It might preach well but you have got to be kidding! How is it possible to live that free?"

To live this way is not only possible, it's what you were made for! And there are three essential and biblical practices you can use to begin your journey: relax in Jesus, detach for Jesus, and listen to Jesus.

Practice 1: Relax in Jesus

The day after Jesus feeds the five thousand and then mysteriously disappears, the crowds come looking for him. When they find him, there is this fascinating exchange:

> They asked him, "What must we do to do the works God requires?"
>
> Jesus answered, "The work of God is this: to believe in the one he has sent." (John 6:28–29)

When the people ask about the "works" God requires, they have in mind things such as prayer, acts of mercy, giving, or Bible study. Surprisingly, Jesus says there is only *one* work—"To believe in the one [God] has sent." This phrase *believe in* [*him*] means to *trust in him*—and not just once but continually—in an ongoing, moment-by-moment, and day-by-day kind of way.

Jesus issues this invitation to trust in him ninety-eight times in the Gospel of John. In fact, John states that the purpose of his entire gospel is "that you may believe [*be trusting, moment by moment*] that Jesus is the Messiah" (John 20:31). Theologian Frederick Dale Bruner captures the richness of this kind of trust when he writes, "'Relaxing in' is a good modern translation of 'trusting in' or 'believing in.'"[20] We relax by allowing ourselves to be held by him, regardless of the storms and circumstances in which we find ourselves.

Relax in Jesus.

If you think about it, isn't this the goal of everything we do in ministry, including worship, preaching, small groups, programming, classes, outreach, serving, giving? To get people to relax in Jesus? Jesus says that if we get this right—if we make it our work to relax in him—he will take care of the rest.

Relax.

This, of course, is easier to talk about than to live, especially when we are surrounded by anxiety or the ministry appears to be going backward rather than forward. And yet, it is precisely what Jesus modeled for us in his own ministry.

We sometimes forget that Jesus experienced a mass defection in which he lost thousands of disciples. After feeding the five thousand, large crowds began to follow Jesus. However, when he subsequently began to teach hard truths about the need for people to eat his flesh and drink his blood, the crowds were offended and quit following him (John 6:66). Thousands abandoned him. Only the Twelve remained, and one of them was Judas!

In responding to the disbelief of the crowds, and then later, the disciples, Jesus makes three statements, each of which offer insights into how he was able to relax in God:

- "All those the Father gives me will come to me" (John 6:37).
- "No one can come to me unless the Father who sent me draws them" (John 6:44).
- "This is why I told you that no one can come to me unless the Father has enabled them" (John 6:65).

Even as thousands turn back, Jesus relaxes, grounded in a deep sense of the Father's sovereignty and plan. He understands that, ultimately, it is the Father who draws disciples, and the Father who keeps them there. Regardless of the outcome, Jesus trusts that the Father is responsible for his mission and will send the right people to him. He models a steady contentment in doing God's will, in God's way, according to God's timetable.

How relaxed would you be in similar circumstances?

Chances are, most of us would probably respond along the lines of what Jesus's brothers did, which was to panic. They tell him to get to Jerusalem as soon as possible to get his numbers back up. But Jesus didn't always work in what we might consider a strategic way. He lived by the Father's strategy, not by what anyone else considered best practices. Jesus simply told his brothers, "The right time for me has not yet come; for you any time is right" (John 7:6).

Jesus rejected popularity, success-ism, and greatness-ism, and embraced suffering and failure—at least in the world's eyes. He knew the disciples who stayed with him were given to him by the Father. The Father was in charge of the mission. Everything was fine—even if things looked like they were falling apart.

He relaxed.

So, what does it look like to "relax" within the context of ministry and leadership? Here are a few of the markers to look for.

I Know I Am Relaxing in Jesus When I Am . . .

- Enjoying communion with Jesus even in the midst of disappointments and storms.
- Experiencing a lack of anxiety in my body.
- Not doing for others what they can and should do for themselves.
- Maintaining my rhythms of *being with* Jesus in seasons of great pressure.
- Less and less triggered by things going awry.
- Present to the beauty and wonder of those around me.
- Enjoying a deep sense of knowing I have nothing to gain and nothing to lose—I want only God's will.
- Experiencing deep contentment in caring for the people God has entrusted to me.
- Receiving God's gift of limits rather than fighting, ignoring, or denying them.
- Discerning and embracing the season in which God has placed me.

Practice 2: Detach for Jesus

The goal of the Christian life is loving union with God, to allow God and his will to have full access to every area of our lives. This loving union with God is a oneness that is best understood by the analogy of a marriage, in which two people become one flesh and yet also remain separate from one another. This is the answer to Jesus's prayer, "Father, just as you are in me and I am in you, may they also be in us" (John 17:21).

The key to sharing this rich life of oneness with God is found in a practice called *detachment*. Unlike the cold detachment that we might expect from a judge or an accountant calculating our taxes, our motive for this kind of detachment is being with Jesus. Jesus speaks of detachment as losing our lives that we might find them (see Mark 8:35–36). Paul describes it as not clinging or holding to anything, whether it be marriage, sorrow, joy, or anything we possess for the sake of Christ. He writes:

> From now on those who have wives should live as if they do not; those who mourn, as if they did not; those who are happy, as if they were not; those who buy something, as if it were not theirs to keep; those who use the things of the world, as if not engrossed in them. For this world in its present form is passing away." (1 Corinthians 7:29–31)

In other words, we relinquish all possessiveness and self-will.

Meister Eckhart (1260–1328), a Dominican monk, pastor, and theologian from Germany, uses the story of Mary, the mother of Jesus, to teach the practice of detachment. Faced with the loss of reputation, security, and her dreams, Mary emptied herself of her will for her life to radically surrender herself to the birth of Jesus in her. In the same way, argues Eckhart, we must be emptied of all created things to be full of God and what he wants to birth in us. He writes, "To be empty of all created things is to be full of God and to be full of created things is to be empty of God."[21]

What does this mean practically? Many things. But here are three to start:

- We are open to the unfolding of events and circumstances in our life, accepting everything, not attaching to any earthly experience or goal, but trusting God is orchestrating all things for our good, his glory, and the good of the world.
- We set goals and direction for our lives and ministry, yet release attachment to any particular outcome. We engage in active service to Jesus with a passionate, yet detached activism, recognizing we cannot manipulate or predict what he wants to do.
- We are prayerful, not to get what we want, but to surrender our will to God's will, recognizing that unhealthy attachments are a reflection of our core spiritual problem: self-will.

Here is how relaxing played out in one of the most difficult decisions I ever had to make in ministry.

I had been the lead pastor at New Life Fellowship Church for twenty-two years when it became clear that I needed to initiate a succession process over the next four years. As we began work with a consultant to execute a solid plan, I was acutely aware that God might not send a candidate we would consider "right" within that timeframe. And so I wrestled with questions: *Might God want the church to wander in the wilderness for some time? Might it be God's will for New Life to fall apart for a season, and to send a message that, even when we practice emotionally healthy discipleship, it's no guarantee that everything works out the way we want? Might God want to scatter the people of New Life to serve and bless other local churches?*

My work throughout the entire four-year process was to release the outcome to Jesus as we worked through the many ups and downs of the process.[22] It wasn't easy. In fact, it required daily, repeated surrender. I am profoundly aware that God's orchestration of a positive transition to a new lead pastor was a grace and gift, enabling New Life Fellowship Church to blossom in ways that might not have happened had we not done the hard work of positioning ourselves to let go and relax—regardless of the outcome.[23]

Practice 3: Listen to Jesus

Even the best of Jesus's leadership team—Peter, James, and John—were not good listeners. We see this clearly when Jesus invites them to a high mountain where he is transfigured and they see the heavenly glory of Jesus, along with Moses and Elijah (Matthew 17:2).

We might have expected Peter to fall on his face before such a jaw-dropping, overpowering, and dazzling sight. Or at least wait and listen. Instead, Peter does what we so often do. He sees a door of opportunity and interrupts with a plan of his own. He suggests they put up three shelters as a witness to what God is doing!

But he doesn't get very far with his plan. God himself interrupts Peter, saying, "Listen to him [Jesus]!" (Matthew 17:5). Jesus had been talking with Peter about his crucifixion and its implications for discipleship, but he wasn't listening.

Why? Because the direction Jesus is going appears counterproductive and doesn't make sense to Peter.

I relate to this particular incident more than I care to admit. I spent many years leading for Jesus but *not* listening to him. Peter didn't think he was doing anything other than following his best thoughts. So did I. The problem was that his best thoughts were leading him and others astray. The same thing happens when we follow our best ideas without listening first—we hurt ourselves and those we lead.

God's word to Peter is God's word to us: *Listen to Jesus.*

Let's face it. We all want a spiritual life, but we prefer to be in charge of it and have it unfold according to our schedule and in our way. But following Jesus is not first doing things for him; it is first listening to him speak and then doing what he says. That is why listening to Jesus is more important than listening to any other person, project, program, or cause in the world.

This kind of listening, however, is not a quick and occasional check-in with God. It is a deep listening that allows God's direction to do its full work in us so that it explodes with power inside us, even if what he asks us to do is as countercultural as rejecting popularity, greatness-ism, success-ism, and embracing failure and suffering.

For the first five-hundred years of the church, this practice of intentional listening was referred to as *discretion* and was considered the most precious spiritual gift, or charism, one could have.[24] It was understood that without discretion, individuals and faith communities could be easily misguided and ruined. In fact, all abbots of monastic communities were to be distinguished by their wisdom in discretion. Spiritual leaders who lacked discretion were considered dangerous because they unknowingly gave people burdens they could not bear, and offered superficial or misguided spiritual counsel.

Discretion is the practice of waiting with prayerful expectation to see what unfolds. It has the humility and patience to discern when to leave things alone, knowing when our interference will only complicate things. Flowing from a space of silence and stillness, discretion gives us, as the apostle Paul wrote, the keen ability to distinguish between good and evil spirits (1 Corinthians 12:10). Moreover, it enables us to exercise self-control, and to wait.

One of the most striking aspects of the classic teaching on discretion is the emphasis to humbly submit our best discernment to wise elders in the faith. Why? So we can "discern what is correct, and in particular, avoid excess of any kind—even of an apparent good."

That is why, both in our decision making in general and when we are considering new exciting opportunities, a commitment to grow in listening and discretion may be one of the most important things we can do.

I had to practice discretion recently when we faced a crucial turning point in the ministry we lead called Emotionally Healthy Discipleship. While the organization is a nonprofit, we function organically as a ministry of New Life Fellowship Church. Geri and I are set apart to bring the riches developed over decades at New Life to the global church. We function with one full-time executive director and seven to eight part-time contract employees who report to her. With this small team, we were surprised when the ministry began to experience explosive growth in North America and around the world, especially after we released *The Emotionally Healthy Discipleship Course.*

This growth put enormous pressure on us to build out the organization as the demands and requests for help far exceeded our limited capacity to respond. A friend who is also a nationally recognized consultant spent time with us and recommended that, even if we kept organizational expansion to a minimum, we should plan to add eight to ten full-time employees with fifteen or more part-timers and target a $6 to $7 million operating budget within a few years. For well over a year, I wrestled with this. The need was banging at the door. We could do it. Yet Geri and I knew our greatest contribution was in developing high-quality content, mentoring, and training churches to implement Emotionally Healthy Discipleship.

Our discretion process culminated in a board meeting in which members shared their clear sense from God that we keep Emotionally Healthy Discipleship as a ministry with only one full-time employee, and that Geri and I concentrate on what we do best, mentoring and content development. After a year of deep listening and communal discretion, we decided to do the best we could with our limited resources and to trust God with the rest. The fruit of that listening has been great peace and fruitfulness beyond anything we could have imagined.

TAKE COMFORT, YOU ARE NOT ALONE

Taking your next steps to relax in Jesus, to detach for Jesus, and to listen to Jesus is countercultural and prophetic, especially since it's unlikely you are living in a monastic community with built-in structure and support. You can expect starts and stops, successes and failures, as you figure out what works best for you in light of your unique calling, responsibilities, limits, and temperament.

What is most important is that you take the long view of the call of God on your life—and on the lives of those you influence—to follow the crucified, not the Americanized, Jesus. *Relax*, allowing Jesus to hold you. *Detach*, surrendering your self-will and plans to him. And *listen*. You can bank on the reality that Jesus's commitment and ability to speak to you is far greater than your commitment and ability to listen to him.

Chapter Five

Embrace God's Gift of Limits

Once upon a time, there lived a man who had given a great deal of thought and effort to determine what he wanted from life. Then one day, a door opened for him to actually live his dream. But the opportunity would be available only for a short time, and he would have to embark on a long journey.

He began walking and grew more and more excited as he envisioned his future dream becoming a reality. As he hurried along, however, he came to a bridge high above a dangerous, rapidly flowing river.

As he started across the bridge, he noticed a stranger approaching him from the opposite direction. The man had a rope wrapped many times around his waist. The rope looked like it might stretch to a length of at least thirty feet.

The stranger began to unwrap the rope as he walked. Just as the two men were about to meet, the stranger said, "Pardon me, sir, would you be so kind as to hold the end of this rope for me?"

Without thinking, almost instinctively, the man reached out and took the rope.

"Thank you," said the stranger. He then added, "Two hands now, and remember, hold tight."

At that point, the stranger jumped off the bridge!

The strong pull from the now-extended rope was so strong it almost dragged the man over the side of the bridge into the treacherous river below.

He shouted over the railing, "What are you trying to do?"

"Just hold tight," the stranger called back.

This is ridiculous, the man thought. He began trying to haul the stranger up, but the task was beyond his strength.

"Why did you do this!?" he yelled in frustration over the edge.

"Remember," said the stranger, "if you let go, I will die."

"But I cannot pull you up," the man cried.

"I am your responsibility," said the stranger.

"I did not ask for it," the man said.

"If you let go, I am lost," repeated the stranger.

The man began to look around for help, but no one was within sight.

He began to think about his predicament. Here he was eagerly pursuing a unique opportunity to fulfill his dream, and now he was being sidetracked for who knows how long.

Maybe I can tie the rope somewhere, he thought. He examined the bridge carefully, but there was no way to get rid of his newfound burden.

Again he yelled over the edge, "What do you want?"

"Just your help," came the answer.

"How can I help? I cannot pull you in, and there is no place to tie the rope while I find someone else who could help you."

"Just keep hanging on," replied the dangling stranger. "My life is in your hands."

The man was stumped. *If I let go, all my life I will always regret I let this stranger die. If I stay, I will never reach my dreams or destiny. Either way, this will haunt me forever.*

Time passed. Still no one came. The man became keenly aware that it was almost too late to resume his journey. If he didn't leave immediately, he wouldn't arrive in time.

Finally, a new idea came to him. "Listen," he explained to the man hanging below, "I think I know how to save you." He could not pull the stranger up solely by his own efforts, but if the stranger would shorten the rope by wrapping it around his waist again and again, together they could do it.

But the dangling man had no interest.

"You mean you won't help?" he shouted to the stranger. "I can't hold on much longer!"

"If you don't, I will die," came the reply.

At this moment, a revelation came to the man on the bridge, an idea that, until this moment, he would never have considered.

"Listen carefully," the man said, "I mean what I am about to say."

The dangling stranger looked up, hopeless and despondent.

"I will not accept the position of choice for your life, only for my own," the man said. "From this moment on, I give the power of choice for your own life back to you!"

"What do you mean?" the stranger asked, clearly afraid.

"I mean, simply, it's up to you. You decide your future. I will be the counterweight. You do the pulling and bring yourself up. I will tug some from here."

The man unwound the rope from around his waist and braced himself to be a counterweight.

"You cannot mean what you say," the stranger shrieked. "You would not be so selfish. I am your responsibility. What could be so important that you'd let me die?!"

After a long silence, the man on the bridge said slowly, "I accept your choice."

He let go of the rope and continued on his journey over the bridge.[1]

THE CHALLENGE OF NAVIGATING OUR LIMITS

It's just a fable, but it packs a punch, doesn't it?

At one time or another, I think every Christian leader has had the experience of being the man on the bridge. For too many of us, it's even become a way of life. We want to help people who have fallen off the bridge, and we understand that following Jesus requires sacrifice. So, we do our best to pull people up, often at the expense of our own emotional and spiritual health. And then, many of the people we thought we had finally rescued end up falling or jumping off another bridge the next month!

For years, I reached out and grabbed people's ropes. Once I had their ropes and they were dangling, I felt stuck. *How could I let go? I'm a Christian. Wouldn't Jesus pull them up? If I don't pull them up, am I being selfish? How long do I need to put my own dreams and hopes on hold? Or does what I want even matter since I am a servant of Christ? Where is everyone else? Why does it have to be me holding on to all of these ropes?*

As it is with so many others who serve in relationally demanding environments, I slowly became resentful toward those who were not "suffering" for God as I was. In Jesus's parable, the Good Samaritan had come upon just one person on the side of the road (Luke 10:29–37). I felt as if I routinely had fifteen at a time lining up on the bridge, each one placing a rope in my hands. And I had many moments when I wished I couldn't see them all. Merely knowing all the needs around me left me feeling like each one was yet another rope that had been laid in my hands.

At one point, a single mom with six children under age ten lived across the street from us. Geri and I would sometimes give her a break and take care of her children. But the needs of that family were intense and seemingly endless, which raised all kinds of questions. *Should we give her a break next week as well, and then the week after that? Should we mentor her children? Support them financially? When is it appropriate for us to stop? How do I know if meeting this need is a "good hard" that comes with following Jesus, or if it's crossed the line into a "destructive hard" that damages my soul and perpetuates immaturity in others?*

I truly had no way to think about answering these questions. What I lacked was an understanding of God's gift of limits, which is essential in discerning what to do, or not do, for a neighbor in need.

A core mark of emotionally healthy discipleship is a deep theological and practical understanding of limits. Without that, we severely compromise our ability to love God, ourselves, and others over the long haul. Healthy limits are important in every area of life—be it the workplace, parenting, marriage, friendships, or dating—but they are especially necessary for those of us who lead in the new family of Jesus called the church.

They're necessary because limits are a deeply spiritual issue. When we surrender to them, we acknowledge that we are not God. God is God and we are not. Instead, we accept that we are his creatures, and we surrender to the reality that he alone is in charge of the world.

LIMITS ARE A DEEPLY SPIRITUAL ISSUE

How we choose to understand and respond to our limits goes to the core of our relationship with God. It's so foundational, in fact, that the Evil One made limits a target of his strategy from the very beginning.

Limits in the Garden

Adam and Eve's original sin was to defy God's gift of limits. Think about it. God gave them enormous freedom in the garden of Eden. They were to enjoy their work and their achievements. Then, without explanation, God set a boundary: "You are free to eat from any tree in the garden; but you must not eat from the tree of the knowledge of good and evil, for when you eat from it you will certainly die" (Genesis 2:16–17). This was no random limit. The tree of the knowledge of good and evil, right in the middle of the garden, confronted them with God's authority.

God wanted Adam and Eve to trust and surrender to his goodness and love. They were to bow before his incomprehensible ways. Knowing this, the serpent crafted a temptation to defy God's limit by convincing Adam and Eve that God was not good after all. In fact, God's limit was an indicator of his stinginess, not his love. "'You will not certainly die,' the serpent said to the woman. 'For God knows that when you eat from it your eyes will be opened, and you will be like God, knowing good and evil'" (Genesis 3:4–5).

So, rather than receive God's limit, Adam and Eve became convinced God might be withholding something good from them. They succumbed to the Evil One's temptation and chose to "be like God," to be *un*limited. The consequences of their choice remain with us to this day.

Fortunately, however, the story doesn't end with the first Adam.

Limits in the Ministry of Jesus

It's no accident that the apostle Paul makes a direct connection between Adam and Jesus, referring to him as the second Adam (Romans 5:12–21). In order to reverse the consequences of the fall, Jesus also had to face temptations from the Evil One around the issue of limits. When he was tempted three times by the devil in the wilderness, trust in his Father required embracing limits—specifically, allowing his immediate needs to remain unmet.

In the first temptation, the devil begins, "If you are the Son of God, tell these stones to become bread" (Matthew 4:3). Jesus had the power to call down manna from heaven or to create bread from stones, but he didn't. Instead, he waits and embraces the Father's timing for him. Limits.

In the second temptation, Satan takes Jesus to the highest point in the holy city and invites him to jump off, demonstrating to the multitudes that God is really with him. Jesus knows he must wait on God for his timing. He embraces God's limits and walks down the temple steps. There is no miracle. No people believing in him. Again, limits.

In the third temptation, Jesus is taken to a high mountain and shown the magnificent kingdoms of the world. These can all be his—now. All Jesus needs to do is skip over the God-given limit of a slow timetable with suffering and the cross. But he doesn't. Instead, he humbly bows to the Father's wisdom. Limits yet again.

Jesus continued to embrace limits during his three-year ministry.

He did not heal every sick and demon-possessed person. He did not build a large ministry in Capernaum when they begged him to remain in that city (Mark 1:21–45). He refused to let certain people follow him, such as the man from whom he had cast out a legion of demons (Mark 5:18–20). He prayed all night and chose only twelve to be closest to him; others were undoubtedly disappointed. Jesus did not go in person to meet the needs of everyone in Europe, Africa, Asia, or the Americas.

Yet he prayed at the end of his life, "I have . . . [finished] the work you gave me to do" (John 17:4).

This extraordinary contentment and peace that we observe in Jesus' ministry as he embraces his limits is also modeled by someone we've already talked about—the towering figure of John the Baptist.

Limits in the Life of John the Baptist

The life of John the Baptist offers us a wonderful example of what it means to embrace God's gift of limits. Massive crowds flocked to him as he began to preach. Yet once Jesus began his ministry, crowds that formerly followed John switched their allegiance. They began leaving John to follow Jesus. Some of John's followers were upset by this dramatic turn of events. They complained to John, "Everyone is going to him" (John 3:26).

John, out of a theology of limits, replied, "A person can receive only what is given them from heaven" (John 3:27). He was essentially able to say, "I accept my limits, my humanity, my declining popularity. I am not the center of the world. God is. He must increase; I must decrease."

As you can observe in these three case studies—Adam and Eve, Jesus, and John the Baptist—what we do with our limits has far-reaching consequences, for good or ill. Imagine the implications, for example, if John the Baptist had refused to embrace God's limits and insisted on leading a large, growing movement? What might have happened, both to him and to those who followed him? Confusion, delays in the larger work of God, and relationship conflicts between the followers of Jesus and John, to name a few, would have been the order of the day.

It is no different in our ministries today.

THE HIGH PRICE OF MINISTRY WITHOUT LIMITS

In my early years of ministry, I had no idea there was such a thing as God's *gift* of limits. I always felt as if I had too little time and too much to do. I felt chronically pressured, frustrated that I had so little margin or flexibility in my life. It seemed like I would never be finished meeting the needs around me. Still, I kept trying. I asked God for help and worked on my priorities and time management. I attended seminars to help me lead and delegate more effectively. None of it helped.

What was the problem?

I had never connected a theology of limits—that limits are a good gift from God—to following and serving Jesus.

Our failure to understand how boundaries and limits apply to serving Christ almost caused Geri and me to leave the pastorate. I know pastors who started out enthusiastically serving others, but later quit because they didn't know how to navigate ministry bridges without accepting every rope people handed them. We had not been trained to help people take responsibility for themselves, nor how to discern our level of responsibility for them.

As a result, I spent years as a leader trying to be someone I was not. I thought if I could become more like other successful leaders, I could finally get my life and my ministry under control. So I attended conferences and read books that peddled "ecclesiastical pornography," to use Eugene Peterson's term.[2] They all promised me a church free from the problems of regular sinners like ours. The best and brightest programs and people were highlighted. The unwritten promise was that if I could be and do as these leaders had done, then our church would be equally large and prosperous.

Or so I thought.

The problem was that God had not given me the abilities, the capacities, or the calling he had given those other leaders. I brought different strengths to the task of leadership. My unwillingness to embrace my own limits led me down paths God never intended for me. I spent years attempting to live out a script for my life that was not mine. While the script needed an actor, I was auditioning for the wrong part.

God has given me three to five talents. He did not give me eight or ten. My parents told me I could be anything I wanted in life—a doctor, musician, professor, writer, a professional athlete. I tried to play basketball like Michael Jordan in high school. I couldn't. We lost most of our games. Yet I didn't get the message. I could *not* do anything I wanted. Yes, I had gifts and potential, but I also had significant limits. And instead of seeing those limits as God's gift, I considered them obstacles to power and control![3]

What I couldn't see was that in bypassing or denying my limits, I was bypassing and missing God as well. And I brought this same dynamic into the church—from the pace of multiplying churches, to the addition of new ministries and small groups, to the expectations we placed on staff and volunteers.

For years, we simply kept up the same feverish level of activity, ignorant of the Bible's teaching on limits as a gift. For that we paid a high price, in our personal lives, in our families, and in the ministry as a whole.

We hadn't yet discovered that there was another way, one that required a discernment process and a nuancing around the two kinds of limits.

DISCERNING THE TWO KINDS OF LIMITS

Receiving the gift of limits requires asking two primary questions on a regular basis:

- What limits do I need to *receive* and submit to joyfully as God's invitation to trust him?
- What limits is God asking me to *break through* by faith so that others might know him, or so that I might become the person he intends?

The first question refers to limits we accept as gifts because we are to surrender to them. This is one of the most counterintuitive, difficult truths in Scripture to embrace, especially for Type-A leaders. The second type of limit offers a different kind of gift because God uses these limits to manifest his power and to do miracles. We love breaking through these limits because they give us the outcomes we want, such as healing and answers to prayer. The ministry expands, our day-to-day life becomes easier, and God's name is glorified—all at the same time!

Let's take a closer look at both types of limits, starting with the first and more difficult—the limits we are to receive.

Limits to Receive

It takes great maturity for a church to identify new ministry opportunities and yet choose *not* to take advantage of them. How many services should we have on Sunday? What about a Saturday night service? If we are two hundred people, why not become four hundred or eight hundred or a thousand? One of the most powerful examples of this is found in the life of David at the height of his ministry.

David's power had been consolidated. He was riding a wave of popularity and was regularly publishing powerful psalms of worship to God. He desperately wanted to build God a temple so that the surrounding nations might know the God of Israel. He had the money, the labor, and the good will of the entire nation behind him. Even Nathan the prophet encouraged him to go for it.

God, however, said no.

This was one of the most critical moments in King David's life. It would either qualify or disqualify him as a true king with a heart for God.[4]

It's not hard to imagine the depth of David's disappointment and embarrassment. What would all the other pagan kings around him think? They had all built magnificent temple structures to their gods. David, and all Israel, looked weak by comparison.

David, the Bible says, sat down and prayed. By the time it was over, he submitted to God's limit, trusting a divine plan he could not see. "Our God is in heaven; he does whatever pleases him" (Psalm 115:3).

David wrestled with the core spiritual issue we all need to face when trying to live within our God-given limits: *Can I trust that God is good and really has a grip on all things?*

David accepted that his knowledge was too limited to perceive God's intent and why God said no to his plans. Meanwhile, David was faithful to his God-given limits and prepared the materials for Solomon, his son, to build the temple in the next generation.

Such moments and decisions are, of course, equally critical for us.

A limit is a gift few of us want. The question is why?

The answer is twofold. First, almost everything in the messaging coming from the wider culture resists this countercultural truth found so clearly in Scripture. And secondly, it touches on the root of our rebellion against God, just as it did for Adam and Eve in the garden.

And yet, limits offer us so many gifts. They protect us so we don't hurt ourselves, others, or God's work. They keep us grounded and humble, reminding us we are not in charge of running the world. They break our self-will. They are God's means to give us, and our ministries, direction—if we will listen. They are one of the primary ways we grow in wisdom. And perhaps most importantly, limits are places we encounter God in ways that would otherwise be impossible.

In order to discern God's will around our limits, we must first identify what our unique set of personal limits looks like. This requires an honest assessment not only of the wide variety of limits we face, but also their degrees of severity. Here are six key areas of life to consider as a start.

What are the limits of your personality and temperament? Do you get more energy from being with people (extrovert) or from being with yourself (introvert)? Are you more spontaneous and creative, or controlled and orderly? Are you more easygoing and relaxed, or focused and driven? On boldness and risk-taking, I scored a ten on a scale of one to ten (with ten being the highest). I was willing to be Robin Hood and take on Nottingham for a grand vision. At the same time, I also scored a ten on sensitivity. The latter would qualify me to be a counselor or social worker, not the CEO of a large company. The Enneagram, Myers-Briggs, and DiSC are all helpful tools to help you discover more about the limits of your personality and temperament.

What are the limits of your current season of life? Your season of life is also a God-given limit. Ecclesiastes teaches us, "There is a time for everything, and a season for every activity under the heavens" (Ecclesiastes 3:1–2). There are seasons when you may be needed at home with small children, perhaps with special needs. There are seasons we experience physical or emotional challenges or external crises that alter our life course. There are seasons when, because of health reasons, our parents need us. There are seasons of financial prosperity and times of struggle. There are seasons for intensive studying and further schooling. There are seasons for high levels of activity. And there are seasons to step back from responsibilities and grieve a significant loss.

What are the limits of your marriage or singleness? If you are married, that is a limit. If you are single, that is a different kind of limit. The marriage vow to be one flesh with another person informs every decision we make. One major reason we did not launch a Saturday or Sunday evening service when I was lead pastor at New Life was because of our marriage and family limits. If you are single, you need to ask: *What do I need to do today to lead out of a healthy singleness for Christ?* And the same question applies to couples: *What do I need to do today to lead out of a healthy marriage for Christ?* Carving out time to give and receive love in healthy community and engaging in self-care are non-negotiables for everyone.[5]

What are the limits of your emotional, physical, and intellectual capacities? Your emotional, physical, and intellectual capacities are also a God-given limit. I have a large capacity for people and complexity in my work. I love reading four to five books at a time. At the same time, if I work all day with people for more than two consecutive days, I find myself lethargic and depressed. I need time to read, pray, and be alone. I cannot work a seventy-hour week physically, emotionally, or spiritually. I also need three to five minutes for transitioning from one meeting to another in order to be centered and attentive.

When we age physically, we find our bodies cannot do what they used to. When we are young and without much life experience, certain doors remain closed to us. If we have a physical or emotional disability or a sickness, we may find this keeps us from going down a path we may have planned.

Anger, depression, and fears often function as "check oil" lights to slow us down, informing us that something is not right on the inside of the engine of our lives. This is one key way God stops me, limits the pace of my life, and gets my attention.

What are the limits of your family of origin? Your family of origin also has God-given limits and gifts. If we will look for the hand of God moving in our family history, even in the most painful moments, we will find golden nuggets in that rocky soil. Abuse, neglect, abandonment, poverty, oppression, and so on may cause us to feel we are "behind," always trying to catch up. God sees it differently.

The limits I inherited from my family turned out to be gifts, once I embraced them. I find myself more dependent on God, more sensitive, and less judgmental of others. I love others better as I encourage them to joyfully live within their God-given limits.

What are the limits of your time? You have only one life to live. You can't do it all. I would like to try living in Asia, Europe, Africa, and a rural area in the United States. I would like to try a few different professions. I can't. My time on earth, like yours, is running out.

Each decade of our lives thrusts us into a different season—our teen years, twenties, thirties, forties, fifties, sixties, seventies, and beyond, each presenting us with different types of limits. Scripture explicitly calls us to pray for wisdom about our limited time: "Teach us to number our days that we may gain a heart of wisdom" (Psalm 90:12).

We discover, as Jacob did during his flight from his brother Esau, that, "The LORD is in this place, and I did not know it" (Genesis 28:16 NKJV). God reveals himself to us, and to the world, through limits in unique yet powerful ways—if we have eyes to see. Consider these examples from Scripture:

- It was within the limit of five barley loaves and two fish that Jesus was revealed as the Bread of Life. The miracle of feeding the five-thousand men (three to four times that many counting women and children)[6] is so important that, except for the resurrection, it is the only miracle included in all four Gospels.
- It was within the limit of a three-hundred-person army that Gideon prevailed against 135,000 Midianites.
- It was within the limits of Moses's slowness of speech (Exodus 4:10–12) and age (eighty years old) that he led two to three million of God's people out of Egypt.
- It was within Jeremiah's melancholy temperament that God gave him insights about God's grief and heart of love for his people.
- It was within Hosea's painful marriage that he was given one of the greatest revelations of God's love for his people that tens of millions ponder to this day.

If any of these biblical heroes had rebelled against God's limits, they would have missed what God wanted to do in and through them. Put simply, limits are often God's gifts in disguise.

We see only a small part of God's plan at any point in time. His ways are not our ways. But what he does in and through our limits is more than we could ever accomplish in our own strength. Allow me to illustrate with one of my favorite stories.

It comes from an ancient Hasidic tale that points out our tendency to want to live out someone else's life instead of embracing the limits of our own. Rabbi Zusya, when he was an old man, said, "In the coming world, they will not ask me: 'Why were you not Moses?' They will ask me, 'Why were you not Zusya?'"[7] The true vocation for every human being is, as Kierkegaard said, "the will to be oneself."[8]

One of the indicators we are on the road to spiritual maturity is when we live joyfully within our God-given limits. The problem is that most of us resent limits—in ourselves and in others. We expect far too much from ourselves and often live frustrated, disappointed, or even angry lives as a result. In fact, much of burnout is a result of giving what we do not possess.

Once we embrace our limits, we can then help our ministry, and those who serve in it, to embrace their limits as well. I've covered a lot of ground on *receiving* the gift of limits because it lies at the root of so much rebellion against God, especially when it is done in the midst of our work *for* God. This remains one of my greatest spiritual challenges to this day. At the same time, Scripture offers us many biblical examples of God's servants *breaking through* their limitations by the power of God. Many (including myself) have failed to understand this second aspect of limits as well and have needlessly stunted the explosive work of God in and through them.

Perhaps you're wondering, "I think I've done that too. But how do I know?"

Once again, I'm glad you asked.

Limits to Break Through

The second way in which we experience limits as a gift is by breaking through them. Here are the crucial discernment questions we need to ask: *Which limits are God asking me to break through by faith for the sake of his name in the world? What are the limits of immaturity that God is asking me to break through in my personal life?*

What does it look like to break through limits by faith? Allow me to illustrate this biblically and then personally.

God called many of his servants to break through their limitations in supernatural ways.

- Sarah was ninety and Abraham "as good as dead" (Romans 4:19). Yet, God made Sarah a mother of nations.

- Elijah was a prophet prone to serious bouts of depression, and yet he was mightily used by God.
- The twelve disciples were not highly educated, naturally gifted, or well networked. They had no prior leadership experience that would have prepared them to lead the most important movement of human history.
- Timothy, apparently fearful and shy by nature, was called by God to lead a large, influential, yet difficult church at Ephesus, which was beset by divisions, problems, and conflicts.
- Mary was a teenager from a poor family, living in a small town of fifty to two-hundred people in Nazareth, at a time when young girls pregnant outside of marriage was beyond scandalous. She could have been subject to stoning. Yet she was God's chosen vessel to give birth to Jesus.

God used each of these individuals in extraordinary ways as they broke through their limits by faith. I wish I had learned this same lesson much earlier in my own life and leadership.

My failure to respond when God invited me to break through a significant limit almost caused me to quit serving as lead pastor of New Life, which meant I would have missed out on leading our church into her best years under my leadership. For years, I struggled with my lack of organizational and administrative abilities as a pastor. Making personnel decisions, managing budgets, following through on details, and writing job descriptions were difficult tasks for me. I excelled in vision casting and teaching. I was told: "You don't have those gifts, so play to your strengths and hire people to your weaknesses. Spend your time in preaching and casting vision. Let others run the church."

We tried several different staff configurations, hiring from the outside, hiring from the inside, dividing the job between different people. Each time we hit a wall. Nothing seemed to work long term. Tension remained until I was willing to confront my own character flaws around our impasse.

While it is true that my primary calling is not to be an executive pastor (I have God-given limits in this area), the real issue related to my character. I preferred (what was for me) the easier work of preaching and praying, and avoided the harder work of managing people. I did not like investing the time needed to thoughtfully prepare for staff meetings and wrestle with strategic planning. I found it easier to be impulsive and vision-driven than to look at hard facts. Why would I want to confront a nonperforming volunteer when I could be spending that time speaking publicly to others and getting validation from them?

This serious weakness in my character was not God-given. My desire for people to like me was so great that I avoided conflicts, especially honest discussions of people's job performance. Laziness prevented me from writing thoughtful job descriptions, taking time to plan carefully for meetings, or following through on project details. Avoiding meetings I knew would be hard or stressful was about my fears, not a better use of my time for God.

Once these immature behaviors came to a head, I broke my twenty-year leadership denial. I acknowledged the church had hit a wall and I was the root cause. This led me into a long, two-year process of taking another hard look deep beneath the surface of my life. It required saying no to outside commitments so I could do the hard work involved in learning the executive tasks of good leadership.

God changed me profoundly in the process. I didn't recognize myself when it was over! Without hesitation, I can say that breaking through that limit was perhaps the most significant, God-transforming season of my entire leadership journey. In addition, God exploded the ministry of New Life, and we saw more fruit in my final six years as lead pastor than the previous twenty.

RECEIVING THE GIFT OF LIMITS AS A CHURCH

Receiving the gift of limits as a church is both essential and challenging. It's essential because, if we don't, we miss the unique and creative ways God wants to move through our communities. And it's challenging because it requires creating a new a discipleship culture that not only affirms limits as a value, but also helps people to integrate limits in practical ways.

Over the years, there are at least four ways that we have worked to intentionally embed the gift of limits into our church: we systematize self-care of leaders, set limits on invasive people, give people freedom to say no, and teach healthy boundaries.

1. Systematize Self-Care of Leaders

As with all the marks of emotionally healthy discipleship, this one begins with the leadership. We seek to model the priority that our personal lives and family—not the ministry—come first. Staff, board members, and leaders are expected to do appropriate self-care and set boundaries based on who God has made them to be and on the limits of their family situation.

Understanding the gift of limits enables us to affirm self-care, and yet it is often a great challenge for those who've been trained to prioritize the needs of others over their own. I love what Parker Palmer says about this dynamic:

> Self-care is never a selfish act—it is simply good stewardship of the only gift I have, the gift I was put on earth to offer to others. Anytime we can listen to true self and give it the care it requires, we do so not only for ourselves, but for the many others whose lives we touch.[9]

This value is so vital to the health of our church that we have crafted a Rule of Life for our pastoral staff that includes weekly Sabbath-keeping, a day alone with God each month, and a commitment to pause for Daily Offices (often called Fixed-Hour Prayer) each day. This is part of how we systematize the value of self-care in our church culture; we essentially make it part of everyone's job description. It's not enough to say, *Take care of yourself*, or *Your family comes first*, at a staff meeting. We want our staff and volunteers to have the time they need alone *with* God so that Christ's life flows out of them into others. When we are able to help both ourselves and those around us with this delicate balance, we find ourselves so deeply rooted in God that our activity *for* him is marked by a rich peace and joy.

2. Set Limits on Invasive People

A critical issue for a church is to create and maintain a culture of love and respect for each person in the community. For this reason, a primary task for every leader is to define the values of their culture and the boundaries of acceptable and unacceptable behavior. That requires intentionally teaching limits and boundaries as well as "reparenting" invasive people.

Invasive people operate on a continuum that ranges from mild to severe. Each of us regularly engages with mildly invasive people. These are the ones who take up too much space at the expense of others, who don't allow others to express themselves, or who damage the community by approaching situations and people in ways that are not biblical. Yet setting limits on them is an important discipleship moment, both for them and the community. What does that look like?

- Matt comes to small group each week seriously depressed over the loss of his job of twenty-five years and his recent divorce. Because of his unwillingness to see a trained counselor or therapist who can give him the undivided, one-on-one attention he needs, he leaves feeling frustrated each week that the group has not met his needs. He complains to others in the church about the group. You meet with Matt outside the group and clarify the limits and purpose of a church small group over and against a Twelve-Step group, one-on-one therapy, or a conversation with a pastor or spiritual director.
- Jane has arrived fifteen to twenty minutes late to the weekly team meeting for the last three weeks. She is unaware, however, of her impact on the group. You take her out for coffee after the third late arrival to see if you can discover any potential underlying issues for the lateness.

Those are the mild cases.

On the other end of the spectrum are the severely invasive people who, like weeds that choke out healthy plants, invade and overtake other people's spaces in destructive ways. They manipulate and use people for their own purposes and are unwilling to change.[10] Too often in churches, they are allowed to set the agenda and exercise a great deal of power behind the scenes. The following is a true story about Paul, who served as an early test case for me in this area.

Paul fasted and prayed regularly. He used his vacations to attend conferences on prayer and prophetic ministry. During small group meetings, he could be found reading his Bible to receive personal words from God for the group. He gave personal words of prophecy anywhere and to anyone—whether or not they wanted them. The problem was that Paul was unteachable and condescending to others (including me) who were not as "spiritual" as he was. Love required setting a boundary around him and confronting him about his pride and critical spirit. Why? He was exercising an unofficial leadership in our midst that was not compatible with our vision and the culture we were building.

This was not the last time I set a limit on a difficult, invasive person. But I discovered, through my meeting with Paul, that setting a limit on difficult people was actually a gift from God—for the larger community, for them, and for me! That level of intense conflict, along with the discomfort of misunderstandings that often follow, contains gifts for our maturity and differentiation that can only be found in challenging situations like these.

3. Give People Freedom to Say No

At New Life, we teach members to use their spiritual gifts in the church and also encourage them to serve in at least one ministry outside of their primary gifting. At the same time, we applaud people for saying no, especially those who work tirelessly or have difficulty taking care of themselves. And we do this by modeling limits in the way we lead and serve.

For example, I am not available for ministry work or phone calls on Sabbaths (from Friday evening at six through Saturday evening at six), during vacations, or during time set apart with God.

When people say to me, *Pete, I know you're busy, but might you be willing to* . . . I allow them to finish making their request. Then I smile and slowly reply, *Well, you see . . . I'm not busy . . . I'm just limited.* My point is that there is plenty of time to do what God has given me to do. The issue, of course, is my discernment of what his priorities are.

Maritza is a multi-gifted, tireless servant whom I have known for almost thirty years. Since she was a child, before she came to faith in Jesus, her role in the family was to care for her younger siblings because her parents were emotionally absent. Our discipleship of Maritza includes encouraging her *not* to jump in to meet the needs around her. Her emotionally healthy discipleship journey gave her permission, for the first time, to feel her feelings, to listen to her desires, and to not do for others what they can and should do for themselves.[11]

She has been on this journey with us for years. And to this day, Geri and I smile when we hear her responding to a request for her help with, *Thank you so much for the invitation, but that doesn't fit for me right now.*

For those who feel guilty when they see an unmet need, it takes great courage and strength *not* to volunteer. In that case, they are actually denying their sinful self (that wants to be like God) and following Jesus. They are trusting that God will meet that need through others.

Without shame, guilt, or pressure, we want to grow mature people who are free to say, *No, thank you.* The result is that the quality of the ministry we do provide is more loving. People are less cranky and stressed. They love and give love freely. Perhaps most important, giving people the freedom to say no helps us to create a culture in which people feel loved rather than used.

4. Model and Teach Healthy Boundaries

Adam and Eve were the first boundary breakers. They crossed the limit God set for them when they ate from the forbidden tree and then ran from God. From that time forward, human beings have been breaking boundaries and crossing lines with God and one another. The Fall distorted for the rest of human history our sense of separateness, boundaries, and responsibility. Ever since, we have been confused about where we end and someone else begins.[12]

Boundaries are an expression of the fact that I am a separate person, apart from others. With proper boundaries, I know what I am and am not responsible for.

If I am a person with poor boundaries, I feel compelled to do what others want even though it is not what I want to do. I live in fear of disappointing someone or being criticized. I want others to like me, and I surely don't want to be seen as selfish. I might make statements such as the following:

- "I said I would lead the sports ministry because the pastor asked. I know I don't have the time right now, but I just couldn't say no."
- "I have to go to men's Bible study on Saturday morning at seven. People really expect me to show up. I know Joe and the others would be let down if I didn't go."
- "Honey, I know you're exhausted, but we *have* to go to dinner with that couple from church. Do you know how hurt and upset they would be if we said no?"

The problem with each of the above scenarios is that I don't know where I end and the other person begins. That is the crux of what boundaries are all about: "Where do I end and where does someone else begin?"

I must define and protect my boundaries with anything that breathes. My boundaries get tested numerous times each day—by a spouse, friends, coworkers, church members, salespeople, and children. People simply want what they want. That is not a bad thing. People will always want things from you and me, such as time, emotional support, and money. This is normal.[13]

The problem is that the world's needs are far greater than my personal supply. And I must now discern what is the best response in the long run rather than what is the easiest to do right now.

The following graphic illustrates healthy boundaries:

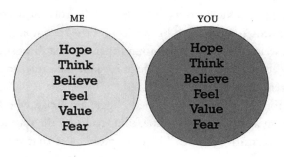

Each circle represents two different people. Each one has thoughts, opinions, feelings, values, hopes, fears, beliefs, abilities, desires, likes, and dislikes. Each person remains inside their own separate circle, not crossing over into the property line or circle of the other person. This is a critical distinction because each of us is a unique individual made in the image of God. He has crowned us with glory and honor (Psalm 8:5). He has stamped on to us uniqueness, sacredness, preciousness, and value. Each individual life is a miracle.[14]

At the same time, the Bible calls us to relate to one another as a family, to be connected to one another in such a loving way that the world will know that Jesus is real and alive (John 13:34–35). However, this connection to others needs to happen without sacrificing our individuality or separateness.

When a church or a ministry implements *The Emotionally Healthy Discipleship Course, Parts 1 and 2*, we carefully train table leaders to model and teach healthy boundaries. We set up guidelines that the table leader gently enforces so people have an experience of the gifts and limits of a healthy community.[15]

My invitation to you is to rearrange your ministry by accepting God's gift of limits. If you do so, you will be engaging in nothing short of a groundbreaking and culture-defying act of rebellion against the contemporary Western way of doing church. But you can rest assured of one thing: When you do God's work in God's way in God's timing, you always bear God's fruit.

REMEMBERING THE
LIMITS OF OUR WORK

Leaf by Niggle is a short story written by J. R. R. Tolkien at a time when he was coming to grips with his limits and the incompleteness of his work as a writer.[16] I find it so profound that I keep a short summary of this story attached to the back page of my journal. I refer to it often as a way to remain grounded and relaxed.

The story is about a man named Niggle, an artist, who has a passion to paint a beautiful landscape, a huge and detailed scene centered around a magnificent tree. The only problem is that Niggle is too distracted to paint the whole tree. Neighbors ask for help with odd jobs, and he finds himself bogged down by the interruptions of everyday life.

"He used to spend a long time on a single leaf, trying to catch its shape. Yet he wanted to paint a whole tree." He is never satisfied with the leaves he has painted, so he works on them endlessly.

One day, Niggles dies and wakes up in an unfamiliar place. He comes upon a bicycle with a yellow label tied to the handlebars that reads, "Niggle." Niggle gets on the bike and begins riding through a meadow. He looks up and sees something so incredible he falls off his bicycle. There it is is—*the* tree! The tree he had been painting his whole life but never finished. And here it is, finished. But it was not a painting; it was a living tree.

Tolkien writes, "Before him stood the Tree, his Tree, finished. If you could say that of a Tree that was alive, its leaves opening, its branches growing and bending in the wind that Niggle had so often felt or guessed, and had so often failed to catch. He gazed at the Tree, and slowly he lifted his arms and opened them wide. 'It's a gift!' he said."

Niggle realizes the work he did in his earthly life was a gift. But even more, he discovers the work he did in his earthly life was only a partial reflection of a greater work that would find its completion only in the life to come.

So it is with us.

Sometimes it can seem as if living within boundaries and limits is not in our best interest or even in the best interest of God's mission. But they are—more than we can possibly imagine.

When we trust in God's goodness by receiving his limits as gifts and expressions of his love, we mature in wisdom. At times, however, this involves grieving the loss of dreams we may have for our lives, a reality that leads us to the next principle of emotionally healthy discipleship: the ability to discover the treasures buried in grief and loss.

Chapter Six

Discover the Treasures
Buried in Grief and Loss

Jerry and Lynda Sittser, along with his mother and their four children ranging from ages two to eight, were driving in their minivan on a lonely stretch of highway in rural Idaho. They had been visiting a nearby Native American Indian reservation as a school project for their two oldest children. They seemed, as friends described them, like the "two-million-dollar" family. They felt as if they were "living on top of the world."

Ten minutes into their drive home, Jerry noticed a car traveling toward them extremely fast. He slowed down at a curve, but the oncoming car, traveling at eighty-five miles an hour, crashed headlong into their minivan. The driver was drunk. In one moment, Sittser lost three generations—his mother, his wife, and their four-year-old daughter. He writes, "In one moment my family as I had known and cherished it was obliterated."[1] Sittser sat on that lonely highway watching them die.

At the subsequent trial, the driver of the other car was eventually declared not guilty and set free because it could not be proven, beyond the shadow of a doubt, that he (not his pregnant wife, who had died in the accident) had been driving the car.

Sittser later wrote a book about his descent into an abyss of grief and incomprehensible pain that changed his life. But he also wrote about the unexpected treasure he found buried in his grief and loss:

It is therefore not true that we become less through loss—unless we allow the loss to make us less, grinding our soul down until there is nothing left. . . . *Loss can also make us more.* . . . I did not get over the loss of my loved ones; rather, I absorbed the loss into my life, like soil receives decaying matter, until it became part of who I am. Sorrow took up permanent residence in my soul *and enlarged it.* . . . The soul is elastic, like a balloon. *It can grow larger through suffering.*[2] (emphasis added)

Sittser discovered the painful truth that loss offers a pathway into God's mysterious way of forming us through "treasures of darkness and riches stored in secret places" (Isaiah 45:3 NIV 1984).

This truth took me a very long time to discover. In fact, I covered over my losses for years, unaware of how they were shaping my relationships and stunting my discipleship. God was seeking to enlarge my soul and deeply transform me; I was seeking a quick end to pain. I saw losses as obstacles I had to overcome in order to mature in Christ; God saw my losses as requirements in order to mature in Christ. Little did I know that the treasures buried deep in my sorrows contained the gifts I needed to grow into an emotional and spiritual adult.

It was the last place I wanted to go.

THE WIDE-RANGING NATURE OF OUR LOSSES

Consider for a moment the vast array of losses we accumulate in a lifetime.

There are devastating losses such as the death of a child, the premature death of a loved one, a disability, divorce, rape, emotional or sexual abuse, incurable disease, infertility, the shattering of a lifelong dream, suicide, betrayal, and so many more.

Sometimes losses come unexpectedly from natural disasters or cataclysmic events. Beginning on September 11, 2001, when suicide bombers flew two planes filled with innocent people into the largest buildings in our city, killing almost three thousand people, our community in Queens experienced daily trauma for over a year. Then there was the Covid-19 pandemic that began in one city in 2019 and has gone on to infect and kill millions across the globe. It changed normal life as we knew it and devastated economies around the world.

Other times, losses come in more natural or expected ways. For example, we might graduate from high school or college and experience a loss in emotional and relational security. Perhaps we move to a new place and our former friendships fade away. Our children become less dependent on us as they grow older. There are leadership changes in our church. Our small group ends. A grandparent dies. All of these might be considered normal losses, but that doesn't make them any less worthy of being grieved. Losses that are not grieved accumulate in our soul like heavy stones that weigh us down. When we fail to attend to them, they prevent us from living freely and honestly with God and others.

However it comes, loss is loss. No one escapes suffering and pain in this life. What may feel like an insignificant loss for you could feel like a catastrophic loss for me. That's because God has made each of us unique, with our own temperaments and our own histories.

The fact that we are affected differently by loss does not change the fact that what we experience as loss is real, even if others don't experience it as we do. Each of us responds differently. Geri, for example, experienced the raising of our children in New York City—a city of over 8.5 million people—as a loss. While there were many benefits to raising our children in a densely populated city filled with people from around the world, she knew our children were missing out on the rich experience of growing up in a smaller community as she had. Having grown up in the New York City area, I didn't carry that same sense of loss.

Leadership has losses all its own, and often a disproportionate number of them—people in whom we invest leave, dreams die, leaders and staff move on or don't work out, betrayals happen, marriages in the church end, relationships shatter, and external crises such as natural disasters and economic downturns take a toll on the community. You can't be a leader in the church and expect to escape loss.

In fact, more than one great writer and poet has described all of life as a growth in the art of loss, culminating in the moment when our earthly life ends and we lose everything.[3] Thus, learning to welcome and hold sorrow and grief before God is central to the work of discipleship.

The question, then, is how did we get the idea that we could grow in spiritual maturity without learning how to deal with loss God's way?

THE CHURCH'S PROBLEMATIC
RESPONSE TO GRIEF AND LOSS

Few Christians in North America and Europe fully understand loss and grief, especially as it relates to God, spiritual maturity, and the expansion of Jesus's mission. We mistakenly believe embracing our grief will slow us down and hinder us in achieving God's mission in the world. Actually, the opposite is true. Embracing our losses, God's way, actually advances his mission.

The question, then, is why are we so allergic to loss and grief and the many treasures buried within them? There are two primary reasons: our resistance to losing control and a faulty theology that interprets losses as interruptions.

We Resist Losing Control

Western culture as a whole devalues loss and grief because it places such a high value on control and continued ascent through life. In contrast, grief and loss require surrender and descent. We like things going "up and to the right"—whether that be the stock market, the economy, the numbers in our ministries, or sense of mastery in the spiritual life.

So, when pain enters our lives, we reflexively deny or minimize it by distracting or numbing ourselves. Sometimes, we blame others. Our defensive maneuvers against loss and grief are endless.

None of us wants to face up to the fact we were never really in control to begin with. It is not an exaggeration to say that our culture, and sadly, our churches as well, are loss denying and grief phobic.

My own fears of losing control were a significant factor in avoiding grief and loss. I was uncomfortable with what might happen if I allowed myself to feel my depression, anger, and doubts about God. I feared letting go of the proverbial steering wheel in my life. Where might God lead me? I didn't have a theology for the dark night of the soul or for hitting a wall,[4] so I kept a tight grip of control on the steering wheel. Unable to mourn, I covered over my losses for years. I feared descending into a bottomless abyss of sorrow, never once imagining that Jesus might be waiting for me there.

Our society has trained us well to pay attention to success but not to loss and pain. And yet, loss demands to be grieved and pain cries out to be felt. In order to keep these feelings at bay, we develop a variety of coping strategies, many of which take the form of substance abuse. That substance could be almost anything—work, movies, drugs, alcohol, shopping, food, busyness, sexual escapades, unhealthy relational attachments, even serving at church—as long as it redirects our attention away from whatever painful reality we might be facing.

Year after year, we avoid the difficulties of life and minimize our failures and disappointments. The result is a widespread inability to face pain.

What we fail to realize in all this is that a refusal to embrace our sorrows and to grieve them fully condemns us, and our churches, to a shallow spirituality that blocks the work of the Holy Spirit in us. It contributes to the overall sense of superficiality in our churches and a lack of profound compassion.

We View Losses as Interruptions

I used to believe that grieving was an interruption, an obstacle in my path to serve Christ. In short, I considered it a waste of time, preventing me from "redeeming the time" (Ephesians 5:16 KJV) for God. "Just get over it," I'd mutter to myself. My counsel for people struggling with bitterness was a flippant, "Forgive and forget, that's what the Bible says!"

After a painful loss, I felt pressure, and pressured others, to return to normal and get back to the work of ministry as quickly as possible. I apologized to my coworkers if I felt sad. Why? As far as I was concerned, grief was a problem to be solved, and my role as a pastor was to solve problems!

One big obstacle to grieving, at least for me, was that I was sometimes the one who had created the situations that caused me and others in the church such pain in the first place. I considered the consequences God's discipline, so I wanted to receive it just as I had taken my father's discipline growing up—stoically, without shedding a tear. After all, what good did it do to dwell in the sadness and frustration of the mess I had made?

Despite the fact that I had spent years reading and studying the Bible—which has much to say about loss and grief—I had never grieved the losses I experienced. Oh, I preached sermons on the book of Job and comforted people by teaching about how Jesus understood their sufferings. But I remained frozen inside. The thought never entered my mind that grief and sorrow were things I needed to experience. My losses—going back to my childhood and family of origin—were locked inside of me. And I had no idea how to free them.

This tendency to view loss and grief as an interruption also happens in our churches. For example, the church moves into a new neighborhood and a new building, yet there is a group of people who struggle with the move. They don't feel right about it somehow and so interpret their unease as a sign from God the church shouldn't have moved. In actuality, however, what they needed was time and an opportunity to grieve leaving a place where God had done many wonderful works. Instead of honoring their loss by going through the old building—to remember those who were transformed in the sanctuary, the babies dedicated on the platform, and wedding receptions in the activities center—we view their resistance as rebellion or an unwillingness to participate in the future work of God.

We celebrate Mother's Day and Father's Day but neglect to be sensitive to those for whom these may be among the most difficult days of the year—infertile couples, singles who long to have children of their own, those who have recently lost a parent or a child, or those whose parents were absent or abusive.

Long-standing and faithful members of our church move away, and we feel guilty about or uncomfortable with our sadness and grief. So we cover over it by glibly quoting verses such as, "Rejoice in the Lord always. I will say it again: Rejoice!" (Philippians 4:4), or "Give thanks in all circumstances" (1 Thessalonians 5:18).

A young man in his twenties begins to explore his past, and for the first time, faces the abuse and abandonment he suffered as a foster child in the city system for eighteen years. He is immediately encouraged to put it behind him and press forward into his new relationship with his heavenly Father. We are not sure what to say and we try to close up the wound as quickly as possible—regardless of an infection that remains and may never heal properly.

All of these are examples of ignoring the painful realities of loss and grief. We prefer to rush through them or give them a drive-by mention as we move on to what is next. Sitting with what we do not understand is hard and heartrending, but necessary. Like most leaders, I discovered it was easier to offer superficial answers that got an amen from an audience.

We prefer to skip what we don't understand. And when we do that, we fail to discover the treasures waiting for us, riches that can only be ours when we trust God with our losses. God, however, has another pathway for us, one he has clearly revealed in Scripture.

GOD'S THREE PHASES FOR PROCESSING GRIEF AND LOSS

Elisabeth Kübler-Ross has made famous five stages of response to death and loss: denial, anger, bargaining, depression, and acceptance.[5] A sixth stage was added later—finding meaning.[6] While Kübler-Ross's work is very helpful, and I commend it to you, God offers us a comprehensive biblical theology as our first and primary framework.

Scripture describes three biblical phases to process grief and sorrow: pay attention to pain, wait in the confusing in-between, and allow the old to birth the new. Each of these three phases has distinct characteristics, and they don't necessarily happen in a step-by-step fashion. In fact, they frequently overlap. And, as we shall see, it is also possible to experience all three phases at the same time! But the process begins with paying attention to and feeling the pain of our losses.

Phase One: Pay Attention to Pain

When a loss enters our life or church, we often become annoyed or angry at God and treat it as an alien invasion from outer space.

We forget that attending to the pain of grief and loss has been a distinctive of God's people since the beginning. Consider a few examples.

- The ancient Hebrews expressed their laments dramatically and physically by tearing their clothes, putting on sackcloth, and sitting in ashes (Esther 4:1–3; Daniel 9:3).
- During Noah's generation, Scripture indicates that God himself was "grieved in His heart" about the wickedness of humanity (Genesis 6:6 NASB).
- Thirty-five chapters in the book of Job describe a man who was anguished, angry, suicidal at times, depressed, and bewildered (Job 4:1–36:33).
- The wisdom writer tells us, "There is a time for everything, and a season for every activity under the heavens," including "a time to weep" and "a time to mourn" (Ecclesiastes 3:1, 4).
- The prophet Jeremiah wrote an entire book in the Bible called Lamentations.
- Jesus himself prayed with "loud cries and tears" (Hebrews 5:7 NRSV). In Gethsemane, Jesus was anguished, sorrowful, and spiritually overwhelmed, not emotionally frozen or shut down (Luke 22:39–44).

From Genesis to Revelation, the Scriptures invite us to integrate seasons of grief and sadness as a central aspect of the spiritual life. To reject these seasons is to live only half of life, and to live a spirituality marked by unreality. And if an authentic spiritual life is anything, it is an absolute commitment to reality, not an escape from it.

Perhaps the most compelling and instructive examples we have of paying attention to loss and grief are found in what has been the most popular book of the Bible throughout history, the book of Psalms.

> **GOD'S 3 PHASES FOR PROCESSING GRIEF AND LOSS**
>
> 1. **Pay attention to pain.**
> 2. Wait in the confusing in-between.
> 3. Allow the old to birth the new.

Learning Lament from the Psalms

The Psalms are loved for good reason, for there is a "psalm for every sigh." This longest book in the Bible includes psalms of adoration, thanksgiving, wisdom, repentance, and even psalms expressing doubt. Most, according to tradition, were written by David.

The majority, however, are far from cheerful. As scholar Bernhard Anderson writes, "Laments far outnumber any other kind of songs in the Psalter."[7] Half to two-thirds of the 150 psalms are classified as laments. They were gifted to God's people in order to teach us how to pray our emotions and struggles back to God.

The laments never flinch in paying attention to the reality that life can be hard, difficult, and even brutal. They decry the apparent absence of God. They take notice when circumstances seem to say that God is not good. They cry out to God for comfort and care, and wrestle with their doubts about God's loyal, faithful love:

- "Tears have been my food day and night" (Psalm 42:3).
- "Why must I go about mourning, oppressed by the enemy?" (Psalm 43:2).
- "You have put me in the lowest pit, in the darkest depths. . . . You have overwhelmed me" (Psalm 88:6–7).

The Psalms operate in the certainty that God does allow his people to experience great pain, even if we don't always understand the reasons why.

David, the author of so many psalms, is well known for being a man after God's own heart (Acts 13:22). However, what few realize is how clearly this is reflected in the way he repeatedly paid attention to his losses, disappointments, and fears. And David didn't just notice these things; he actually wrote songs about the many losses he experienced and sang them back to God as a prayer.

For example, David had a deep love and respect for King Saul even though Saul had hunted him down and sought to kill him for many years. David was also best friends with Saul's son Jonathan. When Saul and Jonathan were killed in battle with the Philistines, David didn't just move on and step into God's plan for his life as the new king. Instead, he set aside time to grieve.

He wrote a song—a moving, beautiful, and detailed lament of the horror that had occurred. It is found in 2 Samuel 1:17–27. He anguished over the catastrophe: "How the mighty have fallen! . . . Saul and Jonathan—in life they were loved and admired." David even addressed his dead friend Jonathan directly: "I grieve for you, Jonathan my brother" (2 Samuel 1:19, 23, 26).

What is perhaps most instructive for us as leaders is not just that David paid attention to his own grief, but that he also ordered that the lament be taught to the people of Judah that followed him (2 Samuel 1:18). Can you imagine? Right when he faced the monumental task of transitioning an entire country to a new government, David commanded that everyone first join him in a communal expression of grief. He wanted his people to *learn* lament by pouring out their grief for the great loss Israel had suffered.

When was the last time your church devoted a whole service to lament or taught how important grieving losses is to spiritual maturity? When was the last time you heard a sermon on the biblical centrality of sadness, sorrow, or lament?

As a leader, David understood how indispensable grieving is to a healthy spiritual life. He knew grieving one's losses before moving on was a choice.[8] But he followed this descent into darkness, trusting God would meet him and his people there.

What this requires from us is that we refuse to live frozen and numb, to put on a mask, or to bottle up our feelings—even if that has been our choice for decades. Until we are willing to learn to feel our emotions, the great revelation and treasure found in God's way of processing grief will be lost to us.

Learning to Feel

When our pain and grief goes unexpressed or unfelt, it gets buried alive. As a result, we lose access to the depth and range of feelings given to us by God and our emotional lives are compressed into a tightly constricted box. Eventually, the feelings we bury claw their way back up through the earth of our lives and manifest in symptoms such as depression, anxiety, emptiness, and loneliness.

When I began the journey of emotionally healthy discipleship, one of the first things I did was to open that box and allow myself to feel. Eventually, I made this part of my daily routine by integrating it into my time with God and recording in a journal what was happening inside me. I listened to my body, which was often way ahead of my mental awareness of emotions. My body "spoke" through things such as tension in my neck, knots in my stomach, or tightness in my throat.[9] I then reflected on *why* I might be experiencing each emotion and how God might be communicating with me through them.

I began to read and pray the Psalms. God used the rawness of David's writings to help the suppressed parts of me come alive. These "feeling workouts" strengthened my awareness of my emotions. Once I befriended these vulnerable parts of who I was, an even wider variety of emotions emerged—astonishment, joy, delight, amazement. My soul came alive in new ways. And I began to experience a greater freedom and peace. While it was difficult at first, identifying and naming my emotions eventually became as natural as breathing.

Over time, we developed a spiritual practice to help all of us learn how to identify and pay attention to our buried emotions. We call it "Explore the Iceberg."[10]

Explore the Iceberg

Listed below are four questions to help you identify and pay attention to your emotions, particularly those that may be hidden beneath the surface. Before engaging the questions, close your eyes and sit quietly for a few moments. Ask God to guide you and speak to you. Be open to anything God may want to bring to the surface.

Allow about two minutes to reflect on and write your responses to each of the four questions. Write down whatever comes to mind. Draw from the present, recent past, or distant past.

What are you *angry* about (a betrayal, a coworker's hurtful comment, a car breakdown, unanswered prayer, etc.)?

What are you *sad* about (a small or big loss, disappointment, or a choice you or others have made)?

What are you *anxious* about (your finances, future, family, health, church)?

What are you *glad* about (your family, an opportunity, your church)?

As an option, you may also consider exploring the iceberg with a safe friend. Your friend simply asks you the questions, one at a time, and listens attentively as you verbalize what is happening inside you.

I meet many people who are afraid to feel; they are worried getting in touch with their emotions will release a torrent of hate, bitterness, or despair from within. Perhaps that's true. But an amazing byproduct of paying attention to our pain is a fresh discovery of God's mercy in the gospel. We discover God actually loves and accepts us where we are. In fact, when I feel my emotions, I not only get connected to his love, but the defensive walls I've built to keep people out begin to crumble. And I realize that if I risk living out of my true self in Christ, I won't die.[11]

For this to happen, however, it is critical we do pay attention to our pain in God's presence as an expression of prayer to him. This both overlaps and leads into the next phase in God's grieving process for us, waiting in the confusing in-between.

Phase Two: Wait in the Confusing In-Between

Loss and grief force us to stop, to wait, to change our plans. That can be especially hard for those of us who live in a culture that esteems busyness, productivity, and predictability. For this reason, learning to wait is perhaps one of the most difficult lessons we learn as followers of Jesus. As a classic New Yorker who likes to finish people's sentences when they speak slowly, I know this only too well. Yet, Scripture is full of examples of those who had to learn to wait on God:

- Noah waited a long time for the rains to come and the waters to recede.
- Abraham and Sarah waited almost twenty-five years for God to follow through on his promise of a son.
- Joseph waited over twenty years—most of which were spent in slavery, servitude, and prison—before realizing God's purposes in, through, and in spite of his great sufferings.
- Moses waited forty years in the desert before receiving God's call to lead his people out of Egyptian slavery, and then waited another forty years before reaching the promised land.
- Hannah waited years for an answer to her prayers for a child.
- Elizabeth waited decades before the birth of her son, John.
- Job waited years, not months, for God to reveal himself and usher him into a new beginning.
- The apostles waited, confused and bewildered, between the cross of Good Friday and Pentecost.

From the beginning to the end of Scripture, we discover stories of God teaching his people to wait. And that waiting season is almost always confusing and disorienting.[12] The temptations are great—to fall into a pit of despair, to medicate or numb ourselves with some addictive behavior, to stop speaking with God out of anger.

> **GOD'S 3 PHASES FOR PROCESSING GRIEF AND LOSS**
>
> 1. Pay attention to pain.
> 2. **Wait in the confusing in-between.**
> 3. Allow the old to birth the new.

What makes waiting so difficult is that we are not sure where God is, what he is doing, or when this waiting will end—if ever. We are helpless and thrust on him in total dependence. We can't see the future and there is no way back to the past where we had a sense of stability and order.

We are face-to-face with the cross, with the refining fire of what sixteeth-century spiritual writer John of the Cross described as the dark night of the soul.[13] A dark night is not merely suffering, but a crisis experience of spiritual desolation. We may feel helpless, weary, empty, and consumed by a sense of failure or defeat. John of the Cross's great insight about this confusing-in-between phase is that it is the ordinary way we grow in Jesus. No exceptions. He writes:

> God perceives the imperfections within us, and because of his love for us . . . is not content to leave us in our weakness, and for this reason he takes us into the dark night . . . no soul will grow deep in the spiritual life unless God works passively in that soul by means of the dark night.[14]

Yet, it is in these confusing in-between times that God uproots our self-will, strips us of layers of our false self, and frees us from unhealthy attachments. It is in these in-between seasons that we are emptied, and this emptying has one primary purpose—to make room for something new and better.

Let's face it: waiting on God in the midst of loss defies human instincts and quick solutions. It runs contrary to Western culture and our own bent toward self-will. That is why we so desperately need the Holy Spirit to sustain us in these times.

In a brilliant essay entitled "Of Patience," Tertullian (AD 160–220) expounds on a theme we rarely talk about today—that it is God's nature to be patient. He reminds us that when the Holy Spirit descends, patience and waiting are always present as well. Why? That is his nature.

Tertullian even argues that the root of the original rebellion of Adam and Eve was rooted in impatience: "For, to put it in a nutshell, every sin is to be traced back to impatience. I find the origin of impatience in the Devil himself."[15] We are on very different timetables than our God for whom a thousand years are like a day (2 Peter 3:9).[16] Is it any wonder why this second phase of waiting in the confusing-in-between during loss is so challenging, if not almost impossible, without the Holy Spirit?

Most of my spiritual growth has come out of these painful, mysterious, and confusing experiences—the in-between times—over which I had so little control. I can identify at least five significant dark nights in my forty-five-year journey with Christ. One of the ways I know I am in a dark night is when my prayers sound something like this: "Lord, I can't go on. You overdid it with me. You have given me more than I can bear—even though you promised not to! Just take me home. Amen."

When I have resisted God by simply getting busier and trying to hold everything together, I short-circuited the preparation I needed in order to receive the new beginnings God had for me. When I have waited with him, I discovered this in-between confusion was rich in insights and mercies. What looked like an empty, blurry, inactive season turned out to be a surprising place of transition and God's powerful, beneath-the-surface work in my life.

The same principle of the confusing in-betweens, or dark nights, applies to groups and churches as well. The following story describes one of those we experienced as a church—and it is one I will never forget.

New Life Fellowship Church, for almost four years, had saved and prayed to buy the building we had been renting for eight years. It was a 60,000-square-foot Elks Lodge in the center of Queens, New York City. We thought we had agreed on terms with the owners, but at the final hour, a large developer came in to offer a deal we could not match. When the building owners broke our agreement, we suddenly went from having a glorious future to possible homelessness with only a six-month window to find a new location. The blow came like a sledgehammer to our congregation, in particular to those of us in leadership who had invested so much time and energy into the purchase.

Many people were confused, angry, hurt, and disappointed in God. *Where is God? Why doesn't he answer our prayers? Why did you allow this, O God?* A sense of weariness, helplessness, and failure descended on us. Our prayers no longer seemed to work. We could no longer see what God was doing. We were forced, against our will, to wait in the confusing in-between.

Another building—larger, cheaper, and with more parking—came up for sale during this time. We prayed about it as an elder board but realized it would take us out of our community and away from our calling as a multiracial church committed to serve the poor in the heart of a difficult part of Queens. So we chose not to pursue it and waited.

Weeks and then months passed.

Throughout this experience, God did something profound in me and in us as a community. He purged a bit more self-will and stubbornness out of us and led us to a deeper place of true peace and rest in his will. Eventually, the developer's deal with the building owners collapsed, and we were able to buy the building two years later.

We thought waiting was a parenthesis. It was not. God was working, but we couldn't see it.

Sometimes, we rebel during confusing in-between periods rather than embrace the waiting period in which we find ourselves. When God seems absent, the temptation is to flee from God, to quit the faith, or to fall into despair. The good news is that even then, God finds us and meets us.

Having lived through multiple confusing seasons such as this, what now enables me to remain faithful when the next disorientating in-between time comes is the truth that nothing is wasted. God uses all things—even the confusing dark nights of the soul—for our benefit, for his glory, and for the good of others.

Running away from God and our sorrows during these seasons of disorientation does not heal our pain; it only makes the pain worse. To heal and grow up, we must walk through the valley of the shadow of death on our way to the light. In the dark, we discover new things, as Barbara Brown Taylor articulates so well:

> I have learned things in the dark I could never have learned in the light, things that saved my life over and over again, so that there is really only one logical conclusion. I need darkness as much as I need light.[17]

When we are faithful to the confusing in-between, we eventually move on to the next phase of responding to grief and loss, allowing the old to birth the new. This is where we allow God to reframe our losses so that we can receive the treasures God has for us.

The Confusing In-Between and Forgiveness

Those who say that the decision to forgive is simply an act of the will, regardless of the severity of the injustice, do not understand the larger biblical teaching on grief and loss. In order to truly forgive another person from the heart, we must first feel the pain of what was lost and allow God to lead us through the confusing in-between phase of grief.

When Jesus gave his life to forgive us, he did not say, "Well, they did their best. They couldn't help it." He was not detached and void of emotions. Rather, Jesus truly felt the pain of our rebellion, our unwillingness to receive him, as he hung alone on the cross and prayed, "Father, forgive them, for they do not know what they are doing."

The process of forgiveness always involves grieving before letting go—both for the person who offers forgiveness as well as the person who asks for it.

I had to wrestle with this aspect of forgiveness many years ago when I was blindsided by a split in one of our congregations. Without warning, two hundred people from the Spanish-speaking congregation whom I had shepherded for four years left with the associate pastor. I had invested a great deal of love, energy, and prayer into them and I felt betrayed. Even though I knew I needed to forgive the associate pastor, the more I tried through sheer force of the will, the more my anger intensified. I was trying to move on—preaching, teaching, leading—but inwardly I suffered under the guilt over my inability to forgive him. At the same time, I was also trying to deny the horrible reality of what had happened, which only deepened my resentment toward him and God.

I didn't understand that there might be a *process* to forgiving. I didn't understand I needed time and space to grieve my loss. I didn't understand this required a journey, and that the deeper the wound, the longer the process would need to be. I didn't understand that forgiveness from the heart is very difficult, that it takes a miracle from God.

What I had been struggling with all along is superficial forgiveness—trying to forgive without doing the grief work required to truly forgive. Lewis Smedes sums up the dangers of superficial forgiveness: "I worry about fast forgivers. They tend to forgive quickly in order to avoid their pain. Or they forgive fast in order to get an advantage over the people they forgive. And their instant forgiving only makes things worse."[18]

Forgiving a person who has hurt us deeply requires a miracle only God can do. But if we wait with him in that confusing in-between, asking him to do what only he can do (such as change our hard hearts into soft ones), something new is released in and through us. And we allow God's third phase to become a reality in our lives.

Phase Three: Allow the Old to Birth the New

The central truth of Christianity is that Jesus died a real death on the cross and rose from the dead. He is risen! This is what enables us to affirm that our losses and endings are gateways to new beginnings—even when we can't see anything good that could possibly emerge from them. Our losses are real. But so is the resurrection our living God brings from our losses.

God invites us to trust him with the many small deaths we experience in our lives. Jesus himself said: "Unless a kernel of wheat falls to the ground and dies, it remains only a single seed. But if it dies, it produces many seeds" (John 12:24).

> **GOD'S 3 PHASES FOR PROCESSING GRIEF AND LOSS**
>
> 1. Pay attention to pain.
> 2. Wait in the confusing in-between.
> 3. **Allow the old to birth the new.**

This certainty of God's promise anchors us even when we feel we have descended into hell and there is no hope for a good future. The following is a story of a pastor friend who found himself in such a situation.

Michael's church had been shaken to its core over a financial scandal that had apparently been going on for a number of years. Tens of thousands of dollars, at the very least, were missing. The hole in which he found himself sinking into only grew deeper by the day. Would the church survive? Would he? While he was not directly involved, he had trusted the wrong people.

He wept in pure and utter anguish.

I listened.

Then I said, "Michael, I know everything in you wants to quit, resign, and run. But hear me on this: 'Jesus is risen.'" Only silence answered me on the phone.

I wondered to myself if he could hear my words. So much was at stake—for him, his family, and those he pastored. I knew paying attention to his pain and waiting in the confusing in-between were going to be very difficult seasons for him.

"You may be in an earthly hell right now," I said. "And yes, this is only the beginning. But remember, Jesus is risen. Much good will come out of this in the long run if you remain with Jesus and lead your chuch through this."

Michael did stay with Jesus, and now, many years later, both he and his church are prospering. His story is just one example that demonstrates how God can bring new life out of death. Because Jesus is alive and the resurrection is a reality, enormous gifts await us on the other side of loss and grief—if we wait on him and abide in him.

What makes this third phase so different from the previous phases is that we actually transition to something new. I know people who are good at paying attention to their pain (Phase 1) and waiting on God (Phase 2), but they do not let go of the old so they can transition into the new God has for them (Phase 3). I know this problem well because it is one of my temptations!

I relate to the prisoners at the end of World War II who walked out of the concentration camps after liberation only to return to their lice infested, restrictive barracks. Why? They were more comfortable in the barracks. They had taken on a learned helplessness that kept them stuck in a bad place.[19]

Often, what appears to be a catastrophic ending becomes instead the foundation of a great new beginning—if we follow God's pathway for our grief. I've experienced this in my own life and witnessed it in the lives of countless others over the years. In fact, miraculous shifts take place in us as we follow God's radical pathway of paying attention to the pain that comes with losses and waiting on him when everything in us wants to run away from him.

The following are five treasures of resurrection that I have experienced in my own life and have seen become a reality in the lives of countless others who have bravely lamented in God's way.

God offers us revelation of himself. Embracing our losses enlarges our hearts to how incomprehensible, untraceable, infinite, transcendent, inexhaustible, and perfect God is. (That is why, as Meister Eckhart said, when some people quit God, they are actually getting closer to the real God—and that is a good thing! The God they are quitting is not the God whom we encounter in Scripture.)[20] God's ways are much higher and more expansive than we can imagine. And like Jeremiah in the midst of the disaster of Jerusalem's destruction at the hand of the Babylonians, we discover the depths of his love and faithfulness that are new every morning (Lamentations 3:22–24). We realize that we will never stop progressing or growing in the inexhaustible life of God.[21]

God makes us softer and more compassionate. Sadness softens our defenses, and people experience us as safer containers of Jesus. Author and theologian Henri Nouwen rightly says that the degree to which we grieve our own losses is in direct proportion to the depth and quality of the compassion we can offer to others. "There is no compassion without many tears . . . To become like the Father whose only authority is compassion, I have to shed countless tears and so prepare my heart to receive anyone, whatever their journey has been, and forgive them from the heart."[22] Absorbing our own pain, we are able to enter the pain of others. We become mature lovers and true mothers and fathers of the faith.

God gives us a greater revelation of ourselves. Grieving reveals to us the extent to which self-will remains deeply embedded in us. I never understood, at least on a heart level, Jesus lying on the ground in Gethsemane struggling and overwhelmed by the will of the Father until I experienced my own grief. Loss cuts something out of us, much as a gardener cuts back a plant for greater fruit. God does something in us through the fire of sorrow that enlarges our capacity to wait and surrender to his will. This breaking detaches and empties us so he can fill us with his life. And then, out of union with Jesus, he can fill us with a new and extraordinary capacity for fruitfulness.[23]

God makes us more of our true self in Christ. Sorrow has a remarkable power to wear away the masks we present to the world. Accomplishments or gifts with which we over-identify, give way and disintegrate. We are more liberated from having to impress others and freed from an adolescent avoidance of pain. We find ourselves able to follow God's plan with a new freedom and can now rid ourselves of the unimportant things in life that others so desperately want. Something truer—Christ in and through us—slowly emerges. We acknowledge our brokenness and vulnerabilities rather than covering them over. And we break free from the illusion there is something richer or more beautiful than the gift of loving God and being loved by him.

God makes us more truly alive to our astonishing world. We enjoy a new, vivid appreciation of the sacredness in all of life—the changing seasons, the wind, the falling of the leaves, the holidays, the inner beauty of people. Our hearts are expanded to experience depths of life beneath the surface. And we find ourselves marveling at the wonder and miracle of life more often.

We are not the same people after this final phase of the grieving process. We finally realize that, just as the risen Jesus showed his wounds to the disciples following his resurrection, he sends us into the world to show our wounds as well (see John 20:19–28).

Three Ideas to Integrate God's Pathway for Grieving into the Church

Equip people to identify and reflect on losses—personally and in the larger world. Offer workshops or ministries that apply the theology of grief and loss to the transitions people experience throughout the seasons of life—a divorce, a retirement, a death, a serious illness, a geographic move, a child becoming a young adult, a job loss, etc. The church is uniquely positioned to serve people during these critical moments of disorientation in their lives.

Teach or preach a message series on biblical expressions of grief. The Psalms, Lamentations, the Book of Job, and the life of David, are all useful in giving people a biblical basis and framework for grieving. I once preached a fourteen-week series on different types of songs in the Psalter. I then invited everyone in the congregation to write their own psalms or poems out of their experiences with God through life. Not surprisingly, we received mostly laments written to God.

Create opportunities such as rituals or grieving spaces to give people permission to grieve. You might offer a half-day or one-day guided retreat on grief. Another option is to visit places of mourning or monuments such as the Vietnam Veterans Memorial, the Holocaust Museum, the Wounded Knee Massacre Monument, the National Museum of African American History and Culture, the National Memorial for Peace and Justice, the 9/11 Memorial Museum, the Hiroshima Peace Memorial, and other important museums and monuments. Invite people who have suffered great losses, along with victims of racism, sexism, and classism, to share their stories.

A STORY OF EMBRACING GRIEF AND LOSS

As we close this chapter on discovering the treasures of grief and loss, allow me to share with you the story of one remarkable woman whom I have known for many years, and the unique ways she has carried her wounds and resurrection into the world. Her name is Bianca.

Bianca's life was difficult right from the beginning. From the age of eleven, she remembers being tormented by sexual nightmares. She would toss and turn, feeling dirty. She was still too young to know her nightmares were the result of years of molestation and rape by a much-loved relative.

She grew older without realizing that she was constantly anxious, and that she was uncomfortable with her sexuality and the sexuality of others. Over the years, Bianca shared what had happened to her in childhood with three people. None asked questions. One commented, "Well, maybe he was just experimenting."

She was conscious of her sexual abuse. She hadn't buried it. She didn't have to remember it; it was always there.

When she started working for the board of education in the largest school district in New York City—in a school where 95 percent of the students lived below the poverty line—her nightmares returned with a vengeance. The lack of protection and safety in the lives of some of her students evoked horrible images of her own childhood. Her dreams became filled once again with violence, rape, and anxiety. Insomnia set in.

By then, she had already been a Christian for twelve years, faithfully attending Bible studies and prayer meetings. Nonetheless, the sense of sadness that had always permeated her life became overwhelming.

The church was interested in her strength and her service. She was gifted in so many ways. But she couldn't share that she was dying on the inside. No one in leadership had modeled vulnerability, weakness, confusion, or extreme pain. Everything was "Praise God, for he is good."

She was serving a God she did not trust, a God she felt was distant and only interested in her strengths. On many Sundays after church, she would cry long and hard, thinking her children would have to visit her under some highway overpass because she would end up a prostitute. She questioned how a life so broken could ever be put together again. She secretly wondered how God could have looked on those nights of abuse and not have moved to protect her.

Out of desperation, Bianca went to a safe friend to talk about her grief, and the friend helped her to find a skilled Christian counselor. Here, she began to explore and grieve the devastation to her wholeness as a little girl. She entered the chaos and darkness of the death of her childhood at the hands of this relative. The floodgates were now open. And things seemed to get only worse as her feelings and frozen rage exploded into anger and depression.

She responded to an altar call at her church for people with sexual brokenness in their past. She began to share her abyss of grief with some close, trusted friends. She stopped working so hard to earn God's approval and began to grasp the love and grace in the gospel. All of this took years.

Bianca has a hole in her soul that will never go away. Something died in her at the hands of her abuser that she cannot get back. She is on a journey, however, toward wholeness. It is a process. Issues related to her sexual abuse come up every so often, and sometimes she stalls a little. Injustices toward children sometimes stir in her painful memories.

But Bianca is walking, loving, and serving Christ. Her journey has given her a depth and clarity about the gospel that few others possess. She carries teachings and insights in many small, powerful ways at New Life—through dance, participation in small groups, and gifts of wisdom, so that "our theology might be clean," as Bianca describes it.

Bianca's story is a powerful reminder of what God can do when we are willing to embrace loss and grief. We discover that God has given us treasures on a pathway through grief that we never anticipated or chose for ourselves. They are treasures hidden in darkness (Isaiah 45:3).

When we make disciples who learn how to grow through pain, the rich fruit of godlike compassion toward others will flow from us to the world. Modeling our lives after Jesus who loved people in extraordinary ways now becomes a real possibility for us.

Chapter Seven

Make Love the Measure of Maturity

In 1914, the year that World War I broke out in Europe, a young man came to visit Martin Buber, a well-known German-Jewish theologian and writer. Here is how Buber later recounted the meeting:

> What happened was no more than that one forenoon, after a morning of "religious" enthusiasm, I had a visit from an unknown young man, without being there in spirit. I certainly did not fail to let the meeting be friendly.... I conversed attentively and openly with him—only I omitted to guess the questions which he did not put. Later, not long after, I learned from one of his friends—he himself was no longer alive—the essential content of these questions; I learned that he had come to me not casually, but borne by destiny, not for a chat but for a decision. He had come to me, he had come in this hour.[1]

Before the war began, Buber considered himself deeply religious, primarily concerned with mystical experiences that lifted him out of the earthly, ordinary experiences of everyday life. Rabbi and theologian William Kaufman characterizes Buber's thought at the time as more concerned with the eternal than with the temporal, more focused on ecstasy than daily existence, and more interested in what lies beyond the world than in the world itself.[2] All that changed after the young man who came to visit Buber that day in 1914 subsequently committed suicide.

The guilt Buber felt was not that he had somehow failed to remove the young man's despair, but that he had failed to be fully present to him. He was so preoccupied by his own experience with God earlier that morning that he failed to bring the full resources of his attention to their conversation. He did not turn to the young man with his whole being. Instead of genuinely listening, he brought the equivalent of leftovers, a courteous but partial engagement.

For Buber, the experience felt like a judgment on his whole way of life.[3] He realized that it is possible to have profound spiritual experiences, a "faith that can move mountains," but that such a faith is worth nothing without a deeply present love for people.

While this was only one of a series of such formational encounters Buber had over the years, it effectively captures the context for his ground-breaking classic, *I and Thou*, which was first published in 1923, just five years after the end of World War I.[4]

I relate to Martin Buber's experience on the day he met with that young man. For the first seventeen years of my Christian life, the presence I brought to other people was distracted and preoccupied. It never occurred to me how badly I was failing at a central teaching of the gospel—that love for individuals made in God's image is inextricably linked to love for God. It exposed the shadow side of the Christian leadership model in which I had been reared, as well as the shadow side of church I was building. Just as Buber had been, I, too, was preoccupied with richer experiences with God and learning more about him. As far as I was concerned, that was the measure of spiritual maturity.

MAKING DISCIPLES YET MISSING PEOPLE

When I became a Christian, I felt an overwhelming burden that my friends and family would come to know the love of Jesus. The message of forgiveness and God's unconditional love set my heart on fire. To that end, I was devoted to learning all I could about prayer, Scripture, evangelism, and disciplemaking. I studied leadership, preaching, and how to build community and multiply leaders. I shepherded people as best I could and sought to lead them into greater truth about the living

God. And yet, what had started out feeling so pure and clear about my motivations to serve others gradually grew muddled and unclear.

My focus and aim was to make disciples and to grow the church. To do that, I needed people to respond, to participate, to join. There was something I needed them to do in order to get Christ's mission done more successfully. There was an entire world out there in need of Jesus—churches to be planted, people to be trained, poor folks to be fed—and I needed laborers to join me in that work.

Over time, it became difficult to distinguish between loving people for who they were versus using them for how they could contribute to the mission. Did I need people to come to faith in Jesus to build our church, or could I simply love them regardless of their decision to follow Jesus and serve in the ministry? I was so deeply involved in getting Christ's work done that the line became impossible to distinguish.

Regardless, I didn't have time to sort it out. There was simply too much to do.

I don't remember anyone ever teaching me that loving people well was the defining characteristic of a mature Christian. I didn't know how to do it, what it meant, or what that might look like practically, especially as a leader. It was not taught in seminary or part of any leadership conference I attended. Instead, the emphasis of everything I'd been taught was that I needed to learn all I could from God and about God so I could lead others better. Wasn't that enough?

No, it wasn't enough.

One of the things that made my inability to love people well so difficult to identify was my high level of commitment to cross racial, economic, cultural, and gender barriers from my earliest days as a Christ-follower. As a young adult, I spent three years on staff working with African American and Hispanic university students, part of which included a four-month stint in the Philippines. I routinely attended churches in which I was the minority.

After graduating seminary, Geri and I moved to Central America. We left our world—physically and culturally. We left behind what was comfortable and familiar so we could immerse ourselves in another culture and become one with the people. We ate their food. We learned their language. We celebrated their customs and traditions. We lived with a large family, sacrificing our privacy and desire for personal space. The house was above a carpentry shop that spewed its sawdust through the holes in our floor promptly at 6:00 a.m., Monday through Saturday.

Upon returning to the United States, Geri and I moved to New York to raise our family and plant New Life Fellowship Church. We bid farewell to the comfortable, middle-class life our families of origin had enjoyed, and moved into the complex, multiethnic, heavily congested world of Queens.

On the small block where we have lived for most of the last thirty-seven years, we have had as neighbors drug addicts, prostitutes, orphans, widows, widowers, single moms, and a fifty-something man who worked as an extra in movies. Our neighbors have been African American, Cypriot, Korean, Chinese, Hispanic, Brazilian, single, married, and retired. We walked our daughters through the gifts and liabilities of being a racial minority at church, in school, and in their neighborhood.

On the face of it, you would think that Geri and I had been pretty intentional about prioritizing people, right? And yet, what is most incredible is that, while we spent so many of our early years with people from different races and cultures, we did not know how to truly be present with them.

How could we? *Geri and I didn't know how to be present with one another, let alone with our neighbors or our wider community!*

Geri tried telling me for years she felt lonely in our marriage, that she did not feel seen or heard. But I had no idea what she was talking about. Her words simply bounced off me.

As I mentioned previously, this led Geri to quit the church in January 1996. We then went away for an intensive retreat with two Christian counselors. In the middle of that week, we learned a simple skill we now call "incarnational listening." I do not even remember the precise content of the conversation. What I will remember—forever—is seeing Geri and being seen by Geri for the first time. It was truly extraordinary. God's presence and love overwhelmed us, and we were dumbstruck with wonder.

I had been a Christian for many years at that point, but nothing prepared me for the glory of God that descended between us. It was so entirely different from an incredible sermon, anointed worship time, powerful prayer meeting, or dramatic healing. I did not have a theological framework for what happened, but I knew we had tasted a bit of heaven that far exceeded any other experience I'd had with God up to that point. And it was that experience that soon after led to a radical shift in how we did discipleship—a shift that ultimately launched the global movement we now call Emotionally Healthy Discipleship.

Prior to this encounter, Geri and I had spent years immersing ourselves in the best of Christian leadership training and discipleship. We grasped what it meant that Christ died for us personally, and we practiced the classic spiritual disciplines—everything from Bible study and prayer to fasting, worship, and living in community.

And yet, something was desperately wrong—in us and in the ministry we were building.

Although people seemed to be growing in love and desire for God, this wasn't translating into greater love for people. Many had zeal for Scripture, but remained defensive, judgmental, critical, unapproachable, and unsafe as people.

We finally had to acknowledge the painful reality that the quality of love expressed inside the church was not really all that different from the way people related outside the church. For example:

- We didn't know what to do with anger or sadness.
- We were afraid of being honest in our relationships.
- We avoided conflicts and wanted to be perceived as nice people.
- We often said yes when we really wanted to say no.
- We made assumptions about what other people were thinking without checking them out.
- We overfunctioned, doing for others what they could and should do for themselves.

It became obvious that a person may be chronologically thirty-five or fifty-five or seventy-five but still function as an emotional infant or child in his or her relationships. That's when we realized a fundamental truth: *Emotional health and spiritual maturity are inseparable.*

It is impossible to be spiritually mature while remaining emotionally immature.

When Geri and I discovered that love—not ministry activities or spiritual practices—is truly the measure of spiritual maturity, we embarked on a journey to close this deadly gap in our discipleship. Along with rediscovering the urgency with which Jesus linked loving God and loving others, we began to disciple people on how to love others well, especially when under stress or in the midst of conflict.

We wanted the quality of relationships in our church to reflect the fact that we belonged to the new family of Jesus. That required a discipleship that could move people from brokenness to greater wholeness in their relationships. To help people understand the radical shift that required, we identified some key symptoms or markers of both brokenness and wholeness.

RELATIONSHIPS IN THE NEW FAMILY OF JESUS

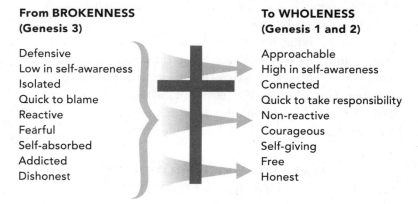

From BROKENNESS (Genesis 3)	To WHOLENESS (Genesis 1 and 2)
Defensive	Approachable
Low in self-awareness	High in self-awareness
Isolated	Connected
Quick to blame	Quick to take responsibility
Reactive	Non-reactive
Fearful	Courageous
Self-absorbed	Self-giving
Addicted	Free
Dishonest	Honest

Over a period of twenty-one years, we also developed eight powerful skills to help people transition from brokenness to wholeness. After refining and testing these skills in a variety of church contexts in North America and around the world, we eventually published them in *The Emotionally Healthy Relationships Course.* Our aim was to equip our people to love like Jesus at home, work, school, with friends, in their neighborhoods, and of course, in the church.[5] The course essentially gave people relationship training wheels, basic skills so they could apply

Scripture and break deeply entrenched, unhealthy relational patterns from their families of origin.

As we began to bring this into churches, we met resistance. For some pastors, the notion of dedicating time and energy to disciple people in healthy relationship skills was too foreign and intimidating. It didn't seem as spiritual and deep as preaching, prayer, or healing services.

One pastor called me and said, "Pete, I'm not really good at the relational thing. But we do have a number of recurring conflicts in our church. Can you just give me the bottom line on that in an hour or so?"

I chuckled, reminding him that equipping people to love like Jesus required the same level of energy he gave to equipping them to love God. If he failed to make that kind of investment, he would be leaving his people emotionally immature. Conflicts would continue, and they would remain severely handicapped in their ability to have the more difficult conversations that divide people, such as race and politics. However, if he were willing to do this work and make love the measure of spiritual maturity, it would unleash a discipleship revolution in his church.

To help pastors like my friend and others better understand the shift we were making, we developed a compelling framework to make plain the link between emotional and spiritual maturity. We did this in two ways: by drawing on Martin Buber's seminal work on the nature of relationships, which itself is steeped in the riches of the Jewish, and particularly Hasidic, tradition; and by taking a deep dive into the incarnation of Jesus as our model for loving well.

MARTIN BUBER: FROM *I-IT* TO *I-THOU* RELATIONSHIPS

Following Martin Buber's encounter with the young man who later committed suicide, he developed a framework for understanding relationships that he defined using two word pairs: *I-It* and *I-Thou*.

Buber proposed that I-It and I-Thou relationships represent two distinct ways of being with another person—that of an "I" toward an "It" or object, and that of an "I" toward a "Thou." When we relate to a person as an object or means to an end, we treat them as an "It."

When we relate to people as sacred or holy, we treat them as a "Thou."[6] The following chart offers five key qualities that distinguish the two.

I-It Relationship	I-Thou Relationship
Distracted, goal-oriented	Fully attentive, listening-oriented
Others are objects or extensions of oneself.	Others are persons, unique and separate.
Judgmental, conditional acceptance	Nonjudgmental, radical acceptance
Monologue, debate, make my point	Dialogue, exploration, curiosity
Withhold myself, limited sharing	Offer myself, vulnerable self-disclosure
Closed, unwilling to learn or change	Open, willing to learn and change

What does it look like to have an I-It relationship in the context of the church? Here are just a few examples from my own life.

- I maintain eye contact while listening to someone, but my mind is focused on what to say next.
- I pass a maintenance worker in our building without saying hello.
- I am more concerned about the flow and quality of my sermon message than I am about loving and connecting with the people in the audience.
- I size up people based on the schools they attended, where they are from, where they work, or their Enneagram number.
- I feel responsible to correct people when faulty views about God come up in conversations.
- I work hard to hide my annoyance when listening to a person with whom I disagree.

Is it any wonder that I often found myself impatient with people who didn't fit into my plans or expectations? My approach was I-It.

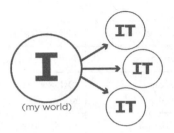

(my world)

I-Thou relationships are completely different.

In I-Thou relationships, we recognize each person as unrepeatable, an inestimable treasure, an image-bearer of the living God. We treat each individual as sacred, as one created from the very breath of God. Most importantly, we welcome their otherness, acknowledging how different they are from us.

In other words, we don't try to get something from them or treat them as an extension of ourselves, the way we might treat an object such as a hammer or a phone. In an I-Thou encounter, we come to the other without preconditions—without masks, pretenses, and, at times, without words. We are completely available to them, seeking to understand them.

We are in a living relationship—a whole person to a whole person—surrendering to the immediacy of the other's presence without an agenda. "All real life is meeting," was how Buber described it.[7]

But true I-Thou relationships, said Buber, can exist only between two people willing to connect across their differences. When that happens, God fills that in-between space. God is not only glimpsed in genuine dialogue between the two persons, but he also supernaturally occupies the space between them, making it sacred space.

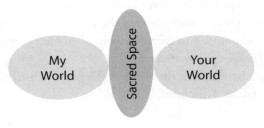

The central tenet of Buber's work was that the I-Thou relationship between persons intimately reflects the I-Thou relationship we have with God. In other words, genuine relationship with any person as a Thou reveals traces of the "eternal Thou." This helps to explain why it is such a powerful experience when two people listen deeply to one another.

This is in fact what had happened between Geri and me in our experience of incarnational listening. We had an I-Thou encounter, our first after eight years of friendship and nearly nine years of marriage!

Let me illustrate this with another example.

Martin Buber was deeply influenced by Eastern European Hasidism and his life as a Jewish man who had suffered pogroms and persecution over decades, including that of Hitler's Germany. When he met with T. S. Eliot, a renowned poet, winner of the Nobel Prize for literature, and a convert to the Anglican church in England, many expected it would be a difficult meeting for Buber. The two men's histories, religious beliefs, and circle of friends could scarcely have been more dissimilar.

At the end of their meeting, Buber was asked if he found his own opinions very different than those of Eliot. His reply offers us a window into what it means to treat another person as a Thou rather than an It: "When I meet a man," he said, "I am not concerned with opinions but with the man."[8]

It's a beautiful story; however, it is often easier said than done, especially in a polarized culture. For a variety of reasons, we often absorb unhealthy and sometimes unspoken messages about loving and relating to people who are different from us:

It is bad that we have differing views.
You must see the world as I do.
I can't stay in relationship with you if you continue believing those
wrong things.

This is part of the reason people often view Christians as judgmental instead of loving and compassionate.

Buber's distinction of I-It versus I-Thou, however, offers us a pathway to break this impasse and help us enter into and remain in authentic, loving relationship with others.

THE POWER OF ASKING YOURSELF
THREE QUESTIONS

How do we live this out in everyday life? How do we practice the presence of people in the same way we practice the presence of God? One tool that has served me well comes from three questions offered by David Benner in his book *Soulful Spirituality*:

1. Am I fully present or distracted?
2. Am I loving or judging?
3. Am I open or closed to being changed?[9]

Our ability to ask ourselves these questions, before and during our time with someone, and to respond in ways that are present, loving, and open, is a great measure of our ability to be with them in an I-Thou posture.

Question 1: Am I Fully Present or Distracted?

I had never experienced someone being fully present to me until I experienced it with a Christian therapist, and with Geri, in the crucible of our marriage and ministry crisis. The therapist offered us an experience of Jesus with skin on—present, unrushed, undistracted.

He modeled what Henri Nouwen beautifully describes as the nature of authentic presence:

> To care means first of all to be present to each other. From experience you know that those who care for you become present to you. When they listen, they listen to you. When they speak, they speak to you. Their presence is a healing presence because they accept you on your terms, and they encourage you to take your own life seriously.[10]

My middle name is "distractable." It is not unusual for me to have three to four ideas floating around my brain at the same time and to miss whatever or whomever is right in front of me. There was nothing in my history that understood how to be present to someone. So, while I have grown a great deal in this area, it remains critical that I ask myself this first question—*Am I fully present or distracted?*—before I even enter a conversation, especially if I hope to understand the other person's experience of the world and share mine with them.

Research has shown that our ability to have face-to-face conversations with eye contact and to connect emotionally has decreased dramatically over the last fifteen to twenty-five years, a fact that only further exasperates our problem. Technology such as smartphones and social media has impacted every area of life, from the workplace to family life to parenting to friendships to classrooms to dating to church communities.[11] This makes it all the more important that we be intentional about being fully present when we are with someone.

Question 2: Am I Loving or Judging?

When people outside the church describe Christians, one of the first words they use is *judgmental*. And they are right.

We judge our spouses for not doing life our way.

We judge our close friends when their politics differ from our own.

We judge our adult children for making choices we think they shouldn't.

We judge our coworkers for not doing their jobs as well as we'd like.

We judge our neighbors for not being responsive to the gospel.

We judge Hindus, Muslims, Buddhists, Sikhs, and other faiths—along with atheists and agnostics—for not following Jesus as Savior and Lord.

We judge younger or older generations for making choices of which we don't approve.

We judge people for their different social class, race, ethnicity, appearance, or education.

We judge them for dressing up or dressing down, for the movies they watch, the cars they buy, or the music they listen to.

We even judge people based on their Enneagram number.

And when I say we *judge* people, I mean we turn our differences into virtues of moral superiority. And in so doing, we create never-ending ways to subtly categorize people and diminish their humanity.[12]

I speak as a recovering judgeaholic. Like most people I know, I don't do well with people who think, act, or believe differently than I do.

I was trained to be judgmental in my family of origin. We simply considered it normal to disapprove of anyone who was different and to try to get them to change so they would see the world as we did.

At this point, you may be wondering, "Isn't it part of our mission as Christians to want people to believe as we do? Aren't we *supposed* to try and get people to change?"

My answer: Yes and no.

Yes, we want people to know the God who so loved the world he gave his only Son. Yes, we want them to participate in Jesus's mission to build his church and expand his kingdom around the world.

But, no, it is not part of our mission to judge people, even in the name of standing up for truth. When we judge, we treat people as objects. Only God, with a knowledge infinitely greater than ours, has the right and the wisdom to judge another person. Crossing that line, as Karl Barth notes, leads us into "the root and origin of sin, the arrogance in which man wants to be his own and his neighbor's judge."[13]

Buber coined the term "mismeeting" to describe any "failure of real meeting between [people]."[14] A mismeeting is what happens when we judge people, treat them as objects, or diminish them in any other way. What Buber described as a "real meeting" can only happen when we see and engage the other as a coequal human being. "Every person born into this world, represents something new," he wrote, "something that never existed before, something original and unique."[15]

So we come to every conversation curious, even when people are making choices we consider biblically wrong, tragic, or foolish. These can range from why a person has had gender reconstructive surgery, left the church to convert to Buddhism, or decided to move in with their partner.[16]

We recognize our first task as a follower of Jesus is to see each person as a Thou, sincerely asking, "Tell me more. Help me understand how you see the world and how you came to that decision or conclusion."

Question 3: Am I Open or Closed to Being Changed?

This question is the deal breaker for many, especially if the other person is not a Christian. Why should we be open to being changed, especially about something we consider a fundamental value or when we "know" the other person is "wrong"? We need to be open to being changed because it's a requirement for dialogue. If we are closed to being changed, the best we can hope for is a one-sided monologue.

You may be wondering, "Pete, are you saying that anything goes, that there is no absolute truth? That we have to be willing to let go of what God says is true?" No, not at all.

As I mentioned earlier, I am passionate to see people come to faith in Jesus. And I am anchored in the historic faith of the church fathers as articulated in faith documents such as the Nicene Creed (see Appendix B).[17]

At the same time, I also consider it biblical to engage another unrepeatable image bearer of God in a posture of openness—to assume I *can* learn from and be changed by them. How? By looking for other gifts to receive from them. Sixteenth-century theologian John Calvin wrote about the "admirable light of truth shining" in the thoughts of ancient Greek and Roman thinkers. Though he considered them pagan, he also commended their insights:

> Whenever we come upon these matters in secular writers, let that admirable light of truth shining in them teach us that the mind of man, though fallen and perverted from its wholeness, is nevertheless clothed and ornamented with God's excellent gifts. If we regard the Spirit of God as the sole fountain of truth, we shall neither reject the truth itself, nor despise it wherever it shall appear, unless we wish to dishonor the Spirit of God.[18]

Nineteenth-century Dutch theologian Abraham Kuyper also affirmed God's Spirit operating through unbelievers, insisting that the activity of the Spirit was a common grace at work in human lives.[19]

Differentness makes us uncomfortable. And so we truly believe that others—not us—are the ones who need to change. Yet, God calls us to be with and to love people who see and experience the world differently than we do. And we can do so without losing or compromising our faith in Jesus. We do this by entering conversations with others as humble learners who are open to the true dialogue required for an I-Thou encounter.[20]

This process can be difficult even when we have a great deal in common with a person.

For example, just recently Geri and I had a conflict. Our interaction ended poorly. As I sat in my office, sulking and blaming her, I journaled. I asked myself the three questions: *Can I be present and not distracted? Can I be loving and not judgmental? Can I be open rather than closed to being changed?* It was the final question that was most difficult. Was I willing to listen to be transformed by her experience and perspective? My pride and self-will shouted no. Jesus inside me nudged me toward yes. Reluctantly, I initiated a conversation with her.

So I listened as she shared her perspective on the workload that came when several of our adult children and young grandchildren moved in with us due to Covid-19, and I did so without interjecting to defend myself. The tension between us dissipated. God came to me through her. And I grew up a little that day.

I mentioned earlier that there are two essential theological components in order to shift culture so that love for people is the measure of spiritual maturity. Martin Buber's work on I-Thou and I-It relationships is the first component, and the second is equally important—making the incarnation of Jesus our model for loving well.

JESUS: THE INCARNATION AS OUR MODEL FOR LOVING WELL

What it means to be a disciple can best be understood around the unfathomable mystery of the incarnation—that God took on human flesh. God knew there was no better way to convey his love to human beings than to fully enter their world. Author and theologian Ronald Rolheiser illustrates why this was so important:

> There is a marvelous story told about a four-year-old child who awoke one night frightened, convinced that in the darkness around her there were all kinds of spooks and monsters. Alone, she ran to her parents' bedroom. Her mother calmed her down, and taking her by the hand, led her back to her own room, where she put on a light and reassured the child with these words: "You needn't be afraid, you are not alone here. God is in the room with you." The child replied: "I know that God is here, but I need someone in this room who has some skin!"[21]

God knew we needed more than words or intellectual assurance that he is everywhere and that he loves us. He knew we needed a God who has some skin, and so he sent us Jesus. Today, God still comes to us in physical form. How? Through his body, the church, in whom he dwells. We are called to be God with skin on for the people around us. That is part of what it means to live out an incarnational faith.

Almost every Christian leader I meet believes in the incarnation of Jesus and in incarnational ministry. But as Basil, the fourth-century bishop of Caesarea, once wrote: "Annunciations are frequent, and incarnations are rare." In other words, bold announcements of what God is doing are common. But people who actually practice being God with skin on are much more difficult to find. Why? Because living an incarnational faith requires a particular type of death to self.

Let me explain.

The life of Jesus teaches us three dynamics that characterize what it looks like to incarnate in order to love people well: we must enter another's world, hold on to ourselves, and live in the tension between two worlds.

All three, while distinct, happen simultaneously. For true incarnation to take place—whether it is with a neighbor, coworker, friend, fellow board member with whom we disagree, a spouse, a parent, or a child—all three dynamics must be active.

Dynamic 1: Enter Another's World

Just as Jesus left his home in heaven to immerse himself in our world, we too must leave our world and enter into the very different world of another person. The best way we do this is through listening. I love how theologian David Augsburger sums it up: "Being heard is so close to being loved that for the average person, they are almost indistinguishable."[22]

> **THE INCARNATION AND DYNAMICS TO LOVE WELL**
>
> 1. **Enter another's world.**
> 2. Hold on to yourself.
> 3. Live in the tension between two worlds.

The only kind of listening I knew, until age thirty-seven, was listening for the purpose of defending, giving an opinion, or advising. My communication style resembled a rapid-fire machine gun. I interrupted others and finished their sentences when the conversation was moving too slowly. The image below illustrates unhealthy togetherness in which we subtly pressure the another person to think and feel like we do.

Unhealthy Togetherness

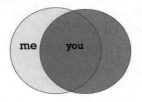

In unhealthy togetherness, there is a lack of recognition and respect for the other person as a separate human being with their own thoughts, feelings, fears, and values. It is not clear where one person ends and another begins.

Jesus, on the other hand, spoke to people clearly and respectfully. The Gospels are filled with accounts of him being fully present with individuals—Matthew, Nathaniel, a prostitute, Nicodemus, a blind man, a Samaritan woman, and many others. When the rich young ruler approached him, Jesus "looked at him and loved him" (Mark 10:21). He took the time to listen. He honored each person's separateness and uniqueness.

Healthy Togetherness

Like many people, I had heard many sermons on the importance of listening and being slow to speak (James 1:19). But listening and speaking like Jesus did not come naturally for me. And yet, as Geri and I began to learn more about emotionally healthy discipleship, we discovered how central listening well is to loving well. This led us to learn—and eventually teach—two key skills: speaking and incarnational listening.

Speaking uses the God-given power of words to bring healing, growth, and the love of Jesus to people. It is indispensable to spiritual maturity and healthy community. In Emotionally Healthy Discipleship, we characterize skillful speaking as words spoken respectfully, honestly, clearly, and in a timely fashion.

Respectfully. Give thought to your words and don't simply blurt them out. Take the other person's feelings into consideration. Instead of, "How could you like that movie? It was terrible," you say, "That is fascinating. Tell me what you liked about that movie."

Honestly. Say what you truly think and feel rather than softpedaling or distorting the truth. Instead of, "I can't volunteer because I have other plans," you say, "I prefer not to volunteer because I want to have some time alone at home."

Clearly. Communicate directly. Rather than being vague or dropping hints, be clear. Instead of, "Are you busy Tuesday night?" you ask clearly, "Would you be willing to attend the class I'm teaching on Tuesday night and give me feedback on how I can improve?"

In a timely fashion. Consider the moment. You understand that some moments are better than others for certain conversations. You notice when the other person is tired, irritated, or short on time, and you choose to wait until they are more relaxed before talking about your concerns.

Few of us have had this modeled in our family. Most of the people we lead have a lifetime of habitually *not* speaking respectfully, honestly, clearly, and in a timely fashion. That is why practice and continual reinforcement is vital, especially when we are in conflict or under stress.

Along with speaking, entering another's world involves incarnational listening. It was this skill that gave Geri and me the communication guardrails and structure we needed so we could truly "attune"[23] to one another. We needed to get beyond facts and information to feelings. This skill, when exercised properly, enables us to hear more than just words. In incarnational listening, the listener also attends to nonverbals such as facial expression, tone and intensity of voice, and posture. This type of holistic listening is what enables us to enter into another person's world so he or she "feels felt." [24]

How to Practice
Incarnational Listening

When we teach incarnational listening, we give people this question to start: *What is the biggest thing impacting you and how are you feeling about it?* We then allow eight to ten minutes for each person when it is their turn to speak. We encourage listeners to pay attention to what is said verbally and non-verbally, such as facial expressions, body posture, tone of voice, eye contact, head movements, and wordless sounds (ooh, ahh, oh, etc.).

We use the following format.

How to begin . . .
• Decide who will speak first and who will listen first.

When you are the speaker . . .
• Speak using "I" statements. (Talk about *your* thoughts, feelings, and desires.)
• Keep your statements brief.
• Stop occasionally to let the other person paraphrase what you've said.
• Include feelings in your statements.
• Be respectful, honest, and clear.

When you are the listener . . .
• Give the speaker your full attention (don't be thinking about what you want to say next).
• Step into the speaker's shoes and try to feel what they are feeling.
• Avoid judging or interpreting.
• Reflect back, or paraphrase as accurately as you can, what you heard them say.
• When you think they may be done, ask, "Is there more?"
• When they are done, ask, "Of everything you shared, what is the most important thing you want me to remember?"

Adhering to the structure and boundaries of incarnational listening may feel awkward or rigid at first (See "Geri's Story of Discovering Incarnational Listening" below). But remember, these guidelines are training wheels—necessary when you begin learning, but unnecessary later as you internalize the skill. We especially need the structure in the beginning to help us break deeply embedded bad habits that go back generations.

When we were first learning this skill, Geri once said to me, "Pete, I felt like you murdered me with your words."

I responded: "So you were a little angry with what I said."

I changed the words to soften Geri's hurt behind them. But the structure of reflecting what she had stated kept me honest and accurate.

A couple of things to note. First, incarnational listening is not a matter of agreeing with what the person is saying. The purpose of incarnational listening is not finding the solution to a problem. (Although research does show that up to 70 percent of problems can be solved through listening.) Problem solving, or clean fighting as we call it, requires a different emotionally healthy skill.

Second, be warned that speaking and listening in order to enter the world of another requires strong character and emotional maturity—especially when the other person is saying something with which we disagree or something negative about us. Our first reaction is often to defend ourselves. God invites us to drop our shields and become more open and approachable.

Geri's Story of Discovering Incarnational Listening

"I will never forget the first time I experienced the fruit of this skill and saw evidence of how God was changing us. Pete and I had practiced incarnational listening on several occasions. Then one day I was at the kitchen sink and Pete walked in and asked me a question. He wanted my opinion about an issue he was struggling with related to the church. In the past, he hadn't really wanted my opinion. Asking me a question was just his way of processing out loud.

> "But on this day, he looked into my eyes and was present with me. And he said, 'I really want to listen to you. Your thoughts and feelings matter to me.'
>
> "I almost fell on the floor. This wasn't just an exercise anymore—something profound was changing in him and in our relationship. It was a holy moment."

Dynamic 2: Hold On to Yourself

The second dynamic—holding on to yourself—may be the most challenging. Why? Because once we enter into someone else's world, it takes great maturity and differentiation to hold on to our sense of self.

Jesus models this for us. In living faithfully to his true self, Jesus disappointed a lot of people. Almost everyone seemed to have expectations and pressures they imposed on his life. He disappointed his family, and at one point, they wondered if he was out of his mind (Mark 3:21). He disappointed the Twelve disciples as they consistently projected on to him the kind of Messiah they wanted Jesus to be. Yet Jesus remained true to himself, even as Judas betrayed him. Jesus disappointed the crowds who wanted an earthly messiah to heal and feed them. And he disappointed the religious leaders who never understood him.

> **THE INCARNATION AND DYNAMICS TO LOVE WELL**
>
> 1. Enter another's world.
> 2. **Hold on to yourself.**
> 3. Live in the tension between two worlds.

Jesus was secure in his Father's love, both in himself and in what he had been given to do. He held on to himself as he loved those around him. As a result, he was able to be a non-anxious presence in the midst of great stress.

Some of us, however, have not done the inner work to know ourselves, and as a result, we too easily take on other people's opinions and expectations. We become chameleons. See if you can relate to any of the following scenarios.

- You are hurt by a coworker's comment, but you don't say anything because you don't want to be thought of as overly sensitive or judgmental.

- You are invited to the wedding of a board member's daughter on a Saturday night three hours away from your home. You do not want to attend, but you go rather than face his disapproval.
- You have a key volunteer working with middle school students who is underperforming and holding back the rest of the team. You hint at the need for change, but she is not getting the message. You cannot bear the thought of causing her to leave the church or be angry with you. You simply find another volunteer and split her group into two.
- A team member uses inappropriate language around you, some of which is racist and demeaning. You say nothing lest he judge you as self-righteous and arrogant.

At times we empathize too much and lose ourselves in the process. We are most susceptible to this when we haven't done the inner work to explore our own preferences, values, feelings, opinions, hopes, and delights. We haven't considered how God is speaking through our life story and unique personality and temperament. As a result, we forget that we have a self to lose.[25]

Remember, Jesus is our model. He knew who he was and where he came from. What I have to give to others—including the way I speak and listen—will always be directly proportional to my degree of self-knowledge. If I don't know myself, the only self I have to offer will be a false self. As a wise mentor taught me years ago, *The degree to which you love and value yourself is the degree to which you will be able to love and value others.*

Here's a true story of what it looks like in practical terms to hold on to oneself while simultaneously entering the world of another.

Two women in our church who were friends recognized there was tension in their relationship. Donna was upset with Allison because it seemed like Allison always declined when Donna asked her to do something. But when Allison suggested an activity, Donna was always willing and available.

Annoyed and angry, Donna finally confronted Allison.

Allison could have felt attacked and responded defensively. However, she had been learning to hold on to herself while entering the world of another. In the past, she always said yes to Donna's invitations because she would have felt like a bad person for saying no. Now, she was respecting herself enough to realize she had a choice to say yes or no. She was finally able to acknowledge that she was an introvert who needed lots of time alone to recharge. Donna, on the other hand, was an extrovert who loved going out—a lot.

So, what did Allison do when Donna confronted her?

First, she listened to Donna's disappointment, sadness, and anger without reacting or defending herself. Then Allison said, "Donna, I appreciate you as a friend. I enjoy spending time with you. I just need the freedom to say no. You see, I need a lot of alone time."

In doing so, Allison held on to herself, honored her own feelings and desires, and also held on to Donna by entering into her world.

Fortunately, Donna responded well and she and Allison were able to navigate a new rhythm for their friendship. But let's imagine that instead Allison had lost herself when confronted by Donna. If she had believed that saying no made her a bad person, she would likely have apologized and then tried to accept every invitation from Donna. Over time, she would probably have grown resentful and it might have ended the relationship. But by holding on to herself, and to Donna, Allison preserved and deepened their friendship.

Dynamic 3: Live in the Tension between Two Worlds

When we choose to incarnate love by moving into the world of another person (Dynamic 1), we must still remain faithful to who we are by holding on to ourselves (Dynamic 2). This leads to the difficult work of living in the tension between our world and the world of another person (Dynamic 3). Living in the tension between two worlds occurs when we listen deeply even though we may not fully agree with what the other person is saying—and doing so without reacting, growing impatient, or becoming defensive.

During his life on earth, Jesus lived in the tension between two worlds: heaven and earth. He left a perfect world to enter our world—a place where he would be misunderstood and persecuted. He experienced suffering on a cross, where he literally hung between heaven and earth.

You and I may not physically die on a cross as Jesus did, but we cannot love incarnationally without embracing our own cross—experiencing some form of death to self. At the very least, the choice to hang between two worlds will cost us time and energy, and almost always cause a disruption to our world.

One of the best illustrations I know of what it means to hang between two worlds is the true story of Sister Helen Prejean, author of the bestselling book *Dead Man Walking*, which was later made into a feature film.

As portrayed in the film, Sister Helen Prejean was working in the St. Thomas housing projects in New Orleans when she received an invitation to be a pen pal with an inmate on death row in the Louisiana State Penetentiary. The condemned man, Matthew Poncelet,[26] had been accused of a terrible crime. Along with his brother, he had found two beautiful teenagers, Loretta and David, in a lover's lane sugar field after a Friday night homecoming game. The men had raped Loretta, shot both Loretta and David execution style in the back of the head, and then left their bodies in the field.

> **THE INCARNATION AND DYNAMICS TO LOVE WELL**
>
> 1. Enter another's world.
> 2. Hold on to yourself.
> 3. **Live in the tension between two worlds.**

Sister Helen initially wonders if Poncelet's claims to innocence might be true. He protests that it was his partner who actually committed the rape and murders, and he wants Sister Helen to work on his behalf to get him off death row. But when Sister Helen enters his world, it is not pretty. Matthew is not a lovable character. He is racist, uses the "n word," and talks of how well Hitler got the job done. He refers to women as the "b word" and talks about how he wants to blow up government buildings. Matthew informs Sister Helen that she missed out by not being married and having sex.

He evokes no sympathy.

Nonetheless, Sister Helen holds on to herself and her convictions, treating him as a fellow human being, not a monster. She repeatedly invites him to make himself right with God by confessing his sin. She tries to get him to take responsibility for what he did. Progress is slow, very slow.

At the same time, Sister Helen initiates a relationship with the grieving families. She enters their world of unfathomable loss and pain.

The parents of the dead children are outraged, and pressures mount for Sister Helen to back off her involvement with Matthew. The families draw a line in the sand. "You can't befriend that murderer and expect to be our friend too," says the father of one victim. He asks Sister Helen to leave his house, saying, "If you really care about this family, you'll want to see justice done."

Newspapers pick up Matthew's racist, pro-Nazi views and also mention his connection with Sister Helen. Her colleagues complain that she is neglecting her work at the St. Thomas projects. "You care more about him than your classes," one of them says.

When the male victim's father asks Sister Helen how she has the faith to do what she does, she replies, "It's not faith, it's work."

She does not give up. Over time, Matthew begins to let down his defenses. Finally, at 11:38 p.m., only minutes before his midnight execution, she asks him, "Do you take responsibility for both of their deaths?"

Crying, he admits his guilt for the first time. A few minutes later, he says, "Thank you for loving me. I never had anybody really love me before."

Sister Helen recalls their walk together toward his execution. "That walk was the first time I had ever touched him. I looked down and saw his chains dragging across the gleaming tile floor. His head was shaved, and he was dressed in a clean, white T-shirt. When they took him into the execution chamber, I leaned over and kissed his back. "Matthew, pray for me."

"Sister Helen, I will."

When he is strapped to the chair to be injected with lethal solutions, she tells him to watch her face. "That way the last thing you will see before you die will be the face of someone who loves you." He does so and dies in love rather than in bitterness.

We observe in Sister Helen what it means to live in the tension between two worlds. It is painful. It requires great character. Yet in this way, we enter the suffering of Jesus who, out of love for the world, hung on a cross between heaven and earth.

Sister Helen hangs between multiple worlds—the condemned killer's world, the grieving parents' world, her colleagues' world, and her own world. She never ceases to be committed to her community, the victims' parents, or Matthew, even though everyone misunderstands and judges her. But like Jesus, she remains faithful out of love for Matthew and the world.

Whenever we make the incarnation our model for loving well, we will experience tension and pain. That tension may be with a spouse, friend, supervisor, child, sibling, coworker, neighbor, or a person from a different race, culture, or social class. But as servants we are not above our master, and as students we are not above our teacher (Matthew 10:24). We too must follow the pattern of the crucified Jesus and die so others may live.

REVOLUTIONIZE HOW YOU MEASURE MATURITY

Jesus refused to accept that people were growing in love for God in a way that did not translate into love for people. We must refuse to accept that as well. The religious leaders of his day knew their Bible, practiced spiritual disciplines, and worshiped faithfully, but they were defensive, judgmental, and unsafe to be around. And so are many people in our churches.

Jesus's integration of love for God and people was revolutionary in the first century, and it remains revolutionary today. "We listen to God about as well as we listen to those we do not agree with,"[27] is something he would have said. His priority was clear: "By this everyone will know that you are my disciples, if you love one another" (John 13:35). We are to be the best lovers of people on the face of the earth.

For this reason, building a countercultural community that relates maturely to one another is truly one of the greatest gifts we can offer the world. Discipling people in how to love others, especially those with whom we disagree or who drive us crazy, needs the same time and energy we give to equipping them to love God. The two loves are, as Jesus said, inseparable.

Martin Buber's I-It and I-Thou—along with Jesus's incarnational model of loving well—offer a powerful framework to create a radically new culture in our churches and communities. And in so doing, we open up a pathway for our people to experience more of God's love, something they can now offer freely to the world.

Chapter Eight

Break the Power of the Past

In the early years of our marriage, Geri often asked me about my family growing up. She noted, for example, that screaming and yelling was a regular part of the way our family communicated.

It seemed perfectly normal to me.

I remember Geri saying, three years into our marriage: "Pete, do you realize that I've yet to have a real conversation with your mother? You know, like, 'Hi, Geri, nice to see you.'"

I reminded her that my mom was warming up to losing her youngest son at the early age of twenty-eight!

Much of my behavior also confused Geri.

I had these strong, charge-the-hill leadership gifts from God, and at the same time, a crippling indecisiveness. I would rally the troops and boldly launch a new initiative, and then fall into a depressive, stay-up-all-night fetal position when I was criticized.

Geri saw that I was consumed to get the church off the ground, regardless of the cost. I'd leave her home alone with a three-year-old and a one-year-old, for example, even when holidays fell on Mondays, because these were strategic times for outreach. It never occurred to me to consult with her.

Another glaring inconsistency she observed was my reaction to angry, complaining, strong women. I'd become silent and shrink back emotionally as if I were a ten-year-old boy, irrationally agreeing to things that were harmful to me, to the church, and to our family.

When Geri asked about my family to try and get to the root of some of these issues, I shut it down: "It's under the blood," I said. "I'm a new creation in Jesus."

She replied with one of her classic one-liners: "No, you're not. I live with you!"

MY MARRIAGE SHAPED BY
MY FAMILY HISTORY

Christ had transformed my life in many ways. As Paul explains in Romans and Galatians, the moment I became a Christian, God declared me pardoned and set free from the penalty of my sins. By grace, I was now a full member of his family.

Yes, my childhood had its ups and downs. Doesn't everyone's?

I certainly wasn't in the business of blaming my parents for all the problems in my life. My attitude was, "I'm in the family of God. My life is guided by my commitment to and love for Jesus. I am doing so many things differently from my family of origin. I don't hold grudges. I do household chores. I change diapers. I'm committed to the world knowing Jesus."

The list was thin, but I felt it reflected the ways in which I had in fact changed. Unfortunately, it also reflected how blind I was to how much the negative legacies I'd inherited from my family of origin still dominated my day-to-day life—especially in my leadership. And sadly, I was resistant to anything that required reflecting on how my past might be affecting me in the present.

I will never forget the first time Geri and I did a very simple exercise to examine our marriage in light of our parents' marriages. We each described our fathers, our mothers, and listed some general characteristics of their marriages, such as how they resolved conflict, expressed anger, understood gender roles, and connected and bonded with one another.

When we finished, Geri and I sat back in our chairs and looked at each other in shock. Although we had prided ourselves on how much further along we were than our parents, we were stunned to discover how much the unhealthy patterns in our parents' marriages nevertheless still marked ours. Wherever Christ was in our lives, he had not transformed—at least in any substantial way—our relationship with one another.

We were saddened and embarrassed. We also had to admit that the problem went far beyond our marriage. Now we could see why people whom we mentored remained stuck at an immature level of spiritual and emotional development—and also why all our Bible studies, prayer and fasting, and small group meetings would not change that.

My resistance to looking at my own past and my unwillingness to wrestle with its implications for my leadership had deeply impacted our church. Our church was one mile wide and one inch deep because I was one mile wide and one inch deep. Few of us were looking at issues beneath the surface of our lives. Even fewer were looking at how our past impacted our present. Looking back, I am embarrassed at how I could have deluded myself into thinking that an immature leader (me) with an immature marriage (us) could possibly grow a mature congregation (ours).

God, in his sovereignty, chose to birth us into a particular family, in a particular place, at a particular moment in history. That choice offered us certain opportunities and gifts. At the same time, our families also handed us other entrenched, unbiblical patterns of relating and living. In fact, Scripture and life teach us that an intricate, complex relationship exists between the kind of person we are today and our past.

For this reason, one of the greatest tragedies in the church is the large numbers of people crippled by their pasts. Unaware that their past impacts their present, they bury or minimize the family history that lives inside them and settle for a constricted Christian life in which they are stuck spiritually and emotionally.

If we are going to help people live into their unique, God-given selves in Jesus, we must equip them to break the power of the past that holds them back. Numerous external forces may impact us, but the family in which we grew up is the primary one and, except in rare instances, the most powerful system that shapes and influences who we are.

For years, Geri and I simply didn't know how to get at the brokenness and wounds deep beneath the surface of our own lives, much less the lives of those we led. To paint a picture of what this dynamic might look like in the life of a person in your church, allow me to share a story about a promising new worship leader who joined the staff at a good friend's church.

A WORSHIP LEADER SHAPED
BY HIS FAMILY HISTORY

Todd, age thirty-five, accepted Christ in high school through the ministry of Young Life. After attending college and earning a degree in music, Todd moved to a new city, married, and worked as a music teacher at a nearby high school. He and his wife, Julie, joined a new church plant of sixty people and immediately got involved. They participated in a small group for young couples and Todd began playing piano and singing on the worship team. His gifts in both music and leadership were evident from the start. Within six months, he began leading worship two to three times a month.

The congregation was thrilled. More new people visited the church. The pastor was in awe that God had dropped such a great talent into their midst.

By year two, however, issues began to emerge in Todd's behavior. It began when Julie called the pastor in tears one evening about the state of her marriage. Todd was rarely home and even when he was physically present, he was absent emotionally. Then, a young woman on the worship team mentioned to the spouse of a board member that Todd had texted her multiple times just to chat. She felt uncomfortable and wondered how to respond. At about the same time, Todd got into a heated argument about politics with one of the elders on social media. After two meetings between Todd and the pastor to clarify what was going on, Todd suddenly announced he was leaving the church. The next day, he wrote a half-hearted goodbye to the congregation on social media, subtly blaming the leadership for a lack of sensitivity to the Holy Spirit.

"What happened?" the church wondered. "He and Julie were such wonderful people and making such a great contribution."

When something like this happens to a member of our team, we generally respond in one of a few ways. We blame ourselves for our lack of wisdom and discernment. We establish new policies to ensure greater accountability in the future so people aren't promoted too quickly. Or, we may conclude that this is simply part of the price we pay for being in ministry. It happened to Jesus; it happens in other churches; it happens to us. Whatever the case, we do our best to pick up the pieces and move on.

While there may be grains of truth in one or more of the above responses, none address the core issue—the church was engaged in a thin discipleship that ignored the impact a person's past has on their ability to follow Jesus in the present.

GOING BACKWARD TO GO FORWARD:
A BIBLICAL FRAMEWORK

Scripture offers us a three-part, biblical framework for discipleship that frees us from the power of the past:

1. Acknowledge how the blessings and sins of your family—going back three to four generations—profoundly impacts who you are today.
2. Recognize you have been birthed into a new family—the family of Jesus.
3. Put off the sinful patterns of your family of origin and culture, and learn how to do life in the new family of Jesus.

This larger approach to discipleship—encompassing a person's past and family of origin—frees people so they can lay hold of God's great plan for their future.

1. **Acknowledge how the blessings and sins of your family—going back three to four generations—profoundly impacts who you are today.**

We are born into families, but biblical writers have a different understanding of the word "family" than we do. Throughout the Old and New Testaments, one's family refers not just to a couple and their children but to the entire extended family over three or four generations. If applied today, that understanding of family would include everyone in your family history going back to the late 1800s.

Scripture also teaches that the consequences of actions and decisions taken in one generation affect those who follow.

Consider the following:

> For I, the Lord your God, am a jealous God, *punishing the children for the sin of the parents to the third and fourth generation of those who hate me*, but showing love to a thousand generations of those who love me and keep my commandments." (Exodus 20:5–6, emphasis added)

An Old Testament scholar once shared with me that the best translation of the Hebrew word *punishing* used in this passage is *tends to be repeated*. In other words, what happens in one generation tends to repeat itself in the next, whether it be alcoholism, addiction, depression, suicide, unstable marriages, unwed pregnancies, mistrust of authority, or unresolved conflict.

Scientists and sociologists have been debating for decades whether this is a result of "nature" (our DNA) or "nurture" (our environment) or both. The Bible doesn't answer this question. It only states that this is a "mysterious law of God's universe."

While it may seem that each person is an individual acting alone, that person is also part of a larger family system going back, as the Bible says, three to four generations. And family patterns from the past are almost inevitably played out in present relationships and behavior.

Consider with me two famous families in Scripture, that of Abraham and that of David.

Abraham, Isaac, and Jacob

This story in Genesis clearly demonstrates how sins and blessings are passed from generation to generation. On one level, the blessings given to Abraham because of his obedience passed from generation to generation—to his children (Isaac), grandchildren (Jacob), and great-grandchildren (Joseph and his brothers). At the same time, we also observe a pattern of sin and brokenness transmitted through the generations.

For example, we observe:

A pattern of lying
- Abraham lied twice about Sarah.
- Isaac and Rebecca's marriage was characterized by lies.
- Jacob lied to almost everyone; his name means "deceiver."
- Ten of Jacob's children lied about Joseph's death, faking a funeral and keeping a "family secret" for more than ten years.

Favoritism by at least one parent
- Abraham favored Ishmael.
- Isaac favored Esau.
- Jacob favored Joseph and later Benjamin.

Brothers cut off from one another
- Isaac and Ishmael were cut off from one another.
- Jacob fled his brother Esau and was completely cut off for years.
- Joseph was cut off from his ten brothers for more than a decade.

Poor intimacy in marriages
- Abraham had a child out of wedlock with Hagar.
- Isaac had a terrible relationship with Rebecca.
- Jacob had two wives and two concubines.

David, Solomon, and Rehoboam

David is referred to as "a man after God's own heart" (Acts 13:22). He passes on enormous blessings to his son, Solomon, which continue for multiple generations. At the same time, he also passes on a pattern of sin and brokenness that continues for generations as well.

Spiritual and moral compromise
- David covers up his adultery and murder of Uriah.
- Solomon mixes worship of the God of Israel with other gods.
- Rehoboam, Solomon's son, rejects wise counsel and follows the gods of surrounding nations.

Sexual sin
- David takes many wives and commits adultery with Bathsheba.
- Solomon takes seven hundred wives and three hundred concubines.
- Rehoboam takes eighteen wives and sixty concubines.

> *Unresolved conflicts*
> - David has tensions with his seven older brothers.
> - Solomon's half-brother Absalom kills his brother and tries to kill his father, David.
> - Rehoboam splits with his brother and divides Israel into two.

God allows stories such as these to be recorded to teach us—we need to take a deep, hard look inside (1 Corinthians 10:6). The implication for those of use who lead and disciple others is clear. It is impossible to help people break free from their past apart from understanding the families in which they grew up. Unless we understand the power the past exerts on who we are in the present, we will inevitably replicate those patterns in relationships within and beyond the church.

2. Recognize you have been birthed into a new family— the family of Jesus.

The great news of the gospel is that your family of origin does not determine your future. God does! We are not only forgiven but freed from the power of sin present in our families over generations.[1] God's very life—in the person of the Holy Spirit—now resides within us. We receive a new heart, a new nature, and a new spirit (Ezekiel 36: 25–27).[2]

When we place our faith in Christ, we are spiritually reborn by the Holy Spirit into the family of Jesus. We are transferred out of darkness into the kingdom of light. What determines our new identity is no longer the blood of our biological family but the blood of Jesus. It is a radical new beginning.

The most significant language in the New Testament for becoming a Christian is adoption into the family of God (Romans 8:14–17). The apostle Paul used the familiar practice of Roman adoption to communicate this profound truth, emphasizing we are now in a new and permanent relationship with a new Father, God. Our debts (sins) are cancelled. We are given a new name (Christian), a new inheritance (freedom, hope, glory, the resources of heaven), and new brothers and sisters (from around the world).

In the ancient world of Jesus, honoring one's mother and father was an extremely high value. Yet, without hesitation, Jesus repeatedly called men and women to leave their biological families in order to follow him, saying, "Anyone who loves their father or mother more than me is not worthy of me" (Matthew 10:37). Jesus defined his new family as those who do his will and listen to him (Luke 8:19–21).

For the believer, the church is now the "first family."[3] Although the New Testament contains ninety-six metaphors for the church—including a body, a house, and a bride—the church as a family is the one most widely used.[4] Scholars Ray Anderson and Dennis Guernsey say it best:

> The church is the new family of God . . . Through spiritual rebirth, we each become a brother or sister of Jesus Christ through adoption into the family of God. Consequently, we are brother and sister to each other. . . . Husbands and wives are first of all brother and sister in Jesus Christ before they are husband and wife. Sons and daughters are also brother or sister to their father and mother before they are sons and daughters.[5]

The New Testament assumes that growing into maturity as a disciple happens within the context of a healthy local church. God's intention is that our local churches and parishes are the communities where, slowly but surely, we are re-parented in doing life Christ's way.

3. Put off the sinful patterns of your family of origin and culture, and learn how to do life in the new family of Jesus.

The extent to which we can go back and understand how our past has shaped us will determine to a large degree our ability to break destructive patterns, pass on positive legacies, and be transformed in Christ so we can offer our lives as a gift to the world. So why isn't this happening in most of our churches? Why is it that most people in our churches are not radically different from their unchurched neighbors, even though they may pray, read the Bible, and attend worship?

The answer: We have not taken seriously Jesus's call to break the power of the past and practically implement the third part of a biblical discipleship framework—putting off the sinful patterns of our family of origin and culture, and relearning how to do life God's way in the new family of Jesus.

Here's another way to think about it: *Jesus may live in your heart, but Grandpa lives in your bones.* In other words, those who precede us in the family tree—our "grandpas"—cast a long shadow, even generations after they are gone. Every disciple, then, has to look at the brokenness and sin of his or her family and culture.

But this is hard work.

SETTING YOUR CHURCH FREE

As we have endeavored to do this in our own congregation, and then with churches around the world, we have developed a five-part approach to help people break the power of the past for a great future—both individually and corporately:

1. Genogram your family, identifying how it has shaped you.
2. Do the hard work of discipleship.
3. Get a great future out of the past.
4. Break the power of the past in every area of life and leadership.
5. Name and tame the negative legacies of your ministry's history.

1. Genogram Your Family, Identifying How It Has Shaped You

Geri and I devoted almost two decades to adapt a tool from family systems theory—the genogram—for discipleship in the local church. We discovered that helping people construct a genogram is one of the most compelling and effective ways to help people with the difficult task of identifying how their family has shaped them.

A genogram, very simply, is a visual tool to look at the history and dynamics of our family relationships and their impact on us over three to four generations. It helps us examine unhealthy patterns from the past that we bring into our relationship with Christ and with others. And because our families are the most powerful, influential group that has shaped who we are today (except in rare instances), examining and understanding them is key to our transformation in Jesus.

It enables people to step out of their current circumstances and get the big picture of their life, much like the experience of astronauts and cosmonauts looking back at the planet from space and seeing the entire Earth for the first time.[6] When they saw the Earth from this perspective—as a tiny, fragile ball "hanging in the void," shielded by a paper-thin atmosphere—the transformation they experienced was so profound that a new term was invented to describe it: the Overview Effect.[7]

A similar transformation can happen to us as we review our family story over three to four generations using the genogram as a tool. We experience the Overview Effect, seeing our lives in an entirely new and holistic way.

The following are the types of questions we ask to get beneath the surface and identify how the past might be impacting the present.[8] We ask people to fill out the genogram through the eyes of their childhood, as if they were between eight and twelve years of age. As part of that process, we also ask them questions such as these:

- How would you describe each family member (parents, care-takers, grandparents, siblings, etc.) with two or three adjectives?

- How would you describe your parents' (or caretakers') and grandparents' marriages?
- How was conflict handled in your extended family over two to three generations? Anger? Gender roles?
- What were some generational themes (for example, addictions, affairs, losses, abuse, divorce, depression, mental illness, abortions, children born out of wedlock, etc.)?
- How well did your family do in talking about feelings?
- How was sexuality talked or not talked about? What were the implied messages?
- Were there any family "secrets" (such as an unwed pregnancy, incest, or financial scandal)?
- What was considered "success" in your family?
- How was money handled? Spirituality? Relationships with extended family?
- How did your family's ethnicity, race, culture shape you?
- Were there any heroes or heroines in the family? Scapegoats? "Losers"? Why?
- What addictions, if any, existed in the family?
- What traumatic losses has your family suffered? For example, sudden death, prolonged illness, stillbirth/miscarriage, bankruptcy, or divorce?
- What additional losses or wounds resulted from those traumatic losses? For example, loss of a nurturing childhood, loss of an emotionally available mother or father, loss of trust, etc.?

Using a set of symbols to describe the relational dynamics between people (such as conflictual, cutoffs, distant/poor relationships, enmeshment, and abuse), we ask people to describe the relationships between those named on their genogram. We then invite them to step back and ponder what they have written, asking: "What themes emerge over generations (noting any addictions, affairs, mental illness, children born out of wedlock, unemployment, family secrets)? This is followed by asking if there were any "earthquake events" in their family history, things that sent shock waves through the family for generations (such as war, suicide, infidelity, immigration from another country, etc.).[9]

After people fill out their genogram, we ask them to prayerfully reflect on these two questions:

- What one or two patterns from your family of origin might have most impacted who you are today?
- What might be one message from your family of origin that God has revealed to you today that you want to change as part of your hard work of discipleship?

We then add a third question for pastors and leaders: What are one or two specific ways this may be impacting your leadership in the church?

At this point, they are ready to consider the specific discipleship issues they need to address as members of the new family of Jesus.

2. Do the Hard Work of Discipleship

Jesus never sugarcoated the cost of discipleship. He said plainly, "Whoever wants to be my disciple must deny themselves and take up their cross daily and follow me" (Luke 9:23). This is an invitation to die to self—and not just once, but as a way of life. Yet when we apply this invitation and start breaking the particular and specific unhealthy patterns of our own past, the pain becomes very real and close.

Inevitably, we resist the hard work of discipleship. It seems too costly. Too difficult. Let's face it: We all want Easter without Good Friday, light without darkness, hope without despair, happiness without suffering. But breaking the power of the past requires a crucifixion—and so everything in us screams against it.

The operative word here is *specific*, applying Scripture to those embedded, unhealthy patterns that live in our bones. For example, I didn't do the vulnerable emotions of sadness and fear as an adult. These were unacceptable in my family of origin growing up, especially for men. So allowing myself to feel sadness and share that with my wife, Geri, for example, was a scary step of faith—at least initially. Why? This clashed with generations of family and cultural gender role messages that I had absorbed growing up.

Consider the following sample of unbiblical family commandments that live inside people in our churches:

EXAMPLES OF
UNBIBLICAL FAMILY COMMANDMENTS

1. MONEY
- Money is the best source of security.
- The more money you have, the more important you are.
- Make lots of money to prove you "made" it.

2. CONFLICT
- Avoid conflict at all costs.
- Don't get people mad at you.
- Fighting with dirty tactics is OK.

3. SEX
- Sex is not to be spoken about openly.
- Men can be promiscuous; women must be chaste.
- Sex is dirty.

4. GRIEF AND LOSS
- Sadness is a sign of weakness.
- You are not allowed to be depressed.
- Get over losses and move on.

5. EXPRESSING ANGER
- Anger is dangerous and bad.
- Explode in anger to make a point is OK.
- Sarcasm is an acceptable way to release anger.

6. FAMILY
- You owe your parents for all they've done for you.
- Don't speak of your family's "dirty laundry" in public.
- Duty to family and culture comes before everything.

7. RELATIONSHIPS
- Don't trust people. They will hurt you.
- Don't ever let anyone hurt you.
- Don't show vulnerability.

8. ATTITUDES TOWARD OTHER CULTURES
- Only be close friends with people who are like you.
- Do not marry a person of another race.
- Certain cultures are not as good as ours.

9. SUCCESS
- Is getting into the "best schools."
- Is making lots of money.
- Is getting married and having children.

10. FEELINGS AND EMOTIONS
- You are not allowed to have certain feelings.
- Your feelings are not that important.
- Reacting with your feelings without thinking is okay.

Since these are not the ways God intends us to live as the new family of Jesus, you can definitely say we have a lot to unlearn! We are like the Israelites who lived four hundred years in slavery under the Egyptians. Their way of viewing themselves, God, and others had been formed by the values and lifestyles of their slavery in Egypt. In a similar way, we have been shaped by forces other than our status as children of God. Yes, God has rescued us by grace—that is our salvation and deliverance. But make no mistake—the hard work of discipleship is necessary in order to let go of unbiblical ways of living and requires surrendering to the slow journey of being formed in new ways by Jesus.

Looking at our family histories brings a high level of awareness around specific areas in our lives that need to be opened to the transformative work of the Holy Spirit. Here are a few examples of what that looks like.

- Charlotte was impacted at a young age by immigration. Once in the United States, both her parents worked twelve-hours days, seven days a week in the food service industry. They moved from restaurant to restaurant around different parts of the country. As a result, Charlotte raised herself, cooking her own meals from an early age, and spending most of her days alone. Her discipleship is now focused on learning how to develop close, healthy relationships with her family, friends, and coworkers.
- Pierre's childhood experience of being wrongly classified as "mentally challenged" instead of dyslexic marked his self-image and caused him to distrust God and others. His discipleship is now focused on learning to take risks. Pierre has enrolled in a community college and said yes to leading a small group in the church. He also asked James, one of the church elders, to mentor him.
- Ted's twelve years at a New England boarding school left him feeling like an outsider in his own family. Even now as a married adult with three children, he struggles with intimacy and family life. His discipleship is now laser-focused on learning to feel his emotions each day, journaling, and seeing a Christian counselor every two weeks with his wife to grow in their connection with one another.

All three individuals are in different places and have different issues, but looking at their pasts has revealed clear areas where they need specific equipping so they can make the counterintuitive choices necessary to grow into more fully formed followers of Jesus.

There were many unhealthy patterns I brought into my leadership and discipleship with Jesus. But the following are the two largest ways God used this genogram work to free me and our church.

Shift 1: I grew in my level of differentiation and began leading more strongly. Differentiation refers to our capacity to define our life's goals apart from the pressures of those around us. High differentiation is about growing in our faithfulness to our true selves without being controlled by the approval or disapproval of others. In the family in which I'd grown up, there was great pressure to think and feel alike. This low-differentiation left little room for us as individuals to assert our own opinions, values, or goals apart from the pressure of the family.

I brought this low level of differentiation into my leadership. I may have held the role of lead pastor, but I didn't feel like one. When I proclaimed a new direction, for example, or had to make a difficult decision, I retreated if others challenged me. I desperately wanted people's validation and approval. I didn't trust that my perspective was good enough apart from others or that it was okay to lead out of how God had uniquely made me.

The answer to my problem was to learn how to lead strongly and clearly, while at the same time, remaining connected to other people. But I had some issues from my past I needed to deal with before I could do that.

My mother's family has owned an Italian bakery business here in New York City since 1923. Her family, and the business, were continually marked by confusion and chaos. Unclear roles and boundaries, unspoken expectations, and outbursts of frustration were normal. Our family simply didn't do well-run workplaces. And so I naturally assumed I didn't either.

But here's where my family of origin issues kicked in. I refused to invest the time to learn the executive skills required to supervise multiple paid and unpaid staff well. Why? I just "knew" those skills weren't inside me, so I always tried to avoid this kind of leadership and delegated it to others. It wasn't until I was able to identify my family patterns that I was finally able to break that unhealthy dynamic and learn the executive skills I needed.

One wise friend described what happened to me this way: "Pete, prior to this, the people in our church were like those described in the book of Judges: 'All the people did whatever seemed right in their own eyes' (see 17:6; 21:25). But once you started leading, there was finally peace in the land." He was right. The chaos and anxiety of my interior life had created chaos and anxiety in my exterior world. Now, a growing peace and rest in my interior was leading to a growing peace and rest in the exterior world of our family and church.

Shift 2: I slowed down in order to prioritize self-care and marriage. Like most leaders, I defined myself and understood my place in the world by what I did. "Produce and perform" was the clear message of my family growing up. And so, once I became a pastor, my self-worth was closely connected to how quickly the church was growing. When Geri complained about my busyness and lack of availability, I brushed it off. Few men in my family had been emotionally available to their spouses and most marriages were unhappy. Rather than seeing Geri's unhappiness as the red flag it was, it simply felt normal to me.

Once I finally slowed down to prioritize self-care and marriage, the impact was revolutionary. For the first time, I asked myself, *"How much time do I need to be alone with God and with myself in order to sustain the leadership responsibilities I carry?"* Then I asked, *"What do I need to shift in my schedule so that Geri and I experience a marriage filled with the passion and love of Jesus? Where can I get equipping to grow in this? What resources might help us?"*

As a result of grappling with those questions, I shifted to a five-day, fifty-hour work week, and Geri and I began implementing weekly, twenty-four-hour Sabbaths. This not only put me on a healthier path personally, it also allowed the rest of the church to function in a more balanced way.[10]

Every leader must wrestle with this difficult question: How much of my family history might be running the church or ministry God has entrusted to my care? You have to ask this question because you cannot change anything of which you are unaware. The good news, however, is that once you do the hard work of acknowledging the negative legacies from your past, you are already well on your way to breaking the power the past has had over your life and your leadership.

3. Get a Great Future Out of the Past

God's intention is that we get a great future out of our past. There is perhaps no biblical character who demonstrates that better than Joseph. As a seventeen-year-old boy, Joseph experienced great loss and tragedy at the hands of his family. As a result, he lost his family, his homeland, his language and culture, and his freedom. For thirteen years, he lived as a slave and then a prisoner.

No one would have blamed Joseph for complaining, "My family ruined my life. They robbed me of my best years!" But he never did that. Instead, he persevered through great difficulty because he believed God's plan and purpose for him was good. We see this clearly when he later declares to the brothers who betrayed him, "It was not you who sent me here, but God" (Genesis 45:8). He reminded them that, while their intentions may have been evil, God intended it for good (Genesis 50:20). Joseph knew, as scholar Walter Brueggemann notes, "the evil plans of human folks do not defeat God's purpose. Instead, they unwittingly become ways in which God's plan is furthered."[11]

In the same way, we can trust that God's plans and purposes for us are good, even when our circumstances are far from good. God placed each of us in a family at a particular moment in history, into a particular set of circumstances, in a particular city or town. Those particulars shape us into people who, like Joseph, might be a blessing to the world.

God works in, through, and in spite of our family and past, often in ways that are hidden and mysterious. Joseph never denies his painful past; in fact, he weeps over his losses. And yet, alongside his grief, he surrenders to God's will and trusts in God's goodness. We must do the same.

God has been at work in your life before you even took your first breath. He wants to take your history and build a great future out of it. God wastes nothing, especially your pain and failures, if you offer it all back to him.

In her classic book *Inner Compass*, author Margaret Silf offers a powerful "prayer picture" of what it looks like to let go of the past in order to live into the future God has for us.[12] The following is my adaptation of her story:

> Imagine yourself standing on the banks of a wide, fast-flowing river. You must cross but there is no bridge. Jesus comes carrying a large stone and places it in the river right in front of you. He then invites you to step out onto it. Every day, he brings another

stone, and then another, and another. You move further out into the water each day.

One day, however, you find yourself in the middle of the river with the water rushing all around you, and no new stone appears. When you cannot move forward, you feel a wave of panic. You look backward to the shore and only then do you realize where the stones are coming from. Jesus has been systematically dismantling the cottage on the shore behind you—that place in the past where you have lived your entire life—and is turning it, one stone at a time, into stepping stones for your future.

You take a deep breath and wait for God. When your heart is still, he quietly places the next stone in front of you. He invites you to take yet another step across the fast-moving river.

You realize now he will always bring one more stone—just one at a time—and then nudge you forward. You realize you can trust him as he continues to take the stones from your past and uses them to lead you into a good future.

God invites us to leave the past behind for a great future. But this too is a slow process. Yet, as we step out in faith to follow him to new places, we discover that he takes the broken parts of our history to create something beautiful we can offer to the world, just as he did with Joseph.

4. Break the Power of the Past in Every Area of Life and Leadership

The implications of breaking the power of the past to embrace God's future are more far-reaching than we initially realize. Everything is fair game—from the way you handle money to how you navigate your relationships with authority figures; from the way you deal with conflict to your views of gender roles and sexuality; from how you understand vacations to how you approach death, and so much more. Not only is the scope comprehensive, it's also ever changing. Every new season of life brings with it new situations and challenges that need to be addressed.

Here are just a few personal examples of the many diverse contexts in which I have worked to break the power of the past:

Preaching and teaching. When I study Scripture, I always ask, "How does the truth this passage teaches differ from the way I was shaped, either in my family growing up or by other influences?" For example, in a message series on the book of James, I prepared one sermon on the issue of showing partiality (James 2:1–13). Part of my preparation involved wrestling with how my family of origin ranked people. How did we view and treat people with great wealth or education? People who were poor and uneducated? How did my culture affect the way I viewed and treated people from different social classes, cultures, or races? How was this different from how God views people? Now that I am in Christ's family, what needs to change in the way I view and treat people?

Parenting. We were recently asked, "What is one of the most important pieces of advice you give to parents of teens and young adults?" Our answer: "You parent the way you were parented. That is why your child's biggest problem is *you*. Just ask any youth pastor!"

Geri and I have raised four daughters whose ages now span twenty-five to thirty-four.

When they were small children, we held more power in the relationship and made many decisions for them. It was a clear parent-child relationship. That power decreased as they grew older. And as they became adults, often with their own families, our relationships have become more peer-to-peer. We try not to give advice unless asked. When we age and are in need of care, the power dynamic will change once again. They will become our "parents" and make decisions for us.

This was an important, and difficult, discipleship issue for me initially because my parents never transitioned from a parent-child relationship with us (telling us which decisions we should make and how to live), even when they were in their eighties before they died! Once I finally made that shift with my own children and focused more on safety and emotional connection, the fruit has been incalculable.

Growing older. I began wrestling seriously with aging when I entered my late fifties and transitioned out of my role as lead pastor after twenty-six years. The narrative of my family and the wider culture was that getting older was something to avoid, a time of physical and mental decline along with the loss of a productive and meaningful life. I realized I needed discipleship in how to grow older in the new family of Jesus.[13] So I read books on the topic and reached out to three of my mentors who helped me to apply Scripture to this new season of life.

What have I learned? I discovered that retirement is an idea not found in Scripture. Every Christian is called by God and for God, and that calling transcends the work we do to pay the bills (our job or career). So I began using the word *transition* instead of retirement to describe stepping out of my role. I also found that the Bible is full of God calling people to new things when they are older. For example, Abraham was seventy-five when God called him to leave his home. Anna was eighty-four in the temple at Jesus's circumcision, Moses was eighty when he was called to lead upwards of two to three million people out of slavery. Even at the age of 120, as he was preparing to die, Moses was bearing fruit and mentoring the next generation about the Promised Land through a series of three powerful messages recorded in the book of Deuteronomy.[14]

When I was in my fifties (I am now in my sixties), one older mentor told me that if we are faithful, our most fruitful decade may be in our sixties, our second-best decade may be our seventies, and we may discover that our third-best decade will turn out to be our fifties. I am discovering this to be true. Getting older is not a crisis at all. In fact, when approached God's way, growing older offers a unique opportunity to release old identities of self-importance and learn God's deep wisdom on how to give away our life, and death, for the sake of the world.[15]

Building healthy teams. When I realized that each of us carries emotional and relational baggage from our family history, my approach to team building was transformed. When we fail to recognize this and do not address the "invisible" people present at that table, confusion often follows.

Consider the following scenario, in which you are leading a meeting with five church board members. In the diagram, the lines and circles radiating out from each person at the table represent the family of origin that shaped that person during the most formative period of their life.

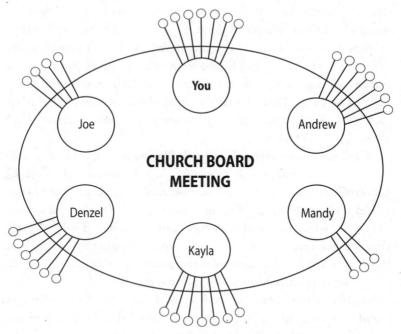

Experiences from each person's family relationships

The difficult decision to be made at this particular board meeting is whether or not to hire an executive assistant for you as a pastor. You have requested that the board authorize payment of salary beginning in two weeks. The hire is going to make the financial situation tight for the rest of the budget year because of other financial commitments the board has already made. So, as you go around the table and ask each board member for their input, you're aware that each person comes from a family system with certain unspoken rules, values, and ways of doing things.[16]

Joe, the chairman of the board, is a high-powered executive with a software company. He loves risk and has already decided to make a personal contribution to cover any potential budget shortfall. He won't say anything to the rest of the board about this decision, however. Joe grew up poor and his dad resented people who were proud and flashy with their money. So that is the last thing Joe will do.

Denzel runs the struggling family hardware store in town. He doesn't like the idea of the church having anything less than six months' worth of reserves in the bank. He would never run his own business that way because his father never ran the business that way before him. He has a pit in his stomach as he listens to you share the reasons why hiring an assistant makes sense. To him, it sounds like a reckless proposal. Denzel wants to delay the decision but also avoid rocking the boat. So he suggests the group pray to get a word from God about this step of faith.

Kayla sits at the table feeling angry. She thinks you made an insensitive comment about single people during your message three weeks ago. *How could a pastor be so insensitive?* Kayla wonders. Kayla has not talked with you about her feelings. Instead, she is thinking of leaving the church when her board term expires in six months. That is the way conflict was always dealt with in her family growing up—avoid and move on. Kayla is not in favor of this expenditure of funds.

Mandy is a pediatrician with a thriving practice. She now has three other doctors and five nurses working with her. They recently bought a building to expand their practice. She joined the church board last year, but she made it clear that, if she joined, she was expecting the board to focus on growth and change. Her father had raised Mandy to "go for it" and not be afraid to take risks and fail. She is glad you are finally taking some initiative to make the changes that will get this church moving.

Andrew functions in two roles. He is an associate pastor and also an elder. This puts him in a particularly powerful position, and he likes that. However, he is perturbed with you. He believes everything is handed to you on a silver platter. Andrew was raised by a single mom and had to work full time to support himself through college and seminary. He is angry you are getting yet another perk. He is sitting at the table thinking, "Why should you get everything you want from the board? I sure don't."

As the leader of this meeting, you will not be privy to the details of each person's family history, but you do know (at least now) that their pasts have a significant impact on the present. You may also sense the tension in the room as the conversation around hiring the assistant begins.

What do you do to bring mature spiritual leadership to the table?
I suggest three things:

- Take a thoughtful look at your own motivations, goals, and
  family dynamics as you consider this decision. You need to
  know what you are feeling and thinking and express that clearly,
  honestly, and respectfully to the board.
- Create safety within the context of the meeting so people can
  honestly express their concerns. This will require time. Be
  curious. Listen. Ask questions. Provide guidelines for differing
  points of view, such as making "I" statements, no fixing, saving,
  or setting other people straight, and turning to wonder rather
  than judgment as you listen.
- Invest in the spiritual/emotional development of this board.
  They need discipling, particularly in how they do relationships,
  how their past impacts their present (genogram), and how to have
  a clean rather than a dirty fight (by negotiating differences).[17]

It's a little overwhelming, isn't it? While it is a fairly accurate picture, it helps us understand the complexity of leading any kind of team, much less a church, and why getting properly equipped is so important.

Name and Tame the Negative Legacies of Your Ministry's History

Just as families pass on patterns and legacies over multiple generations, so do local churches, denominations, parachurch movements, and nonprofits. The great truth that you cannot change what you are unaware of applies to our ministries as well. However, once we name the root causes and expressions of our negative legacies, their power over us is diminished, if not broken.

While speaking with several hundred pastors who were all part of the same family of churches, I had each of them do a genogram of their family and make applications for their personal lives and leadership. Through that exercise, the president of this association of more than 450 churches realized that a number of negative legacies from their history as a group was damaging their churches' health and missional impact. He asked if I might lead an open discussion about this with everyone in the room.

I agreed, and we dedicated a three-hour session to identifying the positive and negative legacies of their family of churches since its inception in the mid-1970s. The list looked something like this:

Positive Legacies	Negative Legacies
Generous to other movements	Distrustful of outside institutions/ training
Marked by a plurality of leadership in each church	Suspicious of strong, visionary leaders
Loyal	Viewing healthy critique as disloyalty
Passionate for the Great Commission	Overly busy and fast moving
Kind and gentle	Unwilling to address conflicts
Marked by humility	Unduly prideful in being different from other churches
Commited to individual discipleship	Indifferent in applying discipleship to racial injustice, the poor and marginalized, the environment and creation care, etc.

This was a courageous exercise. Notice that most of the positive legacies also have a shadow legacy. For example, the positive legacy of being marked by a plurality of leadership also led to an unwillingness to allow gifted people to emerge as point leaders. Yes, they were innovative, but only when innovations arose from within their association; otherwise, they were resistant.

Simply naming and describing the context in which their association was birthed—college campuses in the 1970s with people who had been disillusioned after the debacles of the Vietnam War and Watergate—was eye-opening. They identified how their cynicism toward institutions such as seminaries and Bible colleges, and their reluctance to allow individual visionary leaders to emerge, was rooted more in their history than in Scripture.

Based on what they learned by assessing their positive and negative legacies, the executive leadership team was able to address their negative legacies over the next two years. At the same time, they also maximized their unique charism and calling represented by their positive legacies.[18]

Keep these five pathways before you and your church, following through on at least one of them as a first step:

- leading people to genogram their family;
- committing to do the hard work of serious discipleship;
- ensuring people get a great future out of their past;
- breaking the power of the past in every area of life and leadership; and
- naming and taming the negative legacies of your ministry's history.

These five pathways will serve you well on your journey in the years to come. But most important, listen to Jesus in the process. He is your rudder for navigating these deep waters.

BEGIN WITH YOURSELF

Each time you make a choice to break the power of the past rather than ignore it, you are taking up your cross to follow Jesus. It often begins as an experience of pain, fear, and darkness that appears to be leading you into a bottomless abyss. But let me assure you: the truth will set you and your ministry free. I can promise you that you and your ministry will be reborn into a new place of maturity in Christ. Resurrection is a certainty—if we remain in Jesus, allowing ourselves to be held by him.

But remember the core principle of emotionally healthy discipleship: we always begin by looking at ourselves. Churches will never mature beyond the maturity of their leaders. It is our responsibility to model working on our own "stuff" before pointing out the logs and specks in the eyes of others.

Over the years, I've treasured the following words spoken by an old Hasidic rabbi on his deathbed:

> When I was young, I set out to change the world. When I grew a little older, I perceived that this was too ambitious so I set out to change my state. This, too, I realized as I grew older was too ambitious, so I set out to change my town. When I realized I could not even do this, I tried to change my family. Now as an old man, I know that I should have started by changing myself. If I had started with myself, maybe then I would have succeeded in changing my family, the town, or even the state—and who knows, maybe even the world![19]

God has used these words to keep me grounded. I pray they do the same for you.

Chapter Nine

Lead Out of Weakness and Vulnerability

The English word "vulnerable" is derived from the Latin *vulnerare*, which means "to wound."[1] Everyone alive in our fallen world has been wounded in life.

I was no exception.

Home was not safe. Between Mom's undiagnosed clinical depression and periodic hospitalizations, and my Dad's love mingled with regular and severe physical beatings, I was never quite sure what a new day might bring.

It was confusing, to say the least. But the message was clear: *Be who we want you to be, do what we tell you to do, and make the family proud—or else!*

I entered elementary and high school hoping the rest of the world might be safer. But I had emotional and developmental gaps that caused me to feel different and insecure around other kids. I carried terrible secrets from home and felt out of step with everyone else. While I was extroverted and the life of the party, the slights and rejections of adolescence only deepened these open wounds.

And so I retreated further behind a heavy coat of armor.

When I came to faith in Jesus, my ministry models and authority figures were often gifted and excellent communicators. They taught from a thorough knowledge of Scripture, exhibited the power gifts of the Spirit, and led significant ministries. They exuded a self-confidence and self-assurance I knew I didn't have. I wondered, more than once, if I were an imposter—especially once I started speaking publicly for Jesus.

Before I became a lead pastor, I was taught to share at least one illustration of brokenness in every sermon to connect with the audience, but this was only a means to an end. We talked about the Twelve Steps of Alcoholics Anonymous, but no one I knew actually practiced them. I preached on transparency, but my multilayered protective armor remained solidly in place. I couldn't imagine what genuine vulnerability might look like in a Christian, especially in a Christian leader.

This inability to be weak or vulnerable impacted every area of my life. My ability to bond deeply with people, including Geri, was severely limited. I didn't know myself, so how could I let her, or others, know me? Since I suppressed my own feelings of sadness and fear, I could not share them with others. I attributed people's struggles and weaknesses to a lack of faith or a failure to appropriate God's power and treated them as problems that needed to be fixed.

Is it any wonder I did everything—and I mean everything—to avoid failure?

As I mentioned earlier, it took a full crisis to break through the heavy armor I wore to keep people from seeing the real me. I was like Isaac Cline, the senior weather official in 1900, who refused to evacuate Galveston Island, Texas, before it was pummeled by one of the deadliest hurricanes to strike the United States. Isaac Cline had characterized the fear that a hurricane posed a serious danger to their booming city as "an absurd delusion." In his overconfidence, he never anticipated waves that were ten feet high and fifty feet long, or wind-gusts of two hundred miles an hour. As a result of his arrogance and defensiveness, so many people drowned that bodies washed back up on shore for months.[2]

I was as overconfident and unteachable as Issac Cline. I accumulated a treasure trove of knowledge, skills, and experience to prepare myself for "successful" leadership as best I could. My expectation was that no obstacle could hinder what God wanted to do through me. I reminded myself that greater is he who is in me than he who is in the world (1 John 4:4). I memorized the promise, "With your help I can advance against a troop; with my God I can scale a wall" (2 Samuel 22:30).

I was determined to remain strong and faithful. God had given me zeal, talents, and good ministry experience. I was going to be a warrior and exemplary servant for God and his church. I boasted to myself: *Other people may grow tired, fall apart under pressure, and even quit. But not me—ever!*

My ministry preparation, both formal and informal, left out one of the most important biblical pathways to grow in spiritual authority and leadership—weakness and vulnerability. As a result, when the really big storms hit, I wasn't ready.

I was just as foolish as Isaac Cline of Galveston, Texas.

Cursory emphasis on brokenness in Bible studies, sermons, and seminary did little to penetrate the armor I wore to defend myself against being hurt.[3] Precise and thorough exegesis in Greek and Hebrew did little to break through the weighty layers of self-protectiveness and defensiveness that I wore.

I am sad that it took the equivalent of a destructive hurricane for God to get my attention. It did not have to be that way. I've observed countless people over the years who learned early on about the place of weakness and vulnerability as God's pathway to a flourishing discipleship. This wider, biblical framework enlarged their capacity to surrender to God and stand firm amidst life's hurricanes.

When we live and build entire churches characterized by weakness and vulnerability, something inexplicable happens. People enjoy a taste of God's beauty and presence in Christ. A glimpse of the truth and goodness of heaven shines.[4] God's gentle power flows. People soften.

But the qualities of weakness and vulnerability are rarely encountered in our world, or even more sadly, in our churches.

GOD'S COUNTERCULTURAL PATH TO POWER AND STRENGTH

Western culture places a high value on power and influence. We are dazzled by celebrities, famous artists, and those with thousands of social media followers. We attribute great power to the wealthy and successful and to those who are brilliant intellectually or gifted athletically. We value cutting-edge innovators and entrepreneurs who chart new paths for the future.

Unfortunately, the twenty-first-century church also places a high value on power and influence—especially when ministries attract large crowds, have high impact and visibility, and boast impressive buildings and staff. We are dazzled by our own versions of celebrities, famous artists, and those with highly visible gifts.

Because I didn't know there was an alternative, I allowed myself, and our ministry, to be seduced by the world's definition of power. I worked with all my might to avoid weakness and vulnerability. And it cost me, and many others, dearly.

What I was missing was an understanding of what constitutes power and strength from a biblical perspective—and how radically different that is from the cultural understanding. I needed a revelation of who God is and the way he works. I needed a theology of weakness.

Over the years, I've identified four core characteristics of an emotionally healthy discipleship that embodies weakness and vulnerability:

1. Develop a theology of weakness.
2. Embrace the gift of your limp.
3. Transition to become a church based on weakness.
4. Practice vulnerability daily.

Each of these four characteristics were discerned out of many painful missteps and years of trial and error. Each required I move from a closed and defensive posture to one of openness and intentionality. Let's take a closer look at each one, beginning with the foundation from which all the others follow—developing a theology of weakness.

1. Develop a Theology of Weakness

God's vulnerability is seen in his unrelenting pursuit of humanity, which is evident from the first pages of Scripture when he grants Adam and Eve freedom of choice. Scripture also consistently shows God choosing to work through weak, flawed, and imperfect people. We see this, for example, in the lives of Abraham, Sarah, Rahab, Ruth, and the leader Moses, whom Scripture describes as "a very humble man, more humble than anyone else on the face of the earth" (Numbers 12:3).

Yet it was the model of three biblical characters—Jesus, Paul, and David—that upended my understanding of leadership and completely changed my view of authentic discipleship.

Jesus

Pride and defensiveness in a follower of Jesus, much less a leader or a church, is such a contradiction that I remain incredulous that I, and the churches I served, failed to see it—especially since I invested thousands of hours to be trained as a pastor-leader!

Think about it: God came to earth, not in a flashy show of signs and wonders, but as an infant born into poverty and obscurity. After living as a refugee in Egypt, he returned to grow up in Nazareth, a backwoods town a long way from the big city. He waited thirty years to begin any public ministry, and even then, refused to do miracles on demand or overwhelm people with his brilliant intellect. His ministry was small and almost invisible by the world's standards. Throughout his ministry, Jesus exercised his power carefully so as not to manipulate or force people into following him. He revealed just enough of himself to make faith possible, but hid just enough of himself to make faith necessary.[5]

For his triumphal entry into Jerusalem, he rode not on a magnificent war horse like Alexander the Great, but a humble donkey. And he allowed himself to be arrested and treated as if he were a common criminal.

Then, as he hung on the cross in the worst moment of his earthly life, his final prayer was a question he quoted from the Psalms: "My God, my God, why have you forsaken me?" (Matthew 27:46; Psalm 22:1). What kind of exemplary model of leadership is this? Couldn't he have demonstrated faith and calm by quoting another psalm instead, such as, "The Lord is my shepherd; I shall not want" (Psalm 23:1 KJV)?

Consider the following passage, which describes Jesus as weak in the garden of Gethsemane. Read it slowly, imagining that you are there with Jesus. His raw humanity is on powerful display here. So much so that scholars and preachers throughout history have spilled much ink in an attempt to clean up the weak, broken Jesus we encounter here.[6]

> Then Jesus went with his disciples to a place called Gethsemane, and he said to them, "Sit here while I go over there and pray." He took Peter and the two sons of Zebedee along with him, and he began to be sorrowful and troubled. Then he said to them, "My soul is overwhelmed with sorrow to the point of death. Stay here and keep watch with me."
>
> Going a little farther, he fell with his face to the ground and prayed, "My Father, if it is possible, may this cup be taken from me. Yet not as I will, but as you will." . . .
>
> He went away a second time and prayed, "My Father, if it is not possible for this cup to be taken away unless I drink it, may your will be done." . . .
>
> So he left them and went away once more and prayed the third time, saying the same thing. (Matthew 26:36–39, 42, 44)

Jesus did not approach his death as a superhero. In fact, his anticipation of death stands in stark contrast to reports of later martyrs, such as Bishop Polycarp, who said as he was about to be burned at the stake in AD 155: "Eighty-six years have I served him. . . . Why do you delay? Come, do what you will."[7]

Origin of Alexandria (c. 185–c. 253), the greatest theologian of his generation, was so uncomfortable with Jesus's behavior in Gethsemane that he tried to explain it away, saying: "'Jesus only *began* to be sorrowful and troubled.' His God-head restrained him from consummating the emotion."[8]

After studying this passage in our *Emotionally Healthy Spirituality Course*, Nelson, a young pastor of an influential church, wrote to me, saying, "Pete, I was given secular and church leadership books growing up. I've listened to thousands of hours of church leadership talks. But I honestly believe that, if I did what Jesus did in this passage, I'd feel like a failure and fear for my job in church leadership."

I took the rest of his email and developed a simple chart contrasting the weak and vulnerable leadership modeled by Jesus in Gethsemane, and the proud and defensive way we often lead today. As you read through the characteristics, consider which column you relate to most.

Weak and Vulnerable	Proud and Defensive
I allow myself to be sorrowful and troubled in front of others.	I cover over my feelings of sorrow and confusion in front of my team.
I admit to my team when I am feeling overwhelmed.	I refuse to fall apart, always modeling strong faith and vision, especially in front of my team.
I easily ask for the help and prayers of others.	I rarely appear needy in front of others. While I will be there for others, I don't look for others to be there for me.
I pray in utter dependence to surrender my will to God's will.	I pray how to strategically turn a bad situation around and expand the ministry.
I have no problem falling facedown on the ground in front of others when I struggle to submit myself to the unfathomable will of the Father.	I try to stand tall, being decisive and unwavering in crisis, so others can lean on me for faith and strength.

The column to the right, of course, is the exact opposite of the example we have in Jesus, and it stands in stark contrast to who we are called to be and the kind of churches we are called to build. Is it any wonder that Scripture tells us that "the weakness of God is stronger than human strength," and that God chooses "the weak things of the world to shame the strong" (1 Corinthians 1:25, 27)? Truth, brokenness, and humility release the love and power of God. But lies, boasting, and pride clog that same cardiovascular system.

The apostle Paul understood this, perhaps, better than anyone.

Paul

The apostle Paul is arguably the most influential Christian to have ever lived. He wrote almost half the New Testament and worked to spread the message of Christianity in a way that remains unsurpassed to this day. Even so, Paul's authority and position as an apostle were seriously challenged several times. One primary reason for this was related to his understanding of weakness and vulnerability. A case in point is the church at Corinth.

"Super apostles" had come to the church with a ministry of signs and wonders that seemed to surpass the work that Paul had done. They spoke of revelations and experiences with God and had extraordinary speaking gifts. Claiming a unique anointing from God, they gradually drew the Corinthians' loyalty to themselves and away from Paul.

When he argues for the authenticity of his leadership, Paul appeals not to his visions and revelations from God, not to his successes and gifts, but instead to his weaknesses. He writes about how God had allowed a "thorn in his flesh" to humble him. Although there is debate about the precise nature of the thorn, we can say with certainty that it was a source of torment and discouragement to Paul. Even so, he referred to it as a gift:

> Three times I pleaded with the Lord to take it away from me. But he said to me, "My grace is sufficient for you, for my power is made perfect in weakness." Therefore I will boast all the more gladly about my weaknesses, so that Christ's power may rest on me. That is why, for Christ's sake, I delight in weaknesses, in insults, in hardships, in persecutions, in difficulties. For when I am weak, then I am strong. (2 Corinthians 12:8–10)

Paul considered his great weakness to be his badge of apostleship and authority from God—so much so that he boasted in it, arguing that this was how and why the power of Jesus flowed through him.

If Paul were preaching at a leadership conference today, I suspect his topic would not be "Planting Successful Churches in Asia Minor." Nor would his opening message be, "Six Steps to Raise Up Top-Tier Leaders." He would speak first, perhaps, of how God did *not* answer his prayers for personal healing. He would describe how weak, fractured, and broken he was. "There is a message in this, friends," he might add. "If God can use me, he can use anybody!"

Paul did not want to lead out of weakness, but perhaps God knew that Paul would be overbearing without this thorn. He was brilliant, ambitious, and hard driving. His life prior to his conversion was one marked by privilege, fanaticism, and self-righteous zeal. Without the continual breaking of his self-will, who knows what damage Paul might have done. I know this only too well, because I have my own story of how God loved me too much to allow me to self-destruct.

For a number of years, I traveled and spoke at Christian leadership conferences about our church's successes, focusing on what we were doing right. I conveyed a sense of control and mastery of how to lead a church. I enjoyed sharing my expertise freely over breaks and meals.

But I also glossed over the disappointments and setbacks I'd experienced, both personally and in the church. I exaggerated more than I like to admit. On the surface, it appeared I was succeeding. I hadn't actually lied, but, as I would later understand, focusing on my successes alone was a coping strategy—a way to avoid taking an honest look at how damaged, imperfect, and limited I really was.

I shared about small groups that multiplied, not the ones that died. I talked about the new people who came into our church, not the ones that left or why. I preached from my best one or two messages, never mentioning the ones that were flat. I talked about my best decisions, not my worst.

During that time, I received a last-minute invitation to speak at a church growth conference when a plenary speaker had gotten sick and they needed someone to fill in. But I knew I could no longer go. I finally acknowledged that something in my soul died when I spoke at those conferences. I had a terrible, uncomfortable feeling that I was not telling the whole truth. God had done a number of great things in our church, but there was another side to the story—and to me.

I declined the invitation and stopped speaking outside our church for almost a decade. I knew God was trying to get at something deep in my interior life—though I could not yet name it—and at something deep in the way we were doing church.

God was slowly opening my eyes to what it means to live out of weakness and vulnerability. And it was David, one of my favorite biblical characters, who offered another leadership vision that finally shifted my entire life.

David

The phrase most often used to describe David is that he was "a man after God's own heart." We observe that heart, of course, in the many psalms he wrote as well as the many victories he achieved. But one of the most vivid pictures we have of David's heart is revealed not in a triumph but in a colossal moral failure—when he commits adultery with Bathsheba and then murders her husband, Uriah.

When he is confronted by the prophet Nathan, David does not deny what he's done, cover it up, or try to erase all memory of it from Israel's history. Instead, he repents. And he makes sure his failure is recorded in vivid detail as a lesson for future generations (2 Samuel 12). He even writes a song about it to be sung in worship services and published in Israel's worship manual (Psalm 51)!

How many of us today would do something like that after such a colossal failure?

David understood something significant about who God is and how he works. He wrote:

> You do not delight in sacrifice, or I would bring it;
> > you do not take pleasure in burnt offerings.
> My sacrifice, O God, is a broken spirit;
> > a broken and contrite heart
> > you, God, will not despise. (Psalm 51:16–17)

From David, I learned the importance of speaking about my failures and struggles—in sermons, Bible studies, mentoring, writing, and board meetings. David knew that acknowledging imperfections was critical, not only for his own spiritual health, but also for the health of those he led.

His life embodied God's message that Israel's existence as a people was based on the love and mercy of God alone and not their own performance. And if God can use a person like David, forgiving him of such a massive breach of integrity, God can use anyone—even you and me!

Developing a theology of weakness is essential because the shift required to build a discipleship culture of weakness and vulnerability is so massive, and has so many implications for us, that only a biblical vision will sustain us.

2. Embrace the Gift of Your Limp

I've come to believe that Paul isn't the only one to whom God gave the gift of a "handicap," which is how *The Message* translates "thorn in the flesh." Sooner or later, every believer has something that drives them to their knees on a daily basis. What is it for you? A child with special needs? An addiction? Emotional fragility with a tendency to depression, anxiety, loneliness? Scars on your soul from an abusive past? Childhood patterns of relating to other people that cause you to feel desperate for change? A physical disability? Cancer? Chronic temptations to anger, hate, resentment, or judgmentalism?

Whatever it is, consider yourself in good company.

Vulnerability is something we all share as human beings. According to theologian Jürgen Moltmann, "There is no differentiation between the healthy and those with disabilities. For every human life has its limitations, vulnerabilities, and weaknesses. We are born needy, and we die helpless."[9] And we inevitably become more so as we age, living with increasing degrees of limits and impairments.

God built brokenness and weakness into the fabric of all life when he set in motion the consequences of the fall (Genesis 3:16–19). From that point forward, God declares that all relationships would be marked by pain and misunderstanding, even in the best communities, and all work would be marked by frustration and a sense of incompleteness. He did this so that our weakness would drive us to seek him and recognize our need for him as a Savior.[10] There will be nothing perfect this side of heaven.

While the larger world treats weakness and failure as a liability, God sees our weakness and vulnerability as a gift. His message to us is one of acceptance: "Relax. Weakness and failure cut across all ages, cultures, races, and social classes. I've hidden within them gifts so you can offer to others a broken love, like mine."

Early in my Christian life and ministry, I believed that God wanted to heal my weaknesses and frailties completely. It would never have occurred to me that they might be part of God's design and will for me, as it had been for Paul.

I made a fascinating discovery years ago when I learned that Paul's growth in Christ was matched by an ever-increasing sense of his own weaknesses and sinfulness.

- In his letter written to the church at Galatia, he comments on other apostles this way: "As for those who were held in high esteem—whatever they were makes no difference to me" (Galatians 2:6). Traces of competiveness with the Twelve appear in this statement. The letter is believed to have been written in 49 AD, when Paul would have been a Christian for about fourteen years.
- Six years later, in 55 AD, he writes the Corinthians in a more humble manner: "I am the least of the apostles" (1 Corinthians 15:9).
- Five years after that (about AD 60), and twenty-five years after becoming a Christian, he proclaims, "I am less than the least of all the Lord's people" (Ephesians 3:8).
- Two years before his death, and after walking with Christ for perhaps thirty years, he states clearly, "I am the worst [of all sinners]" (1 Timothy 1:15).[11]

What happened? Over time, Paul grew in his understanding of the love of God, and he became stronger in Christ by embracing rather than shunning his weaknesses.

The world will never comprehend the strange wisdom of Jesus's countercultural kingdom in which the last are first, the weak are blessed, the humble are exalted, the empty are filled, the poor are rich, and where impossibility becomes the occasion for miracles.

Our foundational neediness as human beings is not something to be healed or overcome, but to be embraced as the source of our greatest strength.

One of the best illustrations I know for demonstrating how God uses brokenness is the art of kintsugi. Developed in Japan in the fourteenth century, kintsugi takes broken pieces of pottery and rejoins

them using a lacquer with a beautiful gold powder.[12] The word "kintsugi" literally means "to join with gold." What makes kintsugi art so unique is that it actually emphasizes the broken pieces rather than trying to hide or disguise them, or discarding the object altogether.

The art of kintsugi reflects the Japanese philosophy of wabi-sabi, which calls for seeing beauty in the flawed, the damaged, the imperfect. The idea is to appreciate the whole history of the pottery piece, including it's brokenness. Once reassembled, the piece is considered more beautiful and elegant than the original as the fault lines are now lined with precious veins of gold. It is also stronger and more precious because the repaired breakages make the object more, not less, valuable.

God has a wabi-sabi philosophy of his own—he does kintsugi on his people all the time. Each one of us has places where we are shattered, either by something done to us or wrong choices we have made. Regardless, as we offer our brokenness back to God, he carefully puts us back together in ways more spectacular and beautiful than before. Our cracks remain, but they have been sealed with gold from the Master Artist himself.[13]

This has always been the way God works. Consider the flaws and imperfections of the heroes of Scripture:

- Peter was a loudmouth with a short fuse.
- John Mark deserted Paul.
- Timothy had ulcers and struggled with fear.
- Moses was a stutterer.
- Rahab was a prostitute.
- Amos's only training was farming.
- Jacob was a liar.
- The Samaritan woman had a whole string of divorces.
- Samson was a womanizer.
- Naomi was a poor widow.
- Jonah ran from God's will.
- Gideon and Thomas doubted.
- Jeremiah was depressed and suicidal.
- Elijah was burned out.
- John the Baptist was loud and abrasive.
- Martha was a blamer.
- Noah got drunk.

God has always used cracked pots to "show that this all-surpassing power is from God and not from us" (2 Corinthians 4:7).[14]

This was a paradigm shift theologically—at least for me. The question, then, became, What do I do now? Will people no longer trust my leadership when they see how many cracks I have? Would it be safe? Would the church reject this kind of weakness coming from me?

3. Transition to a Church Based on Weakness

A seismic shift began at our church when, after almost eight years of leading out of strengths and successes, I admitted to the congregation that my personal life and marriage were out of order. Geri and I then made the decision to go public with our struggle and journey of healing and restoration.

It Began with Me

I began to speak freely of my mistakes, vulnerabilities, and failures.

I began to admit in meetings, "I don't know what to do." I talked openly about my insecurities and fears.

I began to take time to listen and be present with people.

I began to share feelings with Geri that, previously, I tended to be ashamed of—anger, jealousy, depression, sadness, despair.

I began to ask forgiveness differently, saying, "Will you forgive me?" and then waiting for a response. Prior to that, I'd say, "I'm sorry" and move on to the next item on the agenda.

When Geri and I led our first marriage retreat and shared painful details of our story as a couple, Jane, a young wife in her early thirties, literally ran out of the room crying. She explained later: "I never expected to see anyone, let alone my pastor, that naked!" The wave of God's love for us in our frailties had so washed over us that we had nothing left to hide.

Not only did I not feel worse, as I initially feared; I actually felt more alive and clean than I had in years. My pretense and protectiveness were dissipating, and I grasped God's love and the Holy Spirit's power in entirely new ways.

If you listen to my sermons before and after 1996, you will notice a sharp difference.

After 1996, I made the radical shift to preach out of my failures, weaknesses, and struggles—not my successes. Initially, this level of vulnerability was very uncomfortable and frightening. I began to wrestle with texts and my own difficulties in obeying them before I applied them to others.

I continued to do exegesis, look for great illustrations, and develop a coherent flow for sermons. But I dropped my perfectionism in this area. Why? I finally realized the most powerful part of the message was the power of Jesus coming through my own struggles to apply the text. Paul was right (see 2 Corinthians 12:7–12)! And while that segment of the message might only last two to ten minutes, space was needed to prepare that well.

We were now all on equal footing, wrestling to obey God's Word in our lives.

Let's face it, creating a healthy discipleship culture flows out of who we are as leaders, which means the stakes are especially high in those moments when our weaknesses and flaws are exposed. And these moments come to all of us.

I Know I Am Being Proud and Defensive When . . .

_____ I am guarded and protective about my imperfections and mistakes.

_____ Those close to me would describe me as defensive and easily offended.

_____ I easily notice the flaws, mistakes, and imperfections of others.

_____ I give my opinion a lot, even when I am not asked.

_____ I am quick to advise or fix things before they fall apart.

_____ I struggle with holding grudges and with asking forgiveness.

_____ I rarely ask others for feedback on how I can improve or change.

_____ I find it hard to ask others for help.

_____ I find it difficult to say, "I don't know" in front of others.

It Rippled through the Leadership

One of the outstanding qualities of New Life Fellowship Church today is that leaders freely share their weaknesses. As one of our pastors recently said, "It's really hard to get fired off staff unless you refuse to be broken." It's simply an expectation to be teachable, vulnerable, and willing to do ongoing work on your own issues. We have no Christian heroes. Just people.

Ministry and small group leaders, as well as board members and volunteers, are encouraged to tell their stories of weakness and failure as they lead others. In fact, it is perhaps the one indispensable quality for serving at New Life. But it was not always that way. It began slowly, coaching one person at a time, encouraging them to trust God's countercultural ways. Consider Drew's story.

Drew, a young and gifted leader, moved to New York City years ago. The following is his account, in his own words, of the cultural clash he experienced at New Life and his journey to embracing weakness.

> I had life all figured out. Ministry? I had that figured out too. I was confident, I was invincible. I had been a Christian for a little over a decade, and in my mind, there was no question too complex or circumstance too deflating to knock over. I was told that I had lots of gifts and natural leadership abilities.
>
> As a result, I was a defensive, feisty, and often unteachable Christian who masqueraded as the humble hero. I would listen to people, but not really listen. I was often impatient with others, and I tended to give advice to anyone and everyone. I valued strength more than weakness, perfection more than brokenness. I was confident in the abilities God had given me."
>
> Hearing about vulnerability and weakness was shattering. It seemed too risky—nice enough to sound good, but at the same time a little too dangerous. To be honest, it was a bit terrifying.
>
> But it was also liberating. It gave me a fresher, newer way of seeing the gospel, of understanding grace. I learned to trust God even when I didn't have the answer to everything, and I learned to listen. I learned to say "I don't know" when really, I didn't know.

In a nutshell, I learned that I was not as whole as I thought. In an odd and mysterious way, I learned that I could only become whole as a leader and friend by being broken and weak and vulnerable before God . . . and, yes, before others too.

That too was liberating.

Drew's story captures a critical lesson. Learning to lead out of weakness and vulnerability takes a long time. By the end of his two-year internship, Drew had experienced significant growth. Then after planting his own church, and multiplying a number of other churches out of that church, Drew's maturity on the weakness-vulnerability continuum progressed even more.

We observe this slow process with Jesus and the Twelve. While Jesus modeled perfect humility and vulnerability, the disciples struggled with pride, power, and status—right up to the crucifixion!

While it takes time to engage in this kind of nuanced discipleship, especially with our teams, the impact is far-reaching. Why? The starting point for change in any church, ministry, or organization has always been leadership. As go the leaders, so goes the church.

It Filtered into the Wider Culture

Once our leaders were making progress, we began to be intentional about developing a wider church culture based on weakness. As you might imagine, it was not a transition that happened quickly.

We began by using every opportunity to invite people to testify about how God meets them in their failures and frailties. We wanted people to acknowledge the cracks in their soul—whether they came as a result of their own sins or of sins committed against them. We used worship services, marriage and singles retreats, equipping classes, baptisms, small groups, and other events to encourage people to tell their stories of weakness. Initially, this was frightening for many people. But we found that our coaching and one-on-one conversations created a safe environment for people to step out by faith and share honestly.

It transformed, and continues to transform, the culture of our community.

Today, it's not uncommon in our services to hear from a recovering heroin addict who leads worship *and* from a respectable, middle-class father of three who struggles with pornography. Weakness and vulnerability runs through every person's story. And so we look for any opportunity to create safe spaces where our people can connect from a place of mutual vulnerability.

4. Practice Vulnerability Daily

Vulnerability as a lifestyle is difficult—I know this only too well. A few of the pressure points where I am tempted to not be vulnerable today include:

- Not learning from young leaders who are breaking new ground with dreams and insights from God. It's easier to say, "Been there and done that!"
- Not creating environments in which people feel free to give me constructive criticism and different points of view. It's easier to say, "It sure seemed great to me!"
- Not integrating limits on a larger scale as I grow older. It's easier to act as if I am not slowing with age physically or emotionally.
- Not treating my four adult daughters as adults, learning from their wisdom and journeys. It's easier to give them answers to questions they are not asking.
- Not dedicating time to continue growing in my marriage with Geri. It's easier to say, "We've done a lot of work and are doing fine. I don't want to change any more."

What helps me to refrain from choosing the easier path is a healthy fear. I never want to end up with a hardened heart—and no one is immune to that.[15]

For this reason, a spiritual practice of surrender is foundational to living in vulnerability and weakness. One of the best illustrations of this principle is captured in the parable of the prodigal son from Luke 15:11–32. I'm particularly drawn to how Rembrandt captured the reunion scene in his painting, *The Return of the Prodigal Son*. It provides a beautiful visual aid to help us choose the pathway of brokenness, weakness, humility, and vulnerability.

As you can see in the painting, the younger son is kneeling, resting his head on the father's bosom. The son is bald, seemingly exhausted and emaciated, without a cloak, wearing only one tattered shoe, and disheveled. He is a picture of a life that has been broken.

The younger son had demanded his share of the estate and ran away from home. He shames his father and disgraces his family. But things eventually go so badly for him that he is reduced to tending pigs. For a Jewish listener in Jesus's day, tending pigs would be the cesspool of all cesspools. Jews who touched pigs were considered as unclean as those who visited a prostitute.

Finally, the son comes to his senses and decides to return home. As he approaches his father's house in shame, the father sees him from a long way off and sprints toward him. He runs to his son and embraces him before the son can even start with his prepared speech.

Then the unimaginable occurs.

The father kisses him repeatedly. "Repeatedly" is conveyed in the original Greek. The father's love is extravagant and excessive. He reinstates his son's position of authority by replacing his tattered clothes with the best robe, giving him a signet ring representing his legal authority, and outfitting him with the shoes of a free man who belongs in the house. The father then throws a huge party filled with music and dancing.

Rembrandt's painting has served me for many years by offering a colorful and stunning picture of what it looks like to practice vulnerability each day.

The Younger Son: A Picture of Brokenness

Take a moment to look at the painting once more, particularly at the younger son. The younger son's brokenness provides a defining picture of the Christian life. We do not kneel in repentance only at salvation. Instead, we endeavor to live in such a way that our posture toward God is one of constant brokenness and vulnerability—one in which we lean into God to be lavishly overwhelmed by his love. To do so, we must be intentional. Otherwise, we will end up being more like the older brother who, in the painting, stands just behind the father.

The key is intentionality.

The son was not shoved to his knees, but chose to kneel. He kneels because he knows the way he was doing life was selfish and that he is very, very needy. We all are.

In his classic book about Rembrandt's painting entitled *The Return of the Prodigal Son*, Henri Nouwen equates the son's act of leaving home with times in his own life when he moved out of the place of the Father's love—a place where he heard in the center of his being, "You are my son whom I love, upon you does my favor rest." Nouwen writes:

Yet over and over again I have left home. I have fled the hands of blessing and run off to faraway places searching for love! This is the great tragedy of my life and the lives of so many I meet on my journey. Somehow I have become deaf to the voice that calls me the Beloved . . . There are many other voices. . . . The dark voices of my surrounding world try to persuade me that I am no good and that I can only become good by earning my goodness through "making it" up the ladder of success.[16]

It's a story many of us in leadership can no doubt relate to. We try hard to please people, achieve success, and be recognized. And yet, in the process, we violate God's gift of limits, leave home—the place of the Father's love—and end up lost.

When I get depressed after someone graciously corrects a comment I made in a sermon, or I find myself envying other people's success, or I am unable to say no without feeling guilty, I am lost. I have left my home of resting in the love of God.

When I attempt to exercise control and power by not greeting someone who has slighted me, I have left home. I am lost and need to make the long journey back to him.

I want to live where the younger brother lives—kneeling with his head resting fully on his father's chest and receiving the father's warm embrace. When I do that, when I am intentional about remaining fully aware of how fragile I am, I gain a small glimpse of "how wide and long and high and deep is the love of Christ" (Ephesians 3:18–19).

The Older Son: A Picture of Lostness

What does it look like to stray from weakness and brokenness? The older son shows us. In Rembrandt's painting, he is well-clothed in a gold-embroidered garment like his father's. However, unlike his father, he appears to be judging, annoyed, and disapproving of his father's lavish reception of his youngest son, who has disgraced the family and squandered the family fortune.

Although the older son has done nothing wrong, his heart is far from right. He is, in fact, more lost than his younger brother because he cannot see how lost he truly is. His devotion to respectability, self-righteousness, and duty have blinded him to his own condition.

He is living in the father's house, but he, too, has left home and remains far from the father's love. The elder brother serves as a warning to me that it is possible to obey God's commands, serve in God's house, and still be lost. I can appear to be near God and yet actually be very far from him. When I am not intentional and purposeful about embracing my weakness and vulnerability every day, I become the older son.

I know I am falling into older son territory when I hold on to my anger rather than process it, when I find myself grumbling and complaining a lot, and when I have a hard time letting go of hurts. These are all sure signs I am the lost older son.

The church is full of both younger sons running away and of older sons who are angry and grumpy. I know. I am both. This is why it is so crucial that I ground my spirituality in practicing vulnerability every day. Jesus's parable of the prodigal son, along with Rembrandt's painting, have helped me to do just that, especially in my times of communion and silence with him.

STAY THE COURSE

You can be sure that when you take steps to live in vulnerability and weakness in leadership, you will have to deal with multiple fears and questions. If you are like me, your mind may be gravitating to worst-case scenarios. When that happens, let me encourage you to stay the course.

In this chapter, we have explored four core characteristics of churches that embody weakness and vulnerability: they develop a theology of weakness, embrace the gift of a handicap, transition to becoming a church based on weakness, and practice vulnerability daily.

As you consider the complexity of such a transition, let me assure you that there really is a resurrection awaiting you and your ministry on the other side of this journey. In fact, you can rest and relax in the truth that this is anchored in the heart of Christianity—life comes out of death, the humble are exalted, the last are the first, and the poor in spirit inherit the kingdom of heaven.

Let me invite you to adjust your expectations in prayer. God has used the following prayer to encourage me to stay on this journey of weakness and vulnerability. I pray it grants you strength as well:

> *I asked God for strength that I might achieve;*
> *I was made weak that I might learn humbly to obey.*
> *I asked for health that I might do greater things;*
> *I was given infirmity that I might do better things.*
> *I asked for riches that I might be happy;*
> *I was given poverty that I might be wise.*
> *I asked for power that I might have the praise of others;*
> *I was given weakness that I might feel the need of God.*
> *I asked for all things that I might enjoy life;*

I was given life that I might enjoy all things.
I got nothing that I asked for, but everything I had hoped for.
Almost despite myself, my unspoken prayers were answered.
I am, among all people, most richly blessed.

Implementing Emotionally Healthy Discipleship

Implementing a discipleship that deeply transforms people for the sake of the world—as described on the preceding pages—requires much more than simply making a few minor tweaks in your ministry. It is more like changing the entire operating system of a computer.

DISCIPLESHIP AS AN OPERATING SYSTEM

Personal computers run on operating systems. An operating system is the software that enables the hardware and other software programs to run. Without it, a computer isn't very useful.

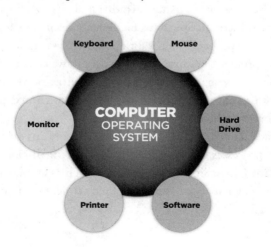

The two most common operating systems for personal computers are Microsoft Windows and Apple's MacOS. Each system has different processes that control how various software programs function together with the hardware. And each of the processes has certain rules and limits. For example, if you download a software program or application from one operating system to a computer that runs the other system, the program will not work.[1] Why? Because it's incompatible with the operating system. Each operating system controls the core processes that allow other programs and applications to run.[2]

That's about the extent of my tech savvy, but I love what the operating system as a metaphor reveals when it's applied to discipleship. Think about it. Just as operating systems are invisible to us, functioning beneath the applications we routinely access each day—such as email, spreadsheets, and word processing programs—every approach to discipleship also has an operating system that remains largely invisible to us.

We think we are simply praying, addressing a conflict, and sharing our faith, but we fail to realize that there is an operating system that informs how we approach these things. That system includes all kinds of assumptions that inform our approach to discipleship and spiritual growth. And many of us have been praying, dealing with conflicts, and sharing our faith in the same way for decades—regardless of how effective they might be.

Why? Because we're using a traditional discipleship operating system that is incompatible with facilitating deep transformation in people's lives. And because it is an operating system, it's invisible to us. That's a problem, because if we don't see it, we can't understand it, and it will not serve us. And we will find ourselves locked into a closed system that prevents us from accessing the breadth and depth of what God has for us—which we desperately need.

The traditional discipleship operating system runs on a set of core beliefs and processes with the objective of growing disciples to impact the world for Christ. It includes practices such as church attendance, small group participation, and giving one's time, talent, and treasure to serve others.

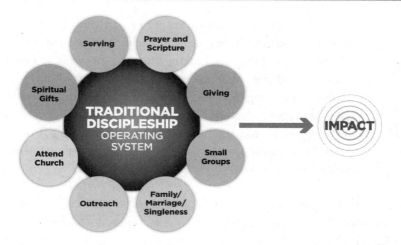

We may add some unique components, like new programs, fresh approaches to worship and outreach, and restudying particular biblical truths. But the core assumptions and processes of the traditional approach remain the same: we expect connecting, serving, and giving to achieve our goal of changing lives so they impact the world.

Here's the problem: we rarely consider the limitations of this traditional discipleship operating system. Emotionally Healthy Discipleship is like a new operating system with three distinctives:

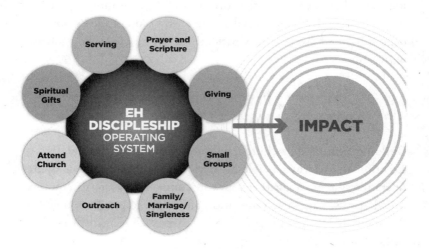

- It integrates biblical truths missing from the traditional discipleship model: the gift of limits, embracing grief and loss, breaking the power of the past, making love the measure of spiritual maturity, and living in weakness and vulnerability.
- It integrates loving God, loving ourselves, and loving others in a way that goes beyond head knowledge to a lived experience.
- It slows us down so we ground our discipleship in the person of Jesus, focusing on who we are on the inside, rather than what we do on the outside.

So, the question that naturally emerges is, "How do I bring Emotionally Healthy Discipleship into our church—and how do I keep it there?" Before we get to specific steps for implementation, it is critical to acknowledge three, beneath-the-surface elements that undergird Emotionally Healthy Discipleship: 1) It is a large, long-term vision for the church; 2) It is a biblical paradigm shift that takes seven to ten years to integrate; and 3) It unfolds from the inside out—from you, to your team, to the wider church.

These components are critical to understand for two reasons. First, you want to set realistic expectations after what is often an initial state of excitement as people get unstuck in their spiritual journey. They need to see that this is only the beginning of a longer journey. Secondly, people need a long-term vision of God's slow discipleship process so that they patiently persevere in this new journey with Jesus.

THREE ELEMENTS TO IMPLEMENT EMOTIONALLY HEALTHY DISCIPLESHIP

Building a ministry, a church, or a non-profit on the foundation of Emotionally Healthy Discipleship is a lot like building a new computer operating system. You gather your core components (such as a motherboard, data storage, and a processor) and begin to put them together. Emotionally Healthy Discipleship has three such elements that must be established before building.

Element 1: Emotionally Healthy Discipleship Has a Large, Long-Term Vision for the Church.

Normally, our goal is to build a church in which people attend worship services, participate in small groups, invest financially, and serve. We assume that active participation in these activities means people are maturing in a vital, personal relationship of loving union with Jesus.

We assume wrongly. It does not.

In fact, I marvel at how many excellent communicators lead as if discipleship takes place primarily through sermons. That is like going to the nursery, spraying the babies with milk, and walking away claiming we fed them.[3]

Emotionally Healthy Discipleship is built on a resolute commitment to make serious disciples of Jesus for the sake of the world. In fact, the scoreboard for success changes from counting numbers (how many attend, participate, give, and serve) to measuring deep transformation and a long-range vision of multiplying disciples who make disciples. To better understand what that looks like, and to see how it differs from traditional discipleship, consider the following graphic.

TRADITIONAL DISCIPLESHIP

TRANSFORMATIVE DISCIPLESHIP

Emotionally Heathy Discipleship provides biblical content, along with a structure, to equip ministry leaders to build, not flippantly or haphazardly, but wisely and intentionally.

Jesus knew that intentional discipling of the Twelve was central to the future of his kingdom mission. The same remains true for us today. As Dietrich Bonhoeffer said so eloquently, "Christianity without the living Christ is inevitably Christianity without discipleship, and Christianity without discipleship is always Christianity without Christ."[4] In other words, while we might resist the long, slow process of transformational discipleship and be tempted to revert to a quick fix program to see the church grow numerically, this will never deeply change people or our churches. It only looks like the real thing on the outside.

Element 2: Emotionally Healthy Discipleship Is a Biblical Paradigm Shift that Takes Seven to Ten Years to Integrate into the Life of a Church.

Yes, you read that correctly. Seven to ten years.

This cannot be rushed. The kingdom of God is, and always will be, a mustard seed that grows slowly, almost imperceptibly (Mark 4:26–32). It takes time for the truth we know intellectually to become truth we know experientially and live out consistently in our everyday lives.

People in our churches have been deeply malformed by three primary forces—Western culture's dictum of bigger, better, and faster; their families of origin; and values attendant to their race and ethnicity. This means that all of these things have to be transformed. There is much to unlearn and much to learn anew about life in the new family of Jesus.

We observe that slow process of transformation in Jesus's work with the Twelve—and he had them full-time, twenty-four hours a day, for almost three years. Emotionally healthy discipleship is introducing people to a new paradigm of discipleship that is so far-reaching not one area of life is left untouched by it.

I sometimes liken the magnitude of the shift required to implement emotionally healthy discipleship to the Copernican Revolution. Do you remember the story? Nicolaus Copernicus, a sixteenth-century

Polish scientist, challenged an assumption that Earth was the center of the universe—which had been the accepted view for over fourteen hundred years. The realization that Earth was only one of many planets orbiting the sun in a vast universe shook the very foundations of society and was deeply unsettling for many. From that point on, everyone began to look at the universe, and their place in it, from a whole new perspective. All kinds of prior information and data could now be considered and analyzed in new ways.

Today, we still use the term Copernican Revolution to describe any significant paradigm shift—an idea that offers a whole new way of looking at life and that shakes the foundations of how we understand the world and our place in it. Implementing Emotionally Healthy Discipleship will certainly result in a Copernican Revolution for many people in your church.

Moreover, it will result in a revolution of your wider church culture over a seven-to-ten-year period, transforming not only the theology around which you frame discipleship, but also how you define everything from healthy community and integrity in leadership, to healthy marriages and families. (See Appendix A for an expanded description of a six-part vision of a church culture that deeply changes lives.)

Element 3: Emotionally Healthy Discipleship Unfolds from the Inside Out—from You, to Your Team, to the Wider Church.

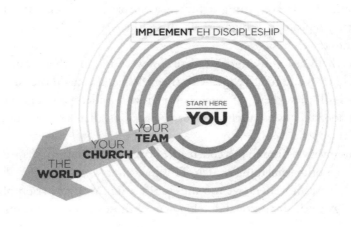

You

Emotionally healthy discipleship is not difficult to understand intellectually. The biblical truths found in this book provide great preaching and teaching material. God intends, however, that we allow ourselves to be deeply transformed by the material. Otherwise, we are simply adding another program and activity to our church. And that is something our people do not need.

Geri sometimes explains this dynamic by comparing it to learning to ride a bicycle. I can read to you from a book about how to ride a bike. I can show you a video on how to ride a bike. I can get on a bike and demonstrate it for you. But you will still not know how to ride a bike. You must get on the bike yourself to learn how to ride a bike. In the same way, each of the seven marks of Emotionally Healthy Discipleship presented in this book must be lived in your context, in your journey with Jesus, and out of your unique temperament and calling.

Remember, what we do matters, but who we are matters more. We cannot give what we do not possess. That is why the most loving thing we can do for the people we serve is to go slowly, allowing God to transform us first before teaching others.

Your Team

We must also invest in the personal development of your team, and not just their ministry skills. They join you in serving as guardians of the values of your ministry culture. I mistakenly expected my team to automatically "do everything right." I was surprised and often upset when they repeatedly brought their unhealthy ways of relating with them into the church.

But what was I thinking? Of course they were bringing their immature behaviors and rough edges with them! What else could they do? That was all they knew. As much as we all wish leaders would arrive on our doorsteps as maturely transformed persons, that is rarely what actually happens.

Jesus invested himself in a core team of twelve who, in turn, shaped the culture of the emerging church. This took time. Lots of it.

As Christian leaders, we too must shift a significant portion of our energy to the intentional development of those on our core team.

Our teams must embody the theology we are inviting our people to live into. They also must learn new relational skills, especially for use when under stress and in conflict. And our teams must master the application of this material as it is nuanced and applied in different life situations so they can intentionally disciple others to do the same. The formula is simple:

**clear theology + new skills + new language +
intentional follow-up = transformed community**

Every time we purposefully and thoughtfully mentor someone, especially in the midst of stress and conflict, we advance the maturity level of our ministry a hundredfold.

Your Church

While Emotionally Healthy Discipleship is not a program, we discovered that long-term, systemic change in a church requires a programmatic element to move people beyond shallow discipleship to deep transformation in Jesus. This means we must drive a stake in the ground to keep high-quality, in-depth discipleship at the forefront and center of our mission, offering a biblical framework to unite the entire community around following Jesus.

This is important because everything in our culture today encourages us to take short-cuts, resorting to a thin discipleship versus the slow, difficult process of developing mothers and fathers of the faith like Jesus. If we hope for our people to be transformed and learn to live in new ways, we have to teach them that discipleship is a life to be lived, not a list of spiritual activities to complete. This is precisely what *The Emotionally Healthy Discipleship Course* is designed to do.

THE EMOTIONALLY HEALTHY
DISCIPLESHIP COURSE

After more than twenty-one years of research, development, and testing, we gathered the core components of what we believed was missing in present-day discipleship into *The Emotionally Healthy Discipleship*

Course: Parts 1 and 2—two, eight-week courses that provide an introductory experience of serious discipleship with Jesus.

the emotionally healthy
DISCIPLESHIP COURSE

PART 1   PART 2

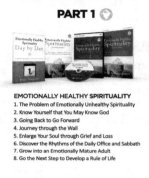 

EMOTIONALLY HEALTHY SPIRITUALITY
1. The Problem of Emotionally Unhealthy Spirituality
2. Know Yourself that You May Know God
3. Going Back to Go Forward
4. Journey through the Wall
5. Enlarge Your Soul through Grief and Loss
6. Discover the Rhythms of the Daily Office and Sabbath
7. Grow into an Emotionally Mature Adult
8. Go the Next Step to Develop a Rule of Life

EMOTIONALLY HEALTHY RELATIONSHIPS
1. Take Your Community Temperature Reading
2. Stop Mind Reading & Clarify Expectations
3. Genogram Your Family
4. Explore the Iceberg
5. Listen Incarnationally
6. Climb the Ladder of Integrity
7. Fight Cleanly
8. Develop a Rule of Life to Implement Your New Skills

We call this a course, rather than a small group curriculum, because the expectations are much higher. The EHD Course requires homework and is led by a trained point person and trained table leaders to ensure consistently high quality. While this course has a pastoral care and community element similar to that of most small groups, it requires an investment of time to read, pray, study Scripture, and gather together weekly. Readings, devotionals, and integration of the material during the week are also required.

This content leads people deep beneath the surface of their lives, introducing them to God, and themselves, on a whole new level. A primary goal is to equip people to cultivate their own personal relationship with Jesus. We guide them to rearrange their days to integrate the practice of being still and silent in God's presence and to develop a rhythm of meeting with Jesus twice a day through the practice of the Daily Office.

We set two conditions for those who want to implement the course. First, we ask that you not bring this to your ministry until you have been trained first (free training is available at www.emotionallyhealthy. org/lead). Second, we ask that the point leader begin living the course *before* teaching it to others. We discovered that, without these two conditions being met, the course inevitably becomes stripped of its key elements (such as the Daily Office and practice of new skills). Follow-up homework is minimized, and little is expected from participants except attendance.

That is not an operating system that will deeply transform people in Jesus.

But as tens of thousands of leaders now testify, getting trained properly and living the course themselves first has resulted in entire churches being dramatically changed. So please, do not be in a rush. We didn't get into the problem of shallow discipleship overnight. And neither will we solve the problem overnight.

Emotionally Healthy Spirituality: Part 1 is about growing in love for God. We cannot be spiritually mature if we are emotionally immature. This provides the theological foundation for emotionally healthy discipleship. It includes reading the book *Emotionally Healthy Spirituality* and learning to cultivate a rhythm of meeting with Jesus twice a day using *Emotionally Healthy Spirituality Day by Day: A 40-Day Journey with the Daily Office*. These devotions correspond with the eight weekly themes of the course. *The Emotionally Healthy Spirituality Course Workbook* is used by participants during the course. The eight sessions include:

1. The Problem of Emotionally Unhealthy Spirituality (Saul)
2. Know Yourself That You May Know God (David)
3. Go Back in Order to Go Forward (Joseph)
4. Journey through the Wall (Abraham)
5. Enlarge Your Soul through Grief and Loss (Jesus)
6. Discover the Rhythms of the Daily Office and Sabbath (Daniel)
7. Grow into an Emotionally Mature Adult (The Good Samaritan)
8. Go the Next Step to Develop a "Rule of Life" (The Early Church)

Many churches, including ours, offer *Emotionally Healthy Spirituality: Part 1* two to three times a year so that it becomes the foundation for the discipleship of the entire community. High-quality training, coaching support, and additional resources are provided on our website at www.emotionallyhealthy.org/lead.

Emotionally Healthy Relationships: Part 2 teaches eight core skills to equip people to love others in a mature way. We call these eight tools "emotionally healthy skills." While they may look simple, each is built on a theological foundation and contains multiple levels of depth to understand and apply. People are taught, for example, how to speak clearly, respectfully, and honestly; how to listen like Jesus; how to clarify expectations and assumptions; how to have a clean, instead of a dirty, fight with someone. Sessions include:

1. The Community Temperature Reading
2. Stop Mind Reading
3. Clarify Expectations
4. Genogram Your Family
5. Explore the Iceberg
6. Incarnational Listening
7. Climb the Ladder of Integrity
8. Clean Fighting

Each skill is anchored in unlocking the application of Scripture for everyday life and relationships.

Participants also cultivate a rhythm of meeting with Jesus twice a day using *Emotionally Healthy Relationships Day by Day: A 40-Day Journey to Deeply Change Your Relationships*. These devotions correspond with the eight weekly themes of this course as well.

I have been teaching Parts 1 and 2 of the *Emotionally Healthy Discipleship Course* for over ten years, both to those in our church and to other pastors and leaders. Every time I do, God meets me in a fresh way. Why? The truths and Scripture texts are bottomless, and every time I come to them, God takes me deeper, applying them differently to where I am in that moment in my following of Jesus.

A PRAYER FOR YOU

Will building deeply-transformed disciples be challenging? Absolutely. You will have to wrestle with a number of important biblical texts and truths for yourself. Will it take a lot of time? Most definitely. Will it cost you? Yes. But the cost will be much greater if you don't.

Jesus promises us that his yoke is easy and his burden is light (Matthew 11:28–30). That is nowhere more true than when we follow him in this slow, disciple-making process.

This pathway of Emotionally Healthy Discipleship will position your people before God so they can be radically changed by the Holy Spirit. And it has the power to produce fruit so wide and deep that it lasts beyond their earthly life into eternity.

May the beauty of that vision compel you forward to engage in the hard work of discipleship.

Allow me to close with a beautiful, Celtic blessing that hangs in the hallway of our home. Geri and I often pray it over visitors, even when we don't expect to see them again in our home. We expect to see them in Jesus's heavenly home one day. As you read this prayer, I invite you to receive this blessing as you embark with Jesus on this new discipleship journey into the unknown.

May the peace of the Lord Christ go with you,
wherever he may send you.
May he guide you through the wilderness,
protect you through the storm.
May he bring you home rejoicing
at the wonders he has shown you.
May he bring you home rejoicing
once again into our doors.[5]

Church Culture Revolution

*A Six-Part Vision for a Culture
That Deeply Changes Lives*

One of the greatest insights I've gained from working with thousands of churches around the world is that creating a healthy culture is a powerful strategy for impacting people's lives as well as the long-term mission of the church. If our goal is to multiply deeply transformed disciples and leaders for the sake of the world, a healthy culture is profoundly important. We have to be intentional about taking the chaos of what people bring with them—from their very different backgrounds, cultures, and families of origin—and shaping it into a radically different culture that operates as the new family of Jesus.

So, what precisely is this thing called culture? Defining it can be challenging because culture consists primarily of unspoken rules about "the way we do things around here."

Culture is that imprecise something, the invisible presence or personality of a place that can be difficult to describe without actually experiencing it. It is often more readily felt than articulated. Perhaps the simplest and best definitions I've come across describe culture as "the sumtotal of the learned patterns of thought and behavior" of any given group,[1] and "what human beings make of the world."[2]

Multinational companies such as Google, Apple, and IBM have very distinct cultures. Ethnic communities, political groups, and countries have cultures. Denominations and parachurch organizations have cultures. Every church, ministry, task force, and team has a certain style that constitutes the spirit or ethos of that particular community. But that doesn't mean culture just "happens." Culture needs to be created, shaped, and maintained. And the responsibility for doing so resides with the leader.

To help you begin thinking about what this might look like in your own church, I've identified six characteristics or qualities of an emotionally healthy church *culture*:

1. Slowed-Down Spirituality
2. Integrity in Leadership
3. Beneath-the-Surface Discipleship
4. Healthy Community
5. Passionate Marriages and Singleness
6. Every Person in Full-Time Ministry

Each characteristic is summarized on the pages that follow. After the description of each characteristic, you will find a brief assessment tool and then questions for personal reflection and team discussion. My prayer is that this process will give you the vision and courage to transform the culture of your ministry so profoundly that its impact will be felt for generations.

QUALITY 1: SLOWED-DOWN SPIRITUALITY

We slow down our pace in order to be with Jesus, and this is the source from which our activity flows.

In a church culture that changes lives, people refuse to allow a hurried world to set the pace for their lives. They choose instead to live by rhythms that are slower and more deliberate. They set aside time each day to immerse themselves in Scripture, silence, and solitude, which are foundational practices for communion with Jesus. Their doing for God flows out of their being with God.

As a result, they consistently embrace other spiritual practices, such as Sabbath-keeping and discernment, in order to cultivate their personal relationship with Jesus and avoid living off of the spirituality of others. They willingly learn about the practices of slowed-down spirituality from two thousand years of church history and the global church. They remain profoundly aware that, apart from abiding in Jesus, it is impossible to bear lasting fruit—both as individuals and as a community.

Assessment

To what degree is your culture characterized by slowed-down spirituality?

Circle the number on the continuum that best describes your response. Then briefly describe the reasons for the number you circled.

1	2	3	4	5	6	7	8	9	10

Not at all true of our culture   Completely true of our culture

Questions for Reflection and Discussion

- In what ways is your current culture an asset that helps people to slow down and cultivate oneness with Jesus? In what ways is it a liability that makes slowing down harder?
- Briefly reflect on your work and leadership over the last month or so. In what ways were the characteristics of slowed-down spirituality most notably evident? For example, in your attitudes, behaviors, demeanor, pace of life, etc. In what ways were these characteristics most notably absent?

QUALITY 2: INTEGRITY IN LEADERSHIP

We do not pretend to be something on the outside that we are not on the inside.

In a church culture that changes lives, leaders—staff and volunteer—are intentional about living out of vulnerability and brokenness.

They refuse to engage in pretense or impression management. They endeavor to be the same person onstage in public as they are offstage in private. They recognize that their first and most difficult task is to lead themselves so that their work for God is nourished by a deep inner life with God.

This ensures that their leadership is not driven by other motives, such as the need for power, approval from others, or success as the world defines and measures it. Through their lives and their leadership, they seek to create an environment in which their people are encouraged to ask questions and give helpful feedback. They also enjoy the freedom to say a healthy "no" as they discern God's will and set appropriate limits.

Assessment

To what degree is your culture characterized by integrity in leadership?

Circle the number on the continuum that best describes your response. Then briefly describe the reasons for the number you circled.

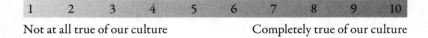

| 1 | 2 | 3 | 4 | 5 | 6 | 7 | 8 | 9 | 10 |

Not at all true of our culture   Completely true of our culture

Questions for Reflection and Discussion

- How would you complete the following sentences?
  - Some of the ways our culture directly and indirectly affirms pretense and subtly encourages impression management are . . .
  - Some of the ways our culture affirms transparency and encourages people to live out of vulnerability and brokenness are . . .
- In what aspect of your life or leadership are you most tempted to skim over truth, to be less than honest about your struggles, to deny negative emotions, or to pretend to be more or better than you are?

QUALITY 3: BENEATH-THE-SURFACE DISCIPLESHIP

We grow in self-awareness because we cannot change that of which we remain unaware.

In a church culture that changes lives, no one assumes people are maturing on the basis of activities such as church attendance, small group participation, and serving. Instead, they understand that maturity results when people engage in the slow, hard work of following the crucified Jesus. Leaders carefully teach people how to break free from unhealthy or destructive patterns in their families and culture of origin, and how to live differently in the new family of Jesus. People understand that their past impacts their present, and they are intentional about identifying and facing their beneath-the-surface issues (such as sinful tendencies, unresolved wounds, triggers, etc.).

They apply the gospel of grace and the truth of Scripture to every area of life, meeting Jesus in their losses and limits and learning how to love other people as Jesus did. They understand they need to die to the less obvious sins—such as defensiveness, detachment from others, and a lack of vulnerability—as well as the more obvious sins, such as lying or coveting. They also pursue the healthy desires God places in their hearts and celebrate God's good gifts, such as beauty, nature, laughter, music, and friendships.

Assessment

To what degree is your culture characterized by beneath-the-surface discipleship?

Circle the number on the continuum that best describes your response. Then briefly describe the reasons for the number you circled.

1	2	3	4	5	6	7	8	9	10

Not at all true of our culture   Completely true of our culture

Questions for Reflection and Discussion

- In what ways, if any, does your culture tend to equate increased levels of participation (in programs, events, or serving) with growth and transformation in Christ?
- What beneath-the-surface issues—a sinful tendency, a weakness, a wound, a past failure, or self-protection—have most impacted your leadership in the past recently?

QUALITY 4: HEALTHY COMMUNITY

We are committed to learning tools and practices in order to love others like Jesus.

In a church culture that changes lives, people recognize that there is a disconnect when those who claim to love Jesus are experienced by others as defensive, judgmental, unapproachable, and unsafe. Thus, leaders teach and train people in how to do relationships as Jesus did. This includes how to speak clearly, respectfully, and honestly; how to listen; and how to clarify expectations. It also includes confronting the elephants in the room, such as "dirty fighting," and equipping people to master "clean fighting" to negotiate conflicts.

As part of living in community, people learn to respect individual viewpoints, choices, and spiritual journeys, allowing each one to take responsibility for his or her own life without blaming or shaming. By sharing and connecting with each other out of their weaknesses and vulnerabilities, they offer a gift of God's grace to one another and to the world.

Assessment

To what degree is your culture characterized by healthy community?

Circle the number on the continuum that best describes your response. Then briefly describe the reasons for the number you circled.

1	2	3	4	5	6	7	8	9	10

Not at all true of our culture   Completely true of our culture

Questions for Reflection and Discussion

- Every culture has a default mode for negotiating conflict and navigating differing viewpoints. What three words or phrases would you use to describe the default mode of your ministry culture when it comes to conflict and differing viewpoints? In what ways are these words/phrases indicative of a healthy culture? An unhealthy culture?
- What three words or phrases would you use to describe your personal default mode when it comes to conflict and differing viewpoints? What similarities and differences are there between your default mode and that of the larger culture?

QUALITY 5: PASSIONATE MARRIAGES AND SINGLENESS

We model God's passionate love for the world by living out of our marriages or singleness.

In a church culture that changes lives, the maturity of each person's marriage or singleness is measured not simply by stability or commitment to Christ, but by the degree to which each is becoming a living sign and wonder of God's love for the world. People live out a vision of love that is passionate, intimate, free, and life-giving, recognizing their oneness with Christ is closely connected to their oneness with their spouses or to their close community.

They talk openly about sexuality, recognizing the intimate relationship between Christ and his church is to be reflected in the sexual relationship between a husband and wife, or in the chastity of those who are single. They carefully differentiate between "using" people and "loving" people by monitoring the movements of their hearts and treating others as unrepeatable and invaluable beings made in the image of God.

Assessment

To what degree is your culture characterized by passionate marriage and singleness?

Circle the number on the continuum that best describes your response. Then briefly describe the reasons for the number you circled.

| 1 | 2 | 3 | 4 | 5 | 6 | 7 | 8 | 9 | 10 |

Not at all true of our culture   Completely true of our culture

Questions for Reflection and Discussion

- In what ways does your culture affirm marriages and singleness as vocations—as two ways of modeling God's passionate love for the world? What, if any, differences are there in the ways your culture equips married adults and single adults to live out their respective vocations?

- Overall, how would you describe the role your vocation (marriage or singleness) plays in your leadership? To what degree does the way you spend your time and energy reflect that your marriage/singleness—not ministry—is your first priority as a leader?

QUALITY 6: EVERY PERSON IN FULL-TIME MINISTRY

We commission every believer to walk in the authority of Jesus at work and in daily life.

In a church culture that changes lives, people reject cultural values that view human beings as spectators and consumers. They affirm that every believer is called to full-time ministry for Jesus. Every sphere of daily activity—paid or unpaid work, or retirement—constitutes a field of ministry. They refuse to compartmentalize work and spirituality, viewing work as an act of worship that brings order out of chaos and builds God's kingdom.

They seek to create community within their spheres of influence, integrating new skills for loving well, and reflecting the generosity of God. In the context of their work and daily activities, they practice Jesus's presence and engage in the slow work of making disciples.

Drawing on the foundation of the gospel, they are active in naming and combating language, attitudes, and behaviors resulting from such evils as racism, classism, sexism, and any other ideology that demeans human beings.

Assessment

To what degree is your culture characterized by every person in full-time ministry?

Circle the number on the continuum that best describes your response. Then briefly describe the reasons for the number you circled.

1	2	3	4	5	6	7	8	9	10

Not at all true of our culture   Completely true of our culture

Questions for Reflection and Discussion

- If you were to ask the people in your church to name their ministry, what percentage would name their volunteer service to the church? What percentage would name their sphere of daily activity? Overall, how would you characterize the degree to which your people tend to compartmentalize work and spirituality?
- In what ways does the truth that every person is in full-time ministry challenge you as a leader? In what ways does it encourage you?

Appendix B

The Nicene Creed (with Notations)

For the first three centuries of its existence, the church found itself in a hostile environment, threatened from without by persecution and from within by ideas that were in conflict with Scripture. In the New Testament, for example, we observe Paul exhorting Timothy to "keep the pattern of sound teaching" he had received (2 Timothy 1:13) and to protect the truth from error. Over the course of three centuries, what the church considered sound teaching was codified into a variety of creeds, the most well known being *The Apostles' Creed*.

When Constantine legalized Christiantiy in AD 313, he discovered that the empire was fractured by theological disputes, especially conflicts over the nature of Jesus Christ. Arius, a priest of the church in Alexandria, had argued that Jesus was created by God, and not fully God. This began to split the church and thus, the empire. As a result, Constantine summoned a council of bishops from all over the empire to settle doctrine for the entire church. This resulted in the Nicene Creed of AD 325. A second council of bishops met to revise and expand the creed at a second council that met in Constantinople (present day Istanbul) in AD 381 to affirm what we now know as the final version of the Nicene Creed.

What makes the Nicene Creed so important is that it has defined orthodox Christian faith for over 1600 years. The three main branches of the Christian Church—Roman Catholic, Eastern Orthodox, and Protestant—agree that this "rule of faith" provides the boundaries of Christian belief and provides a measure, or rule, for the proper reading of Scripture.

Every day, millions of Christians recite this compressed creed in which each word was intentionally chosen and packed with meaning. The Nicene Creed invites us to reflect on the radical nature of what we truly believe about God and the large vision of what he is doing in human history.

THE NICENE CREED

We believe[1] in one God,
    the Father, the Almighty,
    maker of heaven and earth,
    of all that is, seen and unseen.
We believe in one Lord, Jesus Christ,
    the only son of God,
    eternally begotten of the Father,[2]
    God from God, Light from Light,
    true God from true God,
    begotten, not made,
    of one being with the Father.[3]
    Through him all things were made.
    For us and for our salvation
        he came down from heaven:
    by the power of the Holy Spirit
        he became incarnate from the Virgin Mary,
        and was made man.[4]
For our sake he was crucified under Pontius Pilate;
    he suffered death and was buried.
    On the third day he rose again
        in accordance with the Scriptures;
    he ascended into heaven
        and is seated at the right hand of the Father.
    He will come again in glory to judge the living and the dead,
        and his kingdom will have no end.
We believe in the Holy Spirit, the Lord, the giver of life,
    who proceeds from the Father [and the Son].[5]
    With the Father and the Son he is worshipped and glorified.[6]

He has spoken through the Prophets.
We believe in one holy catholic and apostolic Church.[7]
We acknowledge one baptism for the forgiveness of sins.[8]
We look for the resurrection of the dead,
  and the life of the world to come. AMEN.

Notations

1. *"We believe"*: We profess the convictions that bind us together as a community. We stand together and recite them. We are a people defined by these words and truths.

2. *"Eternally begotten of the Father"*: From this point, the language about Jesus is directed to clarify that he was, in the fullest sense of the word, God. They piled phrase upon phrase, most drawn from Scripture, but some not, to assert a simple, but infinitely difficult truth: Jesus is the "only-begotten Son of God." This language and understanding comes from John 1:1, 2, 14, that Jesus was not made by the Father as part of creation, but is rather an extension of the Father's own existence. This is not a making by God but a sharing by the Father out of himself.

3. *"One in being"*: asserting the unity of the Father and the Son

4. This is the heart of the creed. The all-powerful creator of the universe entered our humanity and our history—for our salvation.

5. *"Who proceeds from the Father and the Son"*: This short statement continues to be a source of tension between the Eastern and Western church. It was one of the explicit causes of the schism between Roman Catholic and Eastern Orthodox Christians in AD 1054.

6. *"The Holy Spirit"* is also worshiped and glorified. He is not only a power but a person and is to be thought of in the same manner as the Father and the Son.

7. *"One holy catholic and apostolic church"*: The word *catholic* means *universal* (not the Roman Catholic church). It refers to the reality that the church of Jesus exists around the world and not simply in one denomination or local church.

8. *"One baptism for the forgiveness of sins"*: Ephesians 4:5 states there is "one Lord, one faith, one baptism." While salvation is by grace through faith alone, all agree baptism is an essential mark of our leaving of the world, receiving of forgiveness, and becoming part of the church of Jesus Christ.

Acknowledgments

There would be no Emotionally Healthy Discipleship ministry, much less a book, were it not for Geri, my wife of thirty-six years. Twenty-six years ago, God used her decision to quit our church to get my attention and launch this incredible journey we've been on together ever since. Her integrity and wisdom fill these pages. I am also grateful we get to live this out with our four daughters (Maria, Christy, Faith, and Eva), our two sons-in-law (Jesse and Brett), and our grandchildren (June, Ove, and "Baby M").

This book was birthed in our community at New Life Fellowship Church in Queens, New York, where I served as senior pastor for twenty-six years. Thank you, New Life family, for your vulnerability and for entrusting the pearls of your stories to us. I want to express special appreciation to Rich Villodas who has led the church these last eight years. His creative, thoughtful work in applying Emotionally Healthy Discipleship to this new generation is a gift!

God sent us another gift in Ruth Lugo. Ruth has single-handedly provided the leadership to build a ministry that enables thousands of churches to implement Emotionally Healthy Discipleship. Her growing team—Victoria, Nils, Dale, PlainJoe Studios, Luke, Yolanda, Stephen, Paul—is amazing.

I am grateful also for significant mentors God sent me at key junctures in this journey—Ron Vogt, Steve Treat, Leighton Ford, and Peter and Carol Shrek.

Christine Anderson again served as an outstanding, and exacting, editor in this project. She is a joy to work with.

Finally, I want to thank Ryan, John, Beth, Jesse, and the entire Zondervan team. They are wonderful partners. And a big thank you to Chris Ferebee, my literary agent who provides a steady, stable presence in caring for all emotionally healthy books and my writing life!

Notes

The Difficult Journey to Move Beyond Shallow Discipleship

1. For Geri's full account of the story and her reflections of what she learned over the next fifteen years, see her book *The Emotionally Healthy Woman: Eight Things You Have to Quit to Change Your Life* (Grand Rapids, MI: Zondervan, 2014).

2. To learn more about personal transformation as a leader, see my book *The Emotionally Healthy Leader* (Grand Rapids, MI: Zondervan, 2015).

Chapter 1: The Four Failures That Undermine Deep Discipleship

1. Oliver Sacks, *The Man Who Mistook His Wife for a Hat* (New York: Summit Books, 1985), 63–68.

2. Multiple studies have been done over the years. Among the most well-known in recent decades are the *Reveal* study published in 2008 by Willow Creek Community Church, and *The State of Discipleship: A Barna Report Produced in Partnership with The Navigators* published in 2015. *Worship and the Reality of God* by John Jefferson Davis (2010), and Timothy Tennent's article posted on patheos.com, "The Clarion Call to Watered Down Evangelicalism" (2011) both characterize the North American evangelical church as shallow, thin, and indistinct from the broader culture.

3. Richard Foster's *Celebration of Discipline: The Path to Spiritual Growth* has been a perennial bestseller since it was first released in 1978. He opens the book with this statement: "Superficiality is the curse of our age.... The desperate need today is not for a greater number of intelligent people, or gifted people, but for deep people."

4. I've written an entire book, *The Emotionally Healthy Leader*, addressing the failure that so many of us have not experienced deep discipleship personally and yet now we find ourselves leading others.

5. Another great example is when Jesus is eating at Matthew's house and

he instructs the Pharisees to study again what Scripture says in Hosea, saying, "Go and learn what this means: 'I desire mercy, not sacrifice'" (Matthew 9:13).

6. Frederick Dale Bruner, *Matthew: A Commentary*, vol. 1 (Dallas: Word Publishing, 1987), 177–80.

7. Richard J. Foster, *Streams of Living Water: Celebrating the Great Traditions of Christian Faith* (San Francisco: HarperSanFrancisco, 1998), 189.

8. One of the early church heresies was Docetism, the belief that Christ had not really become human because of the insurmountable difference between the divine and human worlds. Some, therefore, thought that Jesus only seemed to be human but actually never gave up his divine nature or essence. See Helmut Koester, *History, Culture, and Religion of the Hellenistic Age* (Minneapolis: Fortress Press, 1995), 414.

   At the Council of Chalcedon in 451 AD, church leaders declared that Jesus was fully God and fully human—a widespread, historical interpretation of Scripture that I also affirm. The council affirmed that God visited our planet as the Word become flesh and lived among us (John 1:14). They defined the relationship of Christ's two natures as related but without confusion and division. See Henry Bettenson and Chris Maunder, eds., *Documents of the Christian Church*, 2nd ed. (London: Oxford University Press, 1963), 51.

9. For the apostle Paul, the body was not some sort of outer husk covering the human spirit nor some prisonhouse of the soul that might be better discarded. For Paul a person's body is that person. See R.H. Gundry, *Soma in Biblical Theology* (Cambridge: Cambridge University Press, 1976).

10. Dr. Dan B. Allender and Dr. Tremper Longman III, *The Cry of the Soul: How Our Emotions Reveal Our Deepest Questions about God* (Colorado Springs: NavPress, 1994), 24, 25.

11. Throughout church history, one of the seven deadly sins has been sloth or "not caring." Sloth refers not just to laziness, but also to busyness with the wrong things. Which is to say, we are slothful when we choose to be busy with the work of God in order to avoid the effort required for a life of prayer and solitude with God.

12. For an interesting, academic study on the impact of our ignorance, see Daniel R. DeNicola, *Understanding Ignorance: The Surprising Impact of What We Don't Know* (Cambridge, MA: MIT Press, 2018).

13. Tara Westover, *Educated: A Memoir* (New York: Random House, 2018), 238.

14. This is a summary from David Bebbington, *Evangelicalism in Modern Britain: A History from the 1730s to the 1980s*. See also Mark Noll's *The Rise of Evangelicalism: The Age of Edwards, Whitefield and the Wesleys*, and Dale Irvin and Scott Sunquist's *History of the World Christian Movement, Volume II: Modern Christianity from 1454 to 1900*.

15. For an excellent presentation on the various Christian traditions or streams of the church throughout history, see Richard J. Foster, *Streams of Living Water: Celebrating the Great Traditions of Christian Faith.* Foster covers six primary streams: Contemplative, Holiness, Charismatic, Social Justice, Evangelical, and Incarnational.

16. My good friend Scott Sunquist, a global church historian, argues that a fourth branch exists, which is the "Spiritual churches" of Africa, China, and Brazil. He writes, "Other churches . . . that formed in the early decades of the twentieth century were not technically Pentecostal in experience or theology, but they too started up independent of established churches (Protestant, Catholic, or Orthodox), finding their inspiration directly from biblical witness and the Holy Spirit. . . ." Scott W. Sunquist, *The Unexpected Christian Century* (Grand Rapids, MI: Baker Academic, 2015), 31–35. See also Timothy C. Tennent, *Theology in the Context of World Christianity: How the Global Church is Influencing the Way We Think About and Discuss Theology* (Grand Rapids, MI: Zondervan, 2007), 17–20.

17. Orthodox churches are located primarily in the eastern part of the world and include the Coptic Orthodox Church (Egypt), the Syriac Orthodox Church, the Russian Orthodox Church, the Greek Orthodox Church, the Armenian Apostolic Church, as well as other churches located in Iran, Iraq, and throughout the Arab world.

18. There are only seven Church Councils recognized as ecumenical, or universal, in scope: 325AD Nicea; 381AD Constantinople; 431 Ephesus; 451 Chalcedon; 553 2nd Council of Constantinople; 680 AD 3rd Council of Constantinople; 787 2nd Council of Nicea. For a short, accessible introduction to the Church Councils, see Justin S. Holcomb, *Know the Creeds and Councils* (Grand Rapids, MI: Zondervan, 2014).

19. Having studied church history under five different Protestant and Roman Catholic scholars, I consider it essential to also learn from our brothers and sisters in the Orthodox branch of the church. Peter Gillquist, the author of this chart, was a former Campus Crusade staff worker who, along with 300 others, converted to Antiochian Orthodoxy from evangelicalism in 1967. A Russian Orthodox priest in my neighborhood summed up the Orthodox view of Protestantism when he said to me one Sunday, "Pete, I am really glad you found faith in college. But now it is time to come home [to Orthodoxy]. We have never left the apostolic faith. But you are outside the true church. Come back to your roots."

20. For an excellent, and important, example of this, see, John H. Coe and Kyle C. Strobel, editors, *Embracing Contemplation: Reclaiming a Christian Spiritual Practice* (Downers Grove, IL: InterVarsity Press, 2019). They do an excellent job of examining Christian

contemplation–biblically and historically—to demonstate how crucial this is to our spiritual formation today.

21. If you are asking, "Where do I start? I know so little about church history," let me encourage you to begin with, Bruce L. Shelley, *Church History in Plain Language, Fourth Edition* (Nashville: Thomas Nelson, 2008, 2013). To learn more about the early history of the church, see Thomas C. Oden, *The Rebirth of Orthodoxy: Signs of New Life in Christianity*; D. H. Williams, *Evangelicals and Tradition: The Formative Influence of the Early Church*; Bryan M. Litfin, *Getting to Know the Church Fathers: An Evangelical Introduction*; D. H. Williams, *Retrieving the Tradition and Renewing Evangelicalism: A Primer for Suspicious Protestants*.

22. An oft-quoted maxim when navigating theological differences is, "In essentials unity, in non-essentials liberty, in all things charity."

23. See Helmut Koester, *Introduction to the New Testament: History and Literature of Early Christianity*, vol. 2 (New York: Walter de Gruyter & Co., 1982, 2000), 77–78.

Chapter 3: Be Before You Do

1. The contrast between the active (doing) and contemplative (being) life has been written about in every generation of Christian history. For most of church history, the contemplative life (being) devoted solely to love of God was understood to be superior to, and higher than, the active life (doing) of serving others. However, in the fourteenth century, theologian Thomas Aquinas was the first to suggest that the active life flowing out of contemplation was the highest and most difficult calling. Thomas Aquinas, *Summa Theologica*, Second and Revised Edition, "Question 182," Fathers of the English Dominican Province, trans. (1920); revised and edited for *New Advent* by Kevin Knight (2017), https://www.newadvent.org/summa/3182.htm.

2. There is a large, fascinating body of scholarly literature on the early Christian catechumenate. See Michel Dujarier, *A History of the Catechumenate: The First Six Centuries*, trans. Edward J. Haasl (New York: Sadlier, 1979); Alan Kreider, *The Change of Conversion and the Origin of Christendom* (Eugene, OR: Wipf & Stock, 1999); Robert Louis Wilken, "Christian Formation in the Early Church," in *Educating People of Faith: Exploring the History of Jewish and Christian Communities*, ed. John Van Engen (Grand Rapids, MI: Eerdmans, 2004), 48–62; Gerald L. Sittser, *Resilient Faith: How the Early Christian "Third Way" Changed the World* (Grand Rapids, MI: Baker Publishing, 2019), 155–78.

3. For an excellent discussion of how the early church struggled with the "lapsed" in North Africa, see David E. Wilhite, *Ancient African Christianity* (New York: Routledge, 2017), 141–60.

4. "What about the women?" you may ask. Sadly, because of the dominance of the patriarchy, women in the ancient world rarely had the opportunities that men did, and their contributions often went undocumented or unrecognized. However, we do know about a few. For example, Macrina the Younger (324–79), sister of Basil the Great and Gregory of Nyssa, was considered the greatest theologian in her family. Some communities in Egypt had as many as 5,000 women and were led by women. For an excellent treatment of women in the early church, see Lynn H. Cohick and Amy Brown Hughes, *Christian Women in the Patristic World: Their Influence, Authority, and Legacy in the Second through Fifth Centuries* (Grand Rapids, MI: Baker Academic, 2017).

5. See Richard Rohr, https://cac.org/what-is-the-false-self-2017-08-07/.

6. M. Robert Mulholland Jr., *The Deeper Journey: The Spirituality of Discovering Your True Self* (Downers Grove, IL: InterVarsity Press, 2006). See chapters 2 and 3 for a detailed analysis of these consequences. See also my book *Emotionally Healthy Spirituality*, chapter 4, which explores in greater detail the theme of knowing yourself that you may know God.

7. David Benner, *The Gift of Being Yourself: The Sacred Call to Self-Discovery* (Downers Grove, IL: InterVarsity Press, 2004), 91.

8. According to Thomas Merton, those who fled to the desert saw the world "as a shipwreck from which each single individual man had to swim for his life. . . . These were men who believed that to let oneself drift along, passively accepting the tenets and values of what they knew as society, was purely and simply a disaster." See Thomas Merton, *The Wisdom of the Desert: Sayings from the Desert Fathers of the Fourth Century* (Boston: Shambhala, 1960, 2004), 1–2, 25–26. In 323, Pachomius founded the first monastic community and established a clear structure for their life together. Other monasteries gradually arose (some of which numbered in the thousands), culminating with Benedict's founding of a monastery in Italy, which was structured around his "Rule of Saint Benedict."

9. John Wortley, ed. and trans., *The Book of the Elders: Sayings of the Desert Fathers* (Collegeville, MN: Liturgical Press, 2012), 15.

10. Benedicta Ward, trans., *The Sayings of the Desert Fathers: The Alphabetical Collection* (Kalamazoo, MI: Cistercian Publications, 1975), 9.

11. Anselm Gruen, *Heaven Begins within You: Wisdom from the Desert Fathers* (New York: Crossroad, 1999). I am grateful to Gruen for insights into desert spirituality and the phrase "earthy spirituality."

12. For additional information on facing the shadow, see my book *The Emotionally Healthy Leader*, chapter 2.

13. Robert E. Sinkewicz, *Evagrius of Pontus: The Greek Ascetic Corpus* (New York: Oxford University Press, 2003), *Maxims* 2, Maxim 2, 230.

14. For an exhaustive study of emotions in the New Testament, see: Matthew A. Elliot, *Faithful Feelings: Rethinking Emotion in the New Testament* (Grand Rapids, MI: Kregel Publications, 2006).

15. An accessible book written by the director of the Yale Center for Emotional Intelligence gives a large overview of emotions from the perspective of the social sciences and research. See Marc Brackett, *Permission to Feel: Unlocking the Power of Emotions to Help Our Kids, Ourselves, and Our Society Thrive* (New York: Macmillan, 2019).

16. Thomas Keating, *Intimacy with God: An Introduction to Centering Prayer* (New York: Crossroads, 1996), 82–84, 54–55.

17. Among the Desert Fathers, Evagrius is considered the specialist in dealing with thoughts and passions of the heart. His list and exposition on the eight evil, or deadly, thoughts includes gluttony, fornication, love of money, sadness, anger, listlessness, vainglory, and pride. This list was the standard point of reference through the Middle Ages for both the Eastern and Western Church. See William Harmless, S.J., *Desert Christians: An Introduction to the Literature of Early Monasticism* (New York: Oxford University Press, 2004), 311–71.

18. There are a number of excellent resources available to grow in silence and stillness. We regularly update our resources on silence and stillness with God through our website, www.emotionallyhealthy.org. I recommend the following books as well: Cynthia Bourgeault, *Centering Prayer and Inner Awakening* (Lanham, MD: Cowley Publications, 2004), Thomas Keating, *Intimacy with God: An Introduction to Centering Prayer* (New York: Crossroads, 1996).

19. A simple but helpful exercise to begin paying attention to our emotions is to notice our physical reactions in stressful situations—a knot in the stomach, a tension headache, teeth grinding, clenched hands or arms, sweaty palms, neck tightness, foot tapping, or insomnia. Ask yourself, "What might my body be telling me about my feelings right now?" For some, becoming aware of what we experience in our body is a big step in the right direction.

20. For a full explanation of how to begin practicing a weekly Sabbath, see chapter 5 in my book *Emotionally Healthy Leadership*, "Practice Sabbath Delight."

21. For more on the Daily Office, see my books *Emotionally Healthy Spirituality*, 139–50, and *Emotionally Healthy Spirituality Day by Day: A 40-Day Journey with the Daily Office* (Grand Rapids, MI: Zondervan, 2014).

22. For more information on how to craft a Rule of Life, see chapter 8 in *Emotionally Healthy Leadership*, "Go the Next Step to Develop a Rule of Life," and *Emotionally Healthy Leadership*, 135–41, where I also provide a sample Rule of Life.

Chapter 4: Follow the Crucified, Not the Americanized, Jesus

1. See H. Richard Niebuhr, *Christ and Culture* (New York: Harper and Row, 1951) and D. A. Carson, *Christ and Culture Revisited* (Grand Rapids, MI: Eerdmans, 2008).

2. "Americanize," *Merriam-Webster*, https://www.merriam-webster.com /dictionary/Americanize.

3. Frederick Dale Bruner, *Matthew: A Commentary, Volume 2: The Churchbook, Matthew 13–28*, Revised and Expanded (Grand Rapids, MI: Eerdmans, 2004), 147.

4. I am deeply grateful for Lamin Sanneh's work on the translatability of the gospel. Lamin is a brilliant missiologist/theologian from Ghana who taught at Yale for twenty-five years and has written an accessible book on this topic that I recommend: Lamin Sanneh, *Whose Religion is Christianity? The Gospel Beyond the West* (Grand Rapids, MI: Eerdmans, 2003).

5. I am deeply indebted to Frederick Dale Bruner for his outstanding two-volume commentary on Matthew, from which I gleaned countless insights that inform the content in this chapter. See Frederick Dale Bruner, *Matthew: A Commentary, Volume 1: The Christbook, Matthew 1–12*, Revised and Expanded (Grand Rapids, MI: Eerdmans, 2004) and *Matthew: A Commentary, Volume 2: The Churchbook, Matthew 13–28*, Revised and Expanded (Grand Rapids, MI: Eerdmans, 2004). See also Grant R. Osborne, *Matthew: Exegetical Commentary on the New Testament* (Grand Rapids, MI: Zondervan, 2019).

6. "Popular," *Cambridge Dictionary*, https://dictionary.cambridge.org/us/ dictionary/english/popular.

7. This is seen quite clearly in the Sermon on the Mount when Jesus expounds on the foolishness of "play-acting" (hypocrisy) in spiritual practices such as giving, praying, and fasting (Matthew 6:1–16).

8. See chapter 1, "Quit Being Afraid of What Others Think," in Geri Scazzero, *The Emotionally Healthy Woman: Eight Things You Have to Quit to Change Your Life* (Grand Rapids, MI: Zondervan, 2011).

9. See Josef Pieper, *Happiness and Contemplation* (South Bend, IN: St. Augustine's Press, 1998), a translation of the German edition published in 1979. Drawing on the work of Thomas Aquinas, Pieper notes how the human craving for happiness is so boundless that it is almost terrifying. His point is that we have a desire that can only be fully satiated in God.

10. Frederick Dale Bruner, *Matthew: A Commentary, Volume 2: The Churchbook, Matthew 13–28*, 814.

11. The whole book of Galatians makes this point, culminating in the famous text: "There is neither Jew nor Gentile, neither slave nor free, nor is there male or female, for you are all one in Christ Jesus" (Galatians 3:28). Fleming Rutledge does a great job with this truth in her book, *The*

Crucifixion: Understanding the Death of Jesus Christ (Grand Rapids, MI: Eerdmans, 2015), 274–77, 450–53.

12. See Frederick Dale Bruner, *Matthew: A Commentary, Volume 1: The Christbook, Matthew 1–12*, 111–13.

13. Frederick Dale Bruner, *Matthew: A Commentary: The Christbook, Matthew 1–12*, 112.

14. The moral boundaries we cross may include a little pornography, a little emotional affair, a little addictive spending, a little unresolved resentment, a little decline in the quality of our closest relationships. We may skim in our relationship with God because of all we have to do or exaggerate what is happening in the ministry.

15. Gordon D. Fee, *The First Epistle to the Corinthians: The New International Commentary of the New Testament* (Grand Rapids, MI: Eerdmans, 1987), 3.

16. For an excellent exposition of Galatians 6:14 and Paul's understanding that the cross turned the accepted standards of the world's culture upside down, see F. F. Bruce, *The Epistle to the Galatians: A Commentary on the Greek Text* (Grand Rapids, MI: Eerdmans, 1982), 270–73.

17. See Colossians 1:24 where Paul writes, "Now I rejoice in what I am suffering for you, and I fill up in my flesh what is still lacking in regard to Christ's afflictions, for the sake of his body, which is the church." In Philippians 1:29, he writes, "For it has been granted to you on behalf of Christ not only to believe in him, but also to suffer for him." See also 1 Corinthians 4:8–13 and 2 Corinthians 4:7–12 for more on Paul's radical understanding of himself as a disciple and leader.

18. Fleming Rutledge, *The Crucifixion*, 69–70.

19. I explain this more fully in chapter 6 of my book *The Emotionally Healthy Leader*, "Planning and Decision Making."

20. Frederick Dale Bruner, *The Gospel of John: A Commentary* (Grand Rapids, MI: Eerdmans, 2012), 316.

21. Edmund Colledge, O.S.A. and Bernard McGinn, trans., *Meister Eckhart: The Essential Sermons, Commentaries, Treatises, and Defense* (Mahwah, NJ: Paulist Press, 1981), 288. If you're interested in learning more about Meister Eckhart, here are some additional resources: Bernard McGinn, *The Mystical Thought of Meister Eckhart: The Man from Whom God Hid Nothing* (New York: Crossroad, 2001); Cyprian Smith, OSB, *The Way of Paradox: Spiritual Life as Taught by Meister Eckhart*, New Edition (London: Short Run Press, 1987, 2004); and Oliver Davies, trans., *Meister Eckhart: Selected Writings* (New York: Penguin Putnam, Inc., 1994).

22. For a fuller discussion of our succession process, including my internal struggles, see chapter 9 in *The Emotionally Healthy Leader*, "Endings and New Beginnings."

23. For details on our succession process, see Scazzero, *The Emotionally Healthy Leader*, 287–298.
24. See *John Cassian: The Conferences*, translated and annotated by Boniface Ramsey, O.P. (New York: Paulist Press, 1997), 77–112.

Chapter 5: Embrace God's Gift of Limits

1. Adapted from Edwin H. Friedman, *Friedman's Fables* (New York: Guilford Press, 1990), 9–13. Reprinted with permission of Guilford Press.
2. Eugene Peterson, *Under the Unpredictable Plant: An Exploration in Vocational Holiness* (Grand Rapids, MI: Eerdmans, 1994), 17.
3. Nicholas II (1894–1918) found himself at the age of twenty-six installed as tsar of Russia, ruler of almost one-sixth of the world. A reluctant leader, forced by the death of his father into a role for which he was ill-equipped, Nicholas seemed to be just the opposite of his aggressive, strong father, whom he called a "father beyond compare." He lacked his father's experience, authoritative manner, and physical stature. Instead, God had given Nicholas a tender temperament, a deep love for his family, and a sensitive nature. He was continually accused of having an un-tsar-like nature because he was soft-spoken and kind. One historian noted: "In office, the Emperor's gentleness and his lack of self-assertiveness had been weaknesses . . . With his family . . . they were strengths."

  The demands of ruling never suited his personality. He was more suited to be a tailor than an emperor. He much preferred to be with his wife and children in private at home or at one of their summer residences. Meanwhile, the storm clouds of World War I were swirling around him, as was Lenin's Bolshevik Revolution of 1917. Out of a sense of duty, he persevered, but eventually tsarist Russia crumbled. If Nicholas had dared to break with the life script handed to him and let someone else become leader, history may have turned out differently.
4. This story is recounted in full in 2 Samuel 7:1–29.
5. To learn more about honoring limits in marriage and singleness, see chapter 3, "Lead Out of Your Marriage or Singleness," in my book *The Emotionally Healthy Leader*.
6. The text only counts the men (5000 of them). Scholars estimate that, if women and children had been included in that number, it would have been more like 10,000–15,000 or more.
7. Martin Buber, *Tales of the Hasidim: The Early Masters* (New York: Schocken, 1975), 251.
8. Søren Kierkegaard, quoted in Irvin D. Yalom, *Existential Psychotherapy* (New York: Basic, 1980), 285.
9. Parker Palmer, *Let Your Life Speak* (San Francisco: Jossey-Bass, 1999), 30–31.

10. For an excellent story about caging invasive "tigers" in a congregation, see Chapter 6, "Culture and Team Building,"] in my book *The Emotionally Healthy Leader*. See also Edwin H. Friedman's DVD, *Reinventing Leadership* (New York: Guilford, 1996), 42 minutes.

11. See Geri Scazzero, "Quit Overfunctioning," chapter 6 in *The Emotionally Healthy Woman*.

12. Henry Cloud, *Changes That Heal: How to Understand Your Past to Ensure a Healthier Future* (Grand Rapids: Zondervan, 1990), 95.

13. Michael D. Yapko, *Breaking the Patterns of Depression* (Broadway Books: New York, 2001), 282–86.

14. For more on this concept, see Wendell Berry, *Life Is a Miracle: An Essay Against Modern Superstition* (Washington D.C.: Counterpoint, 2000).

15. See "Guidelines for the *Emotionally Healthy Spirituality Course and the Emotionally Healthy Relationships Course*" in *The Emotionally Healthy Spirituality Workbook: Updated Edition* (Grand Rapids, MI: Zondervan, 2017), 11–12, and *The Emotionally Healthy Relationships Workbook: Discipleship that Deeply Changes Your Relationship with Others* (Grand Rapids, MI: Zondervan, 2017), 13–14.

16. J.R.R. Tolkein, *Leaf by Niggle* (New York: Harper Collins Publishers, 1964), 31.

Chapter 6: Discover the Treasures Buried in Grief and Loss

1. Gerald L. Sittser, *A Grace Disguised: How the Soul Grows through Loss* (Grand Rapids, MI: Zondervan, 1995), 18.

2. Gerald L. Sittser, *A Grace Disguised*, 40, 37, 39.

3. See John O'Donohue, *Eternal Echoes: Celtic Reflections on Our Yearning to Belong* (New York: HarperCollins, 1999), 3–9.

4. To learn more about dark nights of the soul—what I call a "wall"—see my book *Emotionally Healthy Spirituality*, chapter 4, "Journey through the Wall."

5. Elisabeth Kübler-Ross, *On Death and Dying* (New York: Simon and Schuster, 1997).

6. See Elisabeth Kubler-Ross, MD and David Kessler, *On Grief and Grieving: Finding the Meaning of Grief through the Five Stages of Loss* (New York: Simon and Schuster, 2005); and David Kessler, *Finding Meaning:The Sixth Stage of Grief* (New York: Simon and Schuster, 2019).

7. Bernhard W. Anderson, *Out of the Depths: The Psalms Speak for Us Today* (Philadelphia: Westminster, 1970), 47. He explains that between 30 and 70 percent of the 150 psalms are laments. He argues that at least fifty-seven of the psalms are individual or community laments (see pages 46–56). Author Eugene Peterson affirms the higher number when he writes that, "Seventy percent of the psalms are laments." See Eugene H.

Peterson, *Leap Over a Wall: Earthy Spirituality for Everyday Christians* (San Francisco: HarperOne, 1997), 115.

8. Victor Frankl said it best: "Everything can be taken from a man but one thing: the last of human freedoms—to choose one's attitude in any given set of circumstances, to choose one's own way." Viktor E. Frankl, *Man's Search for Meaning* (Boston: Beacon Press, 1959, 2006), 66.

9. See Bessel van der Kolk, MD, *The Body Keeps the Score: Brain, Mind, and Body in the Healing of Trauma* (New York: Penguin Random House, 2014); Peter A. Levine, PhD, *In an Unspoken Voice: How the Body Releases Trauma and Restores Goodness* (Berkeley, CA: North Atlantic Books, 2010).

10. See session 4, "Explore the Iceberg" in Peter and Geri Scazzero, *The Emotionally Healthy Relationships Workbook and DVD* (Grand Rapids, MI: Zondervan, 2017).

11. One of my mentors expressed it best: Feelings are like children when you are on vacation. You can't put them in the driver's seat or stuff them in the trunk. You have to listen to them, take care of them, protect them, and at times, put boundaries around them.

12. Theologian and author Walter Brueggemann has said the psalms can be divided into three types—psalms of orientation, disorientation, and reorientation. In psalms of *orientation*, we enjoy a rich sense of well-being and joy in God. In psalms of *disorientation*, we experience seasons of hurt, suffering, and dislocation; the bottom has fallen out and we wonder what is happening. This is the confusing in-between. In psalms of *reorientation*, God breaks in and does something new. This is when joy breaks through our despair. Walter Brueggemann, *The Message of the Psalms: A Theological Commentary* (Minneapolis: Augsburg Publishing House, 1984), 9–11. See also Brueggemann's *The Psalms and the Life of Faith*, Patrick D. Miller, ed. (Minneapolis: Augsburg Fortress, 1995).

13. For a good introduction to the dark night of the soul, see my book *Emotionally Healthy Spirituality*, chapter 4, "Journey through the Wall."

14. St. John of the Cross, *Dark Night of the Soul*, trans. E. Allison Peers (New York: Image, Doubleday, 1959).

15. Tertulian, "Of Patience," *New Advent*, originally published in *Ante-Nicene Fathers*, vol. 3, trans. S. Thelwall, revised and edited for *New Advent* by Kevin Knight, http://www.newadvent.org/fathers/0325.htm. See also Alan Kreider, "Patience in the Missional Thought and Practice of the Early Church: The Case of Cyprian of Carthage," *International Bulletin of Missionary Research*, vol. 39, no. 4 (October 2015) 220–24, https://journals.sagepub.com/doi/pdf/10.1177/239693931503900416.

16. See Alan Kreider, *The Patient Ferment of the Early Church: The Improbable Rise of Christianity in the Roman Empire* (Grand Rapids,

MI: Baker Academic, 2016). He points out that one of the primary reasons the church grew in her first 300 years through persecutions and oppression was because of her commitment to patience. In fact, he argues, the early church fathers wrote more about the Christian virtue of patience than about evangelism.

17. Barbara Brown Taylor, *Learning to Walk in the Dark* (San Francisco: HarperOne, 2014), 5.

18. Lewis B. Smedes, *The Art of Forgiving: When You Need to Forgive and Don't Know How* (New York: Ballantine, 1996), 137.

19. Dr. Edith Eger, *The Choice: Embrace the Possible* (London: Rider, 2017), 223–24. Edith Eger, a psychologist and concentration camp survivor, wrote this book in her nineties, describing her journey out of the Holocaust and the rich insights she gleaned from it over the decades.

20. Cyprian Smith, *The Way of Paradox: Spiritual Life as Taught by Meister Eckhart*, 3rd ed. (London: Darton, Longman and Todd Ltd, 2004), 29–42.

21. Hans Boersma, *Seeing God: The Beatific Vision in Christian Tradition* (Grand Rapids, MI: Eerdmans, 2018), 83–88. Gregory of Nyssa writes about this in his great work, *The Life of Moses*. Even when we reach our heavenly future and see God face-to-face—in and through Christ—we will never stop growing in him.

22. Henri J. M. Nouwen, *Return of the Prodigal Son: A Meditation on Fathers, Brothers and Sons* (New York: Doubleday, 1992), 120–21.

23. For an excellent summary of this, see the work of Meister Eckhart on detaching/birthing/breaking-through. Bernard McGinn, *The Mystical Thought of Meister Eckhart: The Man from Whom God Hid Nothing* (New York: Crossroad, 2001), 131–47.

Chapter 7: Make Love the Measure of Maturity

1. Martin Buber, *Between Man and Man* (New York: Routledge, 2002), 16.

2. William E. Kaufman, *Contemporary Jewish Philosophies* (Detroit: Wayne State University Press, 1976), 62–63.

3. For additional insights on the impact this event had on Buber, see Kenneth Paul Kramer with Mechthild Gawlick, *Martin Buber's I and Thou: Practicing Living Dialogue* (Mahwah, N.J.: Paulist Press, 2003), 174–75.

4. See Martin Buber, *I and Thou*, trans. Walter Kaufmann (New York: Charles Scribner's Sons, 1970). For a fuller treatment of Buber's rich and complex life and philosophy, see also Paul Mendes-Flohr, *Martin Buber: A Life of Faith and Dissent* (New Haven, CT: Yale University Press, 2019).

5. For more information on *The Emotionally Healthy Relationships Course*, visit www.emotionallyhealthy.org/lead.

6. It's important to note that, in the complexity of life, we actually move in and out of I-It moments and I-Thou moments. In fact, some routine

aspects of life are primarily an I-It way of relating—ordering a sandwich at a local deli, paying for groceries, returning a library book, or any other routine transaction. Perhaps a helpful way to consider our relationships is that we live on an I-It to I-Thou continuum, continually moving back and forth between the two ways of being in the world.

7. Martin Buber, *I and Thou*, 5.

8. Kenneth Paul Kramer with Mechthild Gawlick, *Martin Buber's I and Thou*, 32.

9. David G. Benner, *Soulful Spirituality: Becoming Fully Alive and Deeply Human* (Grand Rapids, MI: Brazos, 2011), 127. See also David G. Benner, *Presence and Encounter: The Sacramental Possibilities of Everyday Life* (Grand Rapids, MI: Brazos, 2014).

10. Henri J. M. Nouwen, *Out of Solitude: Three Meditations on the Christian Life* (New York: Ave Maria Press, 1974), 36.

11. For an excellent treatment on the impact of technology on our relationships, see Sherry Turkle, *Reclaiming Conversation: The Power of Talk in a Digital Age* (New York: Penguin Random House, 2015).

12. Fleming Rutledge, *The Crucifixion*, 577–81.

13. Karl Barth, *Church Dogmatics, Volume 3, The Doctrine of Reconciliation: Part One* (Edinburgh: T&T Clark, 1956), 231–34.

14. Martin Buber, *Meetings: Autobiographical Fragments* (New York: Routledge, 1967, 2002), 22.

15. Kenneth Paul Kramer with Mechthild Gawlick, *Martin Buber's I and Thou*, 46, 101. One interesting application of this is in parenting. For example, an introverted parent may find themselves with a highly extroverted son or daughter. This "mismatch" can lead to a lifetime of frustration and annoyance for the parent who may end up treating their child as an It.

16. I highly recommend: Gregory A. Boyd, *Repenting of Religion: Turning from Judgment to the Love of God* (Grand Rapids: Baker Books, 2004). Drawing deeply from Scripture and the work of Dietrich Bonhoeffer, he presents a comprehensive treatment of judgment as core to the original sin in Scripture and love as the central command in Scripture. He concludes with a very helpful chapter on how to balance a concern to love people nonjudgmentally with a concern to become a holy people.

17. See Thomas C. Oden's *The Rebirth of Orthodoxy: Signs of New Life in Christianity* (New York: HarperCollins, 2003) along with his memoir about his journey to an orthodox biblical faith, *A Change of Heart: A Personal and Theological Memoir* (Downers Grove, IL: InterVarsity Press, 2014). See also D. H. Williams, *Evangelicals and Tradition: The Formative Influence of the Early Church* (Grand Rapids, MI: Baker Books, 2005).

18. John Calvin, *Institutes of the Christian Religion*, ed. John T. McNeill, trans. Ford Lewis Battles (Philadelphia: Westminster, 1960), 273–74.

19. See Richard J. Mouw, *Restless Faith: Holding Evangelical Beliefs in a World of Contested Labels* (Grand Rapids, MI: Brazos, 2019), 131–32.

20. The world we live in is increasingly pluralistic. We are neighbors with Muslims, Hindus, Buddhists, atheists, Orthodox Jews, ex-evangelicals, and so on. See, for example, Terry Muck and Frances S. Adeney, *Christianity Encountering World Religions: The Practice of Mission in the Twenty-First Century* (Grand Rapids, MI: Baker Books, 2009). Richard Mouw, former president of Fuller Theological Seminary and a reputable evangelical scholar, has done a great deal of excellent work in dialoging with Mormons and across ecumenical lines. I particularly recommend Richard J. Mouw, *Talking with Mormons: An Invitation to Evangelicals* (Grand Rapids, MI: Eerdmans, 2012). See also "Dialogue Principles" by the Dialogue Institute (https://dialogueinstitute.org/dialogue-principles), which provides excellent guidelines for inter-religious dialogue.

21. Ronald Rolheiser, *The Holy Longing: The Search for a Christian Spirituality* (New York: Doubleday, 1999), 76–77.

22. David Augsburger, *Caring Enough to Hear and Be Heard: How to Hear and How to Be Heard in Equal Communication* (Scottdale, PA: Herald, 1982), 12.

23. To learn more about attunement, which has been widely written about in the field of interpersonal neurobiology, see Daniel J. Siegel, *Mindsight: The New Science of Personal Transformation* (New York: Bantam Books, 2010), 27.

24. To see this modeled and to be guided in actually doing Incarnational Listening, go to: Pete and Geri Scazzero, *The Emotionally Healthy Relationships Course: Discipleship that Deeply Changes Your Relationship with Others* (Grand Rapids, MI: Zondervan, 2017). See Session 5, "Listen Incarnationally," in the workbook, along with the DVD that provides step-by-step guidance.

25. To learn more about developing a healthy sense of self, see Geri Scazzero, *The Emotionally Healthy Woman: Eight Things You Have To Quit to Change Your Life*, 63–87.

26. The names of the actual murderers as well as a number of other details were changed in the movie. I relate the story as portrayed in the movie, but I highly recommend the book to you. Sister Helen Prejean, *Dead Man Walking: The Eyewitness Account of the Death Penalty that Sparked a National Debate* (New York: Vintage Books, 1993).

27. John Paul Lederach, "Advent Manifesto: Does My Soul Still Sing?", *On Being*, December 11, 2018, https://onbeing.org/blog/advent-manifesto-does-my-soul-still-sing/.

Chapter 8: Break the Power of the Past

1. Sin refers not only to our behaviors, but to a power under which we live (Romans 6–8). Sin's power enslaves and is so deeply lodged in us that it required the crucifixion of the Son of God to free us from this demonic power. We ourselves could not overcome it by sheer willpower or any other human capacity. For an excellent exegesis on Paul's description of sin as a power, see Fleming Rutledge, *The Crucifixtion, 167–204.*

2. A few, like myself, have dramatic conversions like Saul of Tarsus; most happen at some point after a long process and period of time. In some cases, especially with children growing up in the church, a particular moment may be difficult to pinpoint. Yet the same reality of a new birth in Jesus has taken place.

3. See Rodney Clapp, *Families at the Crossroads: Beyond Traditional and Modern Options* (Downers Grove, IL: InterVarsity Press, 1993).

4. See Paul Minear, *Images of the Church in the New Testament, New Testament Library* (Louisville, KY: Westminster John Knox Press, 2004).

5. Ray S. Anderson and Dennis B. Guernsey, *On Being Family: A Social Theology of the Family* (Grand Rapids, MI: Eerdmans, 1985), 158.

6. This phenomenon was first described in 1987 by author Frank White in his book *The Overview Effect: Space Exploration and Human Evolution, 3rd ed.* (Reston, VA: American Institute of Aeronautics and Astronautics, 2014). To learn more, see the documentary *The Overview Effect* (https://vimeo.com/55073825), a short film that explores this phenomenon through interviews with astronauts and others who experienced it.

7. Another example is James Irwin who said: "Finally, (the Earth) shrank to the size of a marble, the most beautiful marble you can imagine. Seeing this has to change a man, has to make a man appreciate the creation of God and the love of God." Kevin W. Kelley, conceived and edited for the Association of Space Explorers, *The Home Planet* (Massachusetts: Addison Wesley Publishing Company, 1988), 38. Shuttle astronaut Don. L. Lind said, "There was no intellectual preparation I hadn't made. But there is no way you can be prepared for the emotional impact." See Frank White, *The Overview Effect: Space Exploration and Human Evolution, 3rd ed.* (Reston, VA: American Institute of Aeronautics and Astronautics, 2014), 27. And so it is when we see our histories in the genogram.

8. For fuller treatment, see Monica McGoldrick and Randy Gerson, *Genograms in Family Assessment* (New York: W. W. Norton, 1986).

9. Scazzero, *The Emotionally Healthy Relationships Course,* See Session 3, "Genogram Your Family," in the workbook, along with the DVD that provides step-by-step guidance. See also our team transformational videos at www.emotionallyhealthy.org/team that will lead you and

your team to begin the journey and build a genogram to consider its implications for you, your team, and your leadership.

10. For a discussion of overfunctioning and underfunctioning within the context of the church, see Ronald Richardson, *Creating a Healthier Church: Family Systems Theory, Leadership, and Congregational Life* (Minneapolis: Augsburg Fortress, 1996), 133–37; see also Edwin H. Friedman, *Generation to Generation: Family Process in Church and Synagogue* (New York: The Guilford Press, 1985), 210–12.

11. Walter Brueggemann, *Genesis: Interpretation: A Bible Commentary for Teaching and Preaching* (Atlanta: John Knox Press, 1982), 376.

12. Margaret Silf, *Inner Compass: An Invitation to Ignatian Spirituality* (Chicago: Loyola Press, 1999), 165–66.

13. See *The Emotionally Healthy Leader* podcast on "Growing Older in the New Family of Jesus: Part 1 and 2," at www.emotionallyhealthy.org/podcast.

14. Moses draws on hard lessons learned as he instructs his people about how they are to live in the Promised Land when they arrive. See Peter C. Craigie, *The Book of Deuteronomy: The New International Commentary on the Old Testament* (Grand Rapids, MI: Eerdmans,1976).

15. A few excellent resources on a theology of aging, and aging in general, include J. Ellsworth Kalas, *I Love Growing Older, but I'll Never Grow Old* (Nashville: Abingdon Press, 2013); and David J. Levitin, *Successful Aging: A Neuroscientist Explores the Power and Potential of Our Lives* (New York: Penguin Random House, 2020).

16. The idea behind this illustration is adapted from Dr. Ronald W. Richardson, *Family Ties that Bind: A Self-Help Guide to Change through Family of Origin Therapy* (Bellingham, WA: Self Counsel Press, 1984), 35–39.

17. *The Emotionally Healthy Relationships Course* was developed over an almost twenty-year period for this purpose. It provides a framework to help you establish a shared culture and language, and also teaches eight key relational skills. For more information, visit www.emotionallyhealthy.org.

18. To take this idea to yet another level, we need to also consider the negative and positive legacies of the country in which our churches are located. Beyond that, we might also consider the larger global legacies that impact us—for example, patriarchy, sexism, racial injustice, etc.

19. Quoted in Dr. Ronald W. Richardson, *Family Ties that Bind*, 35.

Chapter 9: Lead Out of Weakness and Vulnerability

1. "Vulnerable," *Merriam-Webster*, https://www.merriam-webster.com/dictionary/vulnerable.

2. Erik Larson, *Isaac's Storm: A Man, a Time, and the Deadliest Hurricane in History* (Westminster, MD: Crown, 1999).

3. Brené Brown, one of the leading researchers on the topic of vulnerability

and imperfection, refers to the twenty-ton shield she used to defend herself. See Brené Brown, *The Gifts of Imperfection: Let Go of Who You Think You're Supposed to Be and Embrace Who You Are* (Center City, MN: Hazelden Publishing, 2010).

4. See Hans Boersma, *Seeing God: The Beatific Vision in Christian Tradition* (Grand Rapids, MI: Eerdmans, 2018).

5. Frederick Dale Brunner, *The Gospel of John: A Commentary* (Grand Rapids, MI: Eerdmans, 2012), 596.

6. For his crime of claiming, based on this text, that Jesus had both a human and divine will, Maximus the Confessor (580–662 AD) had his right hand cut off so he could never write again and his tongue ripped out so he could never teach again. For an excellent account of this, see Robert Louis Wilkins, *The Spirit of Early Christian Thought: Seeking the Face of God* (New Haven, CT: Yale University Press, 2003), 110–35; and George Berthold, *Maximus Confessor: Selected Writings, Classics of Western Spirituality* (New York: Paulist Press, 1983).

7. Polycarp, quoted in *Early Christian Fathers*, ed. and trans. Cyril C. Richardson (New York: Macmillan, 1970), 152–53.

8. Frederick Dale Bruner, *Matthew: A Commentary: The Churchbook, Matthew 13–28*, 649.

9. Quoted in Thomas E. Reynolds, *Vulnerable Communion: A Theology of Disability and Hospitality* (Grand Rapids, MI: Brazos, 2018), 14. Note that it is important to distinguish between a physical or mental disability—as defined by the Americans with Disabilities Act of 1990 (ADA)—and the broader condition of disability we all carry. Thomas Reynolds does an excellent and thorough job of making this distinction in *Vulnerable Communion*. The ADA defines a disability as 1) a "physical or mental impairment that substantially limits one or more of the major life activities of an individual; 2) a record of such impairment; or 3) being regarded as having such an impairment."

10. See Galatians 3:21–25.

11. I owe this observation about the progression in Paul's spiritual development to pastor and theologian Jack Deere, who voiced it at a conference many years ago.

12. There are innumerable articles and videos on the history and methodology of Kintsugi. One very good introduction is Céline Santini, *Kintsugi: Finding Strength in Imperfection* (Kansas City, MO: Andrews McMeel Publishing, 2019).

13. For an outstanding video on kintsugi, go to: https://vimeo.com/330493 356/2dbc2e98c5.

14. An excellent resource on leading out of our weaknesses is Dr. Dan B. Allender, *Leading with a Limp: Take Full Advantage of Your Most Powerful Weakness* (Colorado Springs: Waterbrook Press, 2006).

15. There is a compelling story about this in the life of Bernard of Clairvaux (1090–1153), the abbot of a Cistercian monastery in France, who was perhaps the greatest Christian leader of his day. When his spiritual son, Eugene III, became Pope, Bernard was deeply concerned that his interior life was not sufficiently developed to cope with the level of responsibility he now carried. Bernard warned him: "Remove yourself from the demands, lest you be distracted and get a hard heart. If you are not terrified by it, it is yours already." See, *Bernard of Clairvaux: Selected Works, Classics of Western Spirituality*, ed. and trans. G. R. Evans (Mahway, NJ: Paulist, 1987), 173–205.

16. Henri J. M. Nouwen, *The Return of the Prodigal Son: A Meditation on Fathers, Brothers, and Sons* (New York: Doubleday, 1992), 39–40, 51.

Implementing Emotionally Healthy Discipleship

1. Technically, it is possible to install additional programs that enable one operating system to run the other operating system: But the non-native operating system will not work without this additional program.

2. I'm grateful to Seth Godin for his insights—specifically, the episode of his podcast on "Operating Systems," in which he applies the operating system metaphor to cities, the rule of law, museums, and organizational cultures. I especially love his point that operating systems change over time as they interact with other operating systems. My hope is that this will also be true of emotionally healthy discipleship as an operating system—that it will change in important and needful ways in the years to come. To learn more, see Seth Godin, "Operating Systems," January 8, 2020, in *Akimbo: A Podcast from Seth Godin*, https://www.listennotes.com/podcasts/akimbo-a-podcast/operating-systems-qW5rMNmf3RF/.

3. This analogy comes from Bill Hull, *Conversion and Discipleship: You Can't Have One without the Other* (Grand Rapids, MI: Zondervan, 2016), 184.

4. Dietrich Bonhoeffer, *The Cost of Discipleship* (New York: Touchstone, 1937), 59.

5. *Celtic Daily Prayer: Prayers and Readings from the Northumbria Community* (New York: HarperCollins, 2002), 19.

Appendix A: Church Culture Revolution: A Six-Part Vision for a Culture That Deeply Changes Lives

1. Scott W. Sunquist, *Understanding Christian Mission: Participation in Suffering and Glory* (Grand Rapids, MI: Baker Press, 2013), 244.

2. This is journalist Ken Myers' definition of culture as summarized by Andy Crouch in *Playing God: Redeeming the Gift of Power* (Carol Stream, IL: InterVarsity Press, 2013), 17.

We Help Church Leaders Make Mature Disciples

Move your people from shallow Christianity to depth in Christ.

Developed over the last 21 years, *The Emotionally Healthy Discipleship Course* is a strategy for discipleship that is proven to change lives not just on the surface, but deeply. People in your church begin working out conflicts and grow in unity. You're able to identify and develop your future leaders. And ultimately, your church makes a greater impact in the world for Christ.

EMOTIONALLY HEALTHY SPIRITUALITY

Introducing people to a transformative spirituality with God.

EMOTIONALLY HEALTHY RELATIONSHIPS

Practical skills to launch people into a transformative spirituality with others.

ZONDERVAN®

It's Time to Get Started!
Here Are Your 3 Steps:

GET THE KIT

Includes everything you need to run the course

Emotionally Healthy Discipleship Course Leader's Kit
9780310101352

GET TRAINED

Attend Online Training and discover how to lead the course
emotionallyhealthy.org/lead

RUN THE COURSE

Run a pilot group through both parts of the course

ZONDERVAN®

Leader's Resource Vault

Access a treasure chest of exclusive content designed to equip you to lead *The Emotionally Healthy Discipleship Course* effectively in your church or ministry.

In the Leader's Resource Vault you and your team will receive:

- Planning timelines
- Session schedules
- Training videos and resources
- Presentation decks
- Certificates of completion for participants
- Top 25 FAQ's people ask
- Marketing & promotional graphics

Access to a Certified EH Discipleship Course Coach:

- Customize a plan for your specific ministry context
- Build on areas of strength in your ministry
- Receive specific tools to ensure the Course develops disciple-makers and leaders

Exclusive Resources:

- Have your ministry posted publicly on a national map
- Access to Online Q&A session with author Pete Scazzero
- Networking with other Point Leaders in an EHD Private Facebook Group

Get access today at:

EmotionallyHealthy.org/Vault

The Emotionally Healthy Leader Podcast

Join Pete Scazzero (founder of Emotionally Healthy Discipleship) as he discusses Emotionally Healthy Discipleship in the life of every leader.

What listeners are saying:

"This podcast teaches me to be an agent of change in a culture that is defined by "doing" rather than "being." In a culture obsessed with external success…it's refreshing to hear leaders learn to lead out of their overflow of God's love for them that can only be achieved by slowing down to abide in the love of Jesus."
—Reviewer MarineMike NY

"This stuff can save your life, ministry and relationships."
—Reviewer Brent Squires

"These podcasts are worth listening to each and every time they come out. They cut to the core of issues and give you practical steps to be a better leader and a better Christian."
—Reviewer jhamination

"This podcast is the best resource out there I know for helping me fulfill God's plan for myself and his church!"
—Reviewer Pershing

EmotionallyHealthy.org/Podcast

How Emotionally Healthy Are You?

Take the Personal Assessment

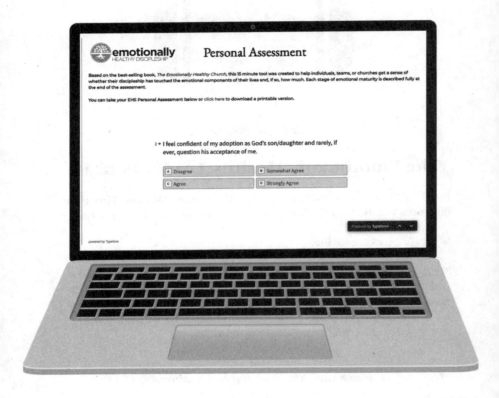

Are you an Emotional Infant, Child, Teen or Adult? This powerful 15- minute diagnostic tool enables you to determine your level of maturity.

This 15-minute tool was created to help individuals, teams, or churches get a sense of whether their discipleship has touched the emotional components of their lives and, if so, how much. Each stage of emotional maturity is described fully at the end of the assessment.

emotionallyhealthy.org/mature